THE

SATURN

DIARIES

This book is a grimoire: a diary of personal spells, elixirs, divination tools, and rituals that aided me in the alchemy of my healing journey.

This book is also a memoir: a reflection of my present recollections of experiences over time. Some names and characteristics have been changed. Some events have been compressed and some dialogue has been recreated. I would like to thank every person portrayed in this book for the impactful roles they played in my evolution. This story is written solely from my memory, with my opinions from my singular perspective.

THE

A MODERN DAY GRIMOIRE

SATURN

BY CARDSY B

DIARIES

LIFE TO PAPER
PUBLISHING

To request permissions, contact the publisher at tabitha@lifetopaper.com.

Hardcover: 978-1-990700-09-5
Paperback: 978-1-990700-08-8
Ebook: 978-1-990700-11-8

First paperback edition October 2022.

Edited by Tabitha Rose, Michelle Kauntz, Jennifer Goulden

Cover art by Mario Manuel

LIFE TO PAPER
PUBLISHING

To all the past versions of myself: even the messy ones... especially the messy ones.

And to Lisa, for your strength, inspiration, and for reminding me of whom to dedicate this book.

CONTENTS

We pushed through the doors, escaping the blustery November cold. I rushed past my mom and headed to the back of Waldenbooks, straight to the Occult section. Long before it was rebranded as Metaphysical, or even New Age, this section, tucked back in the far left corner, was almost always empty aside from the occasional solace-seeking Goth teenager. Paranormal activity books were my current preference, but I had also collected several astrology books, a few on ESP, and two on astral travel.

My mom always said yes to books, even when they cost more than my allowance money. She was proud that I was an avid reader. I'd won the "Book-It" reading competition in my first grade class and finished *Moby Dick* when I was eight, but in fourth grade my TAG (talented and gifted) advanced studies teacher began to voice concerns about the subject matter of the books I was reading. Though not necessarily a student or practitioner of metaphysics herself, my mom was incredibly open-minded. When she was questioned by my teacher, she defended that I was "reading constantly and eager to learn," which she thoroughly supported.

My mom followed behind me to my very favorite shelf, lowered the zipper on her burgundy winter coat, and adjusted the sleeves on her petite frame to adapt to the store's radiator heat.

I didn't want to waste any time getting comfortable. Instead, I chose to leave my coat on along with my pleather backpack—the OG vegan leather—and begin immediately sorting through a pile of books while my mom casually tucked her chin-length blonde bob behind her right ear. Her arctic-blue eyes widened as she spotted the holes in the knees of my black leggings as I sat down.

"Rebecca! Those have holes all over the knees. I threw those in the garbage two days ago! Did you change into them at school? I didn't see them this morning."

I unsuccessfully tried to pull my coat back over my knees.

"Ok. So, I dug them out, and I might have changed into them at school, but they look cool—I like the holes. And they're soooooo comfy."

"I can't believe you wore those to school. People will think we can't afford clothes without holes in them! I went to Penney's *just* to get you new leggings to replace those."

"Mom, who cares what they think? Do they think *Madonna* can't afford new clothes? They look cool. Besides, you got me purple ones. And I REALLY like the black ones."

She shook her head, trying not to crack a smile at my rebuttal.

I sheepishly grinned as I continued to sort my pile of books. *How to Meet and Work with Spirit Guides* by Ted Andrews made its way to the top of my stack. I almost chose this one the week before because I loved the line drawings of the celestial-looking figures in royal purples and greens.

"Oooh, that looks cool. Are you thinking you want that one?" my mom asked encouragingly.

"Yeah... maybe this one."

I liked to take my time deciding. That little dusty occult section in Waldenbooks in the Carlisle, Pennsylvania strip mall was one of the few places where I felt at home. It was obvious that I was different from everyone around me. I felt like a tourist in my own hometown. *"It's okay that you don't belong here,"* a calm, reassuring voice echoed from somewhere inside. The voice felt familiar, but also bigger than me. I wanted to trust it, but I still felt like an outsider. Maybe it was the holey leggings, maybe it was the weird things I sometimes *knew*, but it was clear that I was atypical. I didn't want to grow up and get married to some boy who played on the Varsity football team and, shortly after, have kids that would inevitably go to the same school. I wanted to live in New York City; I wanted to travel the world. Other girls my age had started to care about boys. Other kids belonged to after-school activities and played sports, but not me. Though I excelled academically, I didn't really have any friends, except for one adorable fellow nerd in my advanced studies class. *I wonder if Ellie would like this book too?* I smiled as I thought of my one and only ally, who never judged my weird hobbies and interests.

While contemplating this, the coolest little orange box caught my eye from the shelf just above me. It had a window cut out of the front revealing a mysterious brunette lady on a black background.

"To All Believers," the scripted white text read.

That's me! I thought as I reached upward to grab it. I shoved my initial pile of books to the side and stood up, clasping the little box excitedly.

"This one!! Can I get this one, Mom? It's a little more than my allowance," I admitted, digging my single dollar bills out of my zipped coat pocket. "And I know it's not technically a book, but it says there's a book *inside*," I defended.

"A booklet." My mom enunciated while smiling, clearly seeing through my negotiations. "Ok, let me see."

She picked it up and glanced over the description of the Hanson Roberts Tarot deck and hesitantly said, "Well, I guess so… but the leggings go in the trash when we get home, and permanently this time."

"Thank you! Thank you! Thank you!" I squealed, too excited about my first Tarot deck to mourn the loss of my favorite pants.

My dad walked in promptly at 6:15, just minutes after we got home from the bookstore. He set his brown leather briefcase down next to the kitchen entryway before sitting at the table. His hand smoothed the top of his hair before loosening his necktie.

"How was school today, Sweets?" he asked while opening the newspaper to the stock section.

"It was great!" I beamed. "I got the highest score on the math test. And I got my trophy for winning the invention convention last week. They engraved my name on it, so now I get to keep it!"

"I'm so proud of you, sweetie." He kissed me on top of my head.

"But the best part," I said excitedly, as I dug out the new Tarot deck from my backpack, "is what I got at the bookstore!"

"Ooo, are you going to tell my fortune, like Miss Cleo?" he asked with a laugh.

"Yeah! I mean, I'm learning!" I answered thoughtfully, readjusting the black scrunchie around my ponytail.

In all fairness, Miss Cleo, the infamous television dial-a-psychic, was the only mainstream representation of psychics and energy workers in existence at that time.

"Why don't you get your trophy to show me while Mom finishes dinner?" he asked.

"Sure!" I said as I leapt off the kitchen chair with my Tarot deck still in hand.

In my bedroom, I cleared a special place alongside my gold

light bulb trophy to display my new Tarot deck before carrying them both back to the kitchen table.

"Wow! Look at that!" my dad smiled proudly.

"The judges said she nailed the presentation piece: one of the only kids who didn't use any notes or cue cards," my mom added while swirling spaghetti in a pot of boiling water.

"You're gonna make an amazing executive or lawyer," my dad said as he patted me on the head.

I was always rewarded for my academic accomplishments and those jobs were what smart people did to make money as far as I knew. No one else seemed to find much value in the metaphysical world I loved so much. But I couldn't blame them, really. They didn't know the lure behind the astrology books I pored over, tracing the patterns of the constellations, imagining the stories behind each one. They didn't know that there was something magical about those books, something that made me feel like I belonged to something bigger than myself.

As my school years progressed, the scholastic trophies and framed awards began to crowd out my once-treasured mystical books. These achievements brought a different kind of recognition and sense of inclusion. My allowance was eventually spent on other things. Even though I remained a weird little bullied outsider, I continued to excel academically and discovered a love of art and design. The astrology books and Tarot deck were gradually moved to less and less prominent places in my bedroom, until they were unceremoniously relegated to a Rubbermaid storage container that I wouldn't revisit for decades.

PART ONE

THE TOWER

The Tower: Upheaval, Chaos, Collapse

"The dark night of the soul is when you have lost the flavor of life but have not yet gained the fullness of divinity. So it is that we must weather that dark time, the period of transformation when what is familiar has been taken away and the new richness is not yet ours."

— Ram Dass

CHAPTER I

THE TEN OF SWORDS
A SPOONFUL OF INTUITION

Ten of Swords: Endings, Deep Wounds, Loss

"I failed gay marriage! Like, mere seconds after it was legalized. RuPaul should sashay in here and beat me with a rainbow-studded baton," I groaned, as I woke up in my best friend's hotel room in Midtown.

My head was pounding from polishing off an entire bottle of Cabernet the night before. I was sweating, partially from the wine, and partly due to the thick gauge wool scarf I fell asleep wearing.

"No one's going to beat you," Lindsay calmly stated from the bathroom. She flipped her raspberry-tinted brunette locks behind her shoulders before applying her signature cat eye liner.

Lindsay had an even-keeled, emo, hipster-girl vibe that was incredibly comforting in a crisis.

2

We'd met in our first year of college, bonding over the fact that even though we were both majoring in fashion design, we were both equally challenged by our terrible sewing skills. As an awkward outsider who'd worked tirelessly to be at the top of the class, win every competition, and gain people's approval and affections while growing up, I was instantly attracted to Lindsay's seemingly effortless cool girl attitude.

"Saturn Returns are no joke," Lindsay noted in a motherly tone.

"Huh?" I asked as I attempted to focus my eyes.

"When Saturn returns to the place it was when you were born, it will basically disrupt or remove the areas of your identity and lifestyle that are out of alignment. It occurs every twenty-seven to thirty-one years. Since we're the same age, that means your Saturn is probably also in Scorpio. Scorpio highlights your relationship and understanding of money, power, and sex. It's no joke," Lindsay reiterated.

"Uggggh," I moaned. "If that's your way of telling me the cosmos hate me, thank you. That's already pretty apparent. Anyway, should I just go straight to Bed Bath & Beyond or go home? I mean, almost all the kitchen stuff was hers…" *And I don't really know what my life is supposed to look like after she leaves,* I thought, but that was too scary to vocalize; it was much easier to obsess over new espresso cups.

Lindsay walked out of the bathroom and sat down on the bed beside me, handing me a sad little paper cup of hotel coffee.

"Let's start with coffee and then, eventually, home. Probably better to assess the damage first," she said, reaching into her purse and pulling out a small container of cinnamon, tapping a few brown lumps into the cup.

Lindsay was part rockabilly badass and part Polish grandmother, and her purse was consequently filled with more random shit than the lost and found department at Penn Station.

"What is that?" I asked with an irritable growl.

"It's good for hangovers," she said as she patted my leg. "From a medical standpoint, it helps stabilize blood sugar. It's also said to heighten intuition. You could use a little of both these days," she explained as she tapped another pile into my coffee for dramatic effect.

"You carry cinnamon in your *purse*?"

"Hey, if Beyoncé can carry hot sauce, I can carry cinnamon," Lindsay said as she shoved the container back into her overflowing Marc Jacobs handbag.

I shook my head and took a sip. As much as I didn't want to admit it, she was right. My now ex-wife had moved out the previous evening, and as a result, I was avoiding accessing my intuition *and* my apartment. She'd been living with a friend in Brooklyn for the past two months since our relationship had deteriorated, and yesterday she texted to let me know she would be coming by to grab the last few boxes of her things and officially move out. I'd decided to sequester myself in Lindsay's hotel room in order to avoid the entire thing. Thankfully, the Universe had sent my best friend from college to New York on a work trip at the exact time I needed an escape.

On the surface, my life had been picture perfect: Global Vice President at Playboy by age twenty-eight and married to a quintessential girl-next-door type who everyone adored. We had a fabulous apartment in a luxury high rise in the heart of Chelsea. We chose it because of my love of the downtown skyline view and Amanda's excitement over the design of the kitchen. We hosted lavish dinner parties nearly every week. Amanda was an impeccable cook, who counted on me to bartend and create the perfect ambiance: murder mystery dinners in October and Easter parties with actual egg hunts. We were even photographed for an equal rights campaign and featured as one of NYC's favorite lesbian couples. Friends and family simultaneously complimented and rolled their eyes at our modern-day fairy tale. But, after almost six years, everything was falling down around me, even though I proclaimed to anyone who would listen that my life was better than perfect. It *was* great, but the cracks below the surface were showing. I wasn't sure how long I could keep piling concealer on a relationship that was admittedly in need of serious surgery.

I unwrapped myself from the scarf I'd been sleeping in. The charcoal gray Yohji Yamamoto scarf had belonged to Justin, my mentor and one of my very best friends, who had died of HIV-related complications a year prior to my waking up in Lindsay's hotel room. I'd slept with that scarf every night since his mom gifted it to me as part of a package of his belongings. Aside from clinging to that scarf like a security blanket, I mostly dealt with the loss like a true New Yorker: through workaholism, alcoholism, and countless other "isms" that shaped the backbone of the city's survival culture. Shortly after Justin died, my Global VP fashion executive job began to unravel. My marriage was also falling apart and I was unbearably lonely. Justin was the person I'd leaned on to help navigate so many aspects of my life and career both emotionally and mentally, and he was gone. Instead of facing the darkness, I drank away most of my feelings. And when that wasn't enough, I popped Xanax like Pez from a *Valley of the Dolls* pill case. If I made it campy and ironic, it wasn't REALLY a problem, right?

At least that's what I told myself.

Amanda was extremely patient for most of it. She tolerated my annoying habit of sleeping with my work phone under my pillow in order to answer emails from Asia at 3 a.m., but she slowly lost hope in our marriage when the drinking and pill popping reached a whole new level. Amanda refers to the last year of our marriage as "the baby bottle & sweatpants times." I not only began consuming wine out of glass baby bottles so that I could drink in our bed without getting scolded for spilling, but also convinced several friends to take part. As an innate leader and trendsetter, I discovered the "vin en baby bottle" fad at a little bistro in Montmartre that was cleverly avoiding the French wine glass tax. I, of course, claimed it was "all the rage in Paris" and quickly developed a whole following of Chelsea fashionistas drinking their Pinot Grigio from baby bottles, allowing me to dismiss Amanda's concerns entirely.

Amanda used to love that I could get people to go along with my most insane plans. She didn't even shame me for the ridiculous "Carb-balah" movement I started years ago. When everyone was doing the Atkins and South Beach diet in the early 2000s, I began wearing a Tiffany blue, woven string on my right wrist to ward off the "evil carb." I got at least twenty other people to jump on board.

My friend Travis looked at his blue string one day at my apartment and asked, "But when do we get to take it off?"

I rolled my eyes and tossed my hair extensions back and said, "We don't take it off, Travis! Unless you're so skinny it falls off!"

"She's kidding!" Amanda comforted, smoothing over my outburst, as she would for many years when I acted destructively.

In the beginning of our relationship, she joked that I would have made a good cult leader because of my inherent ability to spot trends and convince others to join me.

Amanda and I met in our early twenties and had been inseparable ever since. I fell instantly in love with her infectious charm and quick wit. We met through a mutual friend, a men's underwear designer by day and comedian by night. I often accompanied him to dingy stand-up bars where he provided me with complimentary martinis in exchange for my contagious laughter. Most of the comics were boring at best, and awkwardly offensive at worst. But Amanda was smart and witty, and she possessed the one quality I simply adored: she was GENUINELY funny, on stage and in real life.

We made plans as a group to have dinner one night at the restaurant where Lindsay's boyfriend worked as a bartender. That night, Lindsay wound up leaving early, and Amanda and I ended up on a completely unplanned first date. Amanda had the crystal blue eyes of a true seeker and a beautiful infectious smile to match. More than that, I was drawn to her genuine kindness and complete lack of jadedness that I, and nearly every New Yorker I had dated, seemed to wear proudly. We ate edamame dumplings and discussed everything from the irony of our day jobs—she was a censor at ABC while I was the Lingerie Director of Playboy—to our shared love of Madonna and our belief in the law of attraction. I felt like I had always known her, and she was finally reappearing after being gone for the first act of my life. I never wanted to spend a moment without her again.

Amanda was attracted to my blonde ambition, but she also saw—beneath the gloss veneer I'd created for myself and loved— the nerdy girl from rural Pennsylvania who still lived deep inside of me. She never shamed me for telling everyone I met that I was Dutch-Canadian, even though I'd only spent a few years in both Amsterdam and Toronto. Amanda was my best friend, and the only person who truly knew me. I didn't want to acknowledge that our marriage was over. I couldn't lose my best friend, and I didn't want to admit to myself that I was letting down the person who had been the kindest to me. I especially couldn't stand the thought that I was destroying the perfect image of our highly public, seemingly enviable, very gay marriage.

I tried the quick fixes of booking us yoga classes and

meditating together at Canyon Ranch. More accurately, Amanda meditated while I made to-do lists and beat myself up for sucking at meditation. Eventually, Amanda suggested we try marriage counseling. The first counselor we saw asked us to fill out a "happiness in the relationship" survey, which had questions that included such gems as: Has your partner ever caused physical harm to you? Has your partner ever pulled a gun or knife on you?

My score came out to a solid eight. I mean, I wasn't ecstatic about things, but no weapons were drawn on either side.

Amanda? She gave us a three. Her somber score should have told me everything I needed to know, but at the time, I was too oblivious and self-centered to read the writing on the wall.

We tried another, highly reputable—aka EXPENSIVE—therapist, a middle-aged psychologist with a severe, angled bob and a perfectly trained, neutral expression who reminded me of an annoying librarian. She proceeded to ask us both what the ideal future looked like for each of us. Amanda said she pictured a stable and secure relationship: a Range Rover with a matching pair of car seats already installed. That image, plus the previous night's liquid supper made me want to vomit in my mouth. I, on the other hand, wanted the "glamorous" Candace Bushnell-esque life I came to Manhattan to claim as my own: the high-powered career, the parties, the fancy friends.

Annoying Librarian then asked us to describe what we thought the other person's life would look like if we stayed together and what it would look like if we split up. We both concluded that staying together looked pretty much like how things were, which I was okay with—I could stay at an eight out of ten—but Amanda clearly was not. When she asked what we thought the other person's life would look like if we separated, I looked up from my watch; I'd been busily calculating exactly how much Librarian was costing me.

"Oh, my turn?" I stammered, flashing Amanda the smile that used to fix everything, at least momentarily. "Um, without me... Yeah, Range Rover and car seats... and like every weekend in New Jersey."

Amanda loved to spend the weekends at her parents' home in New Jersey, whereas I struggled with even the occasional holiday trips to my family's home in suburban Pennsylvania.

Amanda rolled her eyes and continued.

"If Bec and I went our separate ways? She'd probably end up in an expensive Upper East Side apartment, most likely with an older woman. Surrounded by luxurious things, but... kinda lonely... and kinda sad," Amanda said as she looked off in the distance and fidgeted in her chair.

I remained silent while I mentally calculated the pros and cons of this scenario. It sounded like my new lady had great taste and no kids, which struck me as far better than lugging a pair of screaming babies to New Jersey. Pro.

No Amanda. Con.

"What?" Amanda prodded, knowing my silence carried more weight than most of the words I had spoken in the therapy session up until this point.

Her questioning tone pulled me out of my mental exploration of my fictional Upper East Side apartment.

"Nothing," I said. "That's... interesting."

Amanda gave me the side eye and crossed her legs to shift her body away from me and towards the door.

In those therapy sessions, it became clear we had grown too far apart from one another, and as a result, our futures just couldn't align. Though we had once loved each other deeply, we ultimately concluded that the kindest thing we could do for ourselves and each other was to go our separate ways.

Apparently, in the end, having the restraint to not pull weapons on each other wasn't enough to hold the marriage together.

I sighed out loud, still clutching the worn down, under-stuffed pillow, forgetting for a second that Lindsay was still there as I recounted the past few months in my mind.

"I have to head to a 9 a.m. meeting, but stay as long as you like."

Lindsay, perfectly poised in her burgundy sweater dress and kitten heels, looked at me, attempting to smooth my disheveled hair with a mixture of pity and genuine love. She hugged me goodbye before heading for the door. Before her hand had even touched the doorknob, she stopped midway and turned back to look at me.

"Maybe add cinnamon to your shopping list," Lindsay said with a smirk.

"Right, for the Saturn Return supplies section of the list," I retorted.

Pour Myself a Cup of *Intuition* Latte

For divorces, hangovers, and other times when coffee alone won't cut it.

- **4 ounces of espresso or matcha**

- **4 ounces milk of choice** (I prefer almond for this one)

- **½ teaspoon cinnamon**
  + *Medicinally: blood sugar stabilizer/digestion aid*
  * *Magically: increases intuition*

- **½ teaspoon nutmeg**
  + *Medicinally: antioxidant*
  * *Magically: increases luck and well-being*

- **½ teaspoon vanilla**
  + *Medicinally: digestion aid*
  * *Magically: amplifies personal empowerment, mental clarity*

Froth milk, cinnamon, nutmeg, and vanilla together and pour over espresso or matcha.

If you don't own a frother, you can add the spices and milk to a saucepan and heat on medium for 2 to 3 minutes, whisking occasionally.

If you don't own a working stove (see Chapter VIII for why I know what that's like), you can heat the milk and spices in a glass jar in the microwave for one minute, remove, shake, and pour over the cup of espresso or matcha.

Top with an extra sprinkle of cinnamon for additional third eye awareness.

CHAPTER II

THE DEVIL
WEARS GAULTIER... AND DRINKS BLUE MARTINIS

The Devil: Temptation, Vice, Attachment

As amicable as it was, even the kindest divorce is no disco dance party. I just wanted to pretend it wasn't happening and crawl back under my bestie's Marriott room comforter on that cold February morning. But the Aries rising in me never procrastinates for very long; I always have to be DOING something.

I grabbed my coffee to go after Lindsay left and went back to my apartment. Hesitantly, I investigated each room. I took in the empty space in the living room where Amanda's black and white photo of the Flatiron building once hung. The photo grid of our mutual friends looked like a jack o' lantern's smile from all the missing photos of the individuals that she seemed to have claimed as "Team Amanda." I made a mental note of the replaceable items she took and braved the cold to purchase new kitchen appliances and cutlery as quickly as possible. Why feel things when you can shop, do, and drink?

My cell phone jingled loudly as I entered Bed Bath & Beyond with the custom ringtone of my friend, Gia Gallows. The guy behind me in the cookwares section smirked as her "hit single" played from my iPhone's speaker.

"Good morning, mi amor. How are you?" she cooed.

"Ugh—I've been better… She took the Keurig," I grumbled.

"That bitch! Well, why don't you come by my place for lunch today. Would you mind picking up some ciggies? Besos!"

Gia was everything I wanted to be at that point: a beautiful, glamorous, wealthy actress who was unapologetically sensational. THIS was the life I wanted. Fuck Range Rovers and car seats. I wanted my very own autotuned single on iTunes and throngs of adoring gay male fans. Gia had also gone through a divorce as well as a recent breakup with a gentleman who "couldn't handle the spotlight." She made me feel like *we* were the cool ones; *they* were just boring and couldn't keep up. Gia helped me to believe that life as a divorcée would not only be ok, but absolutely fucking fabulous!

I rolled up to Gia's townhouse with my aesthetician friend Andy, a bottle of rosé, and a pack of American Spirits. We caught up as Andy did Gia's makeup for an upcoming interview, and the two of them started grilling me about potential suitors.

"I mean, Amanda JUST moved her stuff out—she's been living at a friend's place for the past two months or so, but the divorce papers aren't even finalized yet—so basically, Andy *is* my love life," I said, rolling my eyes.

He looked up from Gia's brows and blew me a kiss.

"Gia, are you going to Alicia's *Park Avenue Blues* book signing party tonight?" Andy asked.

"Oh, yeah, I forgot about that! I'll probably swing by with Jocelyn," she said. Alicia and Jocelyn were cast members—slash—frenemies of hers.

Andy Bealls was THE go-to makeup artist of Manhattan's elite. He was also good friends with Alicia, who was hosting the event. Andy finished Jo's makeup and turned to me.

"You should totally come, Bex! I'm going too."

Gia and Andy always called me Bex. When you have a lengthy name, people give you eleventeen different nicknames. Professionally, I went by Rebecca while a lot of close friends called me Bec. My college friends all called me Becca. But I *am not* a Becky; it doesn't suit me. My mom told me that when I was little, I used to cry if anyone called me Becky. So, when a group of friends started calling me Bex in my twenties, I thought it was the most glamorous of my nicknames. "Bex… like sex with a 'B,'" I'd explain seductively to the baristas at Starbucks who could never seem to master the spelling. When I left my corporate job at Playboy and launched my own line, I decided to call it BEXnyc, as opposed to my super long and far-from-exotic sounding full name. Amanda thought Bex was the most trendy and pretentious of my nicknames and refused to call me that. So, naturally, post-divorce, I embraced it with a vengeance.

As we left Gia's place to head back downtown, Andy opened the door to my Uber.

"So… I didn't want to say this in front of G—" he began as I slid across the leather seat further into the car, "But I was out with her friend Melissa the other night and Mel kept asking if I knew any hot bi girls because she wants to have a 'lady experience.' I was like, 'HELLLLLLLO, I have THE hottest lesbian bestie.' She was practically drooling over your Instagram pics!"

"Wait, was that what the drunk dial I got was all about?" I asked.

He giggled with a guilty expression as he swiped to her Instagram page.

"She's this incredible marketing tycoon—you will love her!"

I grabbed his phone for a closer look. She wasn't necessarily my type, but I wasn't looking for anything serious. I was intrigued.

"She's kinda hot," I said as he nodded and zoomed in.

"She's coming tonight—I'll hook it up," Andy smiled devilishly.

I met up with Andy at his place a few hours later to go through our standard pre-event routine. He'd touch up my makeup, take an array of selfies, and have a glass of champagne before heading out.

"So, are you nervous?" Andy prodded.

"About what? Oh, your curious friend? Not really. I mean, in my experience, the bi-flexi girls tend to be really timid and meek. Excited to hang with you and G, though," I said, playing it cool while attempting to re-blot my lipstick. He swatted my hand away.

The minute we walked into the party, we instantly spotted Gia. She had that Scandinavian model look that was impossible to miss.

"Hello, my lovieeees," she purred as we air kissed and then headed over to coat check.

"Melisssaaaaa!" I heard Andy squeal behind me.

I turned around to see an older yet sprightly woman with raven-black hair, in a Jean Paul Gaultier leather mini skirt, wearing too much blush. As she moved closer, I noticed that one of her false eyelashes had come slightly unglued, giving her an endearing quality. There was something vulnerable and genuine about her.

"You must be Bex. Can I get you a drink?" she asked, and without waiting for a response, she grabbed my hand and led me to the bar. A blue martini, the signature drink of the evening's launch party, appeared almost instantly in front of her. She reached into a bowl of cobalt jelly beans next to the bartender and handed them to me.

"For you," she giggled.

Melissa reminded me of Marilyn Monroe, my first childhood crush. Her voluptuous curves and in-your-face sex appeal seemed juxtaposed with a kind of childlike innocence.

"Thank you... that's a first," I smiled and deposited the jelly beans into my patent leather clutch.

"What's a first?" she asked flirtatiously.

"Oh, the jellybeans... and the drink... you're quite the gentlewoman. That's usually my role. I'm impressed."

Melissa giggled again.

"This is really good. I wonder what makes it blue?" I asked, staring down into the glass.

"Maybe they put the jelly beans in it?" Melissa answered with wide eyes.

I later discovered this cocktail was made with butterfly pea flower leaves, a flower from East Asia also called clitoria ternatea for its resemblance to female genitalia. It is known magically for its transformative properties due to its color changing abilities when mixed with other liquids.

The irony of this being our first drink will never be lost on me.

Much to Gia's dismay, Melissa and I ended up deeply immersed in conversation while huddled in a corner, isolating ourselves from the rest of the party. Gia eventually broke through our private bubble when she rounded up Alicia and Andy and proposed that we all go downtown for drinks. The five of us squeezed into a booth for four, with Melissa conveniently positioning herself between me and Andy.

"So, would you only be with... um... women who are like... 100% gay?" Melissa whispered in my ear as she grabbed my thigh under the table.

"I mean, I was married to a woman… I'm really comfortable with my sexuality… so in terms of a relationship, I'd only date someone who was out."

"But if it wasn't like… a serious relationship? What then?"

As Gia's charcoal lined eyes narrowed in on me, I could feel Melissa's lips on my ear, distracting me. I felt incredibly drawn to Melissa, but I simultaneously had a sinking feeling from the look in Gia's eyes. Her gaze conveyed that going any further was a terrible idea.

"I have to go to the bathroom… too many blue martinis, I guess," Melissa said suddenly.

I stood up to make way for her when she grabbed my hand and said, "Don't YOU have to go too, Bex?"

"Uh, yeah, sure," I said, following her in a daze.

We entered the private bathroom and had barely closed the door when Melissa shoved me up against the wall and kissed me. Hard. I looked up, breathless and stunned. I was used to being the initiator in romantic pursuits.

"More," she begged softly in a breathy, seductive voice.

I eagerly complied, kissing her back even harder. It was a foreign but euphoric sensation, a combination of danger and undeniable magnetism that I had never felt before. From the moment Melissa had walked into the party, I'd been captivated and consumed by her. I had never kissed someone in a bathroom stall before, and now, here I was with her leather skirt twisted in my hands.

She squirmed in delight. The bathroom door opened. Apparently, we had forgotten to lock it. She quickly shoved it closed. Neither one of us wanted to stop. I was even more turned on by the fact that the intrusion didn't deter her.

Catching my breath, I realized we had been gone for an

inexplicable period of time. Reluctantly, I sighed, "We should probably go upstairs."

She gave me a pouty look and we quickly both adjusted our hair and makeup. I stole a side glance at her and quickly assessed my partner in crime—a sexy girly-girl who reapplied lipstick more incessantly than I did. *Is she even real?*

As we walked upstairs to our dinner table, Katy Perry's *Dark Horse* was playing in the background.

"I hate Katy Perry," she said, flippantly tossing her long, shiny black locks behind her shoulder.

"I love the lyrics to this song, though," I said coyly.

"Never really listened to the lyrics," she admitted.

"You should sometime," I added. *You have no idea what you're in for, you little temptress,* I thought.

We got back to our seats and Gia grabbed my hand, "Where WERE you? I need a cigarette."

It was never an invitation with Gia. It was more of a command, like taking a dog out for a walk, and for some reason I always obliged.

"I asked Andy where the hell you two were and he said, 'They're probably fucking in the bathroom.' Can you believe that? Such a gay boy answer!" She rolled her eyes and handed me an American Spirit.

I laughed nervously. "The line took forever and then Melissa lost her lip gloss."

"Whatever. Should we do karaoke after this?" Gia fancied herself a singer, and in addition to spontaneously crooning acappella happy birthday songs for anyone celebrating in the nearby vicinity, she loved to end a night of debauchery with a round of karaoke on Christopher Street.

I texted Andy under the table to say that his assessment of the long bathroom break was correct and asked a favor. Could he please take one for the team and take Gia to sing her heart out for her downtown karaoke fans, so I could sneak home with Melissa?

He looked up, both shocked and proud, and then mouthed "You owe me!"

The following morning at 7 a.m. Madonna's *Hung Up* blared ceremoniously on my iPhone to remind me that it was Thursday— ass and abs day—and I had exactly thirty minutes to get dressed, caffeinated, and transport myself to Barry's Bootcamp. My head was throbbing. There was the incredibly delicious scent of warm wood and vanilla on my pillow, and I realized that the most erotic dream of my life might actually have happened.

I looked at my phone and saw that in addition to missed calls, there were four texts from Andy, all peppered with countless dirty emojis and question marks.

A final text in all caps read:

SO... YOU... AND MELISSA??!!

Butterfly Peaflower Transformation-tini

For periods of deep transformation: *use with caution*

- **1 cup of water**
- **3 to 4 ice cubes**
- **2 ounces desired alcohol of choice**:
  Vodka or gin work nicely
  Non-alcoholic: use an additional 2 oz of tea
- **1.5 teaspoons dried butterfly pea flower tea**
  + *Medicinally: antidepressant, nootropic, relaxant*
  * *Magically: transformation*
- **1 teaspoon of wildflower honey**
  + *Medicinally: antiseptic, antibacterial*
  * *Magically: love, beauty, abundance*
- **1 lemon wedge / 1 ounce of fresh squeezed lemon juice**
  + *Medicinally: vitamin c, antibacterial, antioxidant*
  * *Magically: clarity, happiness, solar plexus boosting*

Boil 1 cup of water (208 degrees Fahrenheit on an electric kettle).

Add 1.5 teaspoons of dried butterfly pea flower. Steep for 5 min and strain.

Add 1 teaspoon of wildflower honey.

Refrigerate at least 30 min before use.

In a martini shaker, combine chilled butterfly pea flower tea, 3 to 4 ice cubes, and alcohol of choice (or 2 oz of additional tea for non-alcoholic).

Shake and serve with a lemon wedge or with a sidecar of fresh lemon juice to be combined before drinking (adjust the amount of lemon juice to taste).

CHAPTER III

THE TWO OF WANDS

THE *OTHER* ADELAIDE THOMSON LOVES SPA WATER

Two of Wands: Collaborations, Decisions, Crossroads

After my workout, I lit a cigarette and walked the five blocks back home. My doorman looked up as I stamped out the butt on the walkway.

"I mean, you put so much effort into the gym, Bex," he said in a big brother tone, shaking his head.

"Listen, I just got divorced... I'm gonna quit, I just need a minute," I said, exhaling wearily.

I was tossing my gym clothes into the hamper in my bedroom when I noticed a lock of hair sticking out from under a pillow. I laughed as I pulled out a long, black, clip-in extension. Melissa must have left it behind when she rushed to get home before her teenage daughter noticed she was missing.

After Googling her address, I wrapped the glossy strands in tissue paper and packed it up along with a pair of new black lace panties from my line and a note that said, "I'd love to take you, your weave, and these panties out for dinner if you're free tomorrow night. Xx—Bex."

As I was handing the package to a messenger, my phone rang. When I glanced over at it from across the room, I saw it was Adelaide Thomson calling. Not the famous child actress, but the fashion blogger of the same name. When we were married, Amanda always referred to her as "The Other Adelaide Thomson," which Addy hated. It annoyed Adelaide that she shared a name with someone *currently* more famous than herself, but it had actually also helped her and her business partner Erica break into the NYC fashion scene. They'd moved to the city straight out of college and launched a fashion blog at the height of the blogging buzz. Struggling to get into New York Fashion Week shows under their newly formed *Gallivanter Girls,* they started reaching out to designers as "Adelaide Thomson's assistant," and before they knew it, they were front row at Alexander Wang and being dressed by Marc Jacobs. Addy was about the same height and build as the actress so it worked long enough to get some fab shots, and soon *Gallivanter Girls* was one of the top fashion blogs, known for posting some of the best runway photos on the internet.

I first met Addy and Erica at a burlesque bootcamp class two years prior. The workout garnered a lot of buzz due to its super sexy ads showing toned women doing squats in heels to Christina Aguilera remixes on Instagram and on the TVs in the back of cabs. I arrived at my first burlesque bootcamp class to discover it looked more like a standard cardio class in a public dance studio. Erica, Adelaide, and I showed up in fishnets, sequins and feathers while the rest of the women sported Lululemon leggings and tanks. When I spotted two tall, gorgeous blondes covered in feathers and glitter, I scooted over next to them where at least my sparkly booty shorts made a little more sense.

"Hey. I love your outfits," I said with a conspiratorial grin. "Looks like we didn't understand the assignment here. Are you two models?"

The tall blondes giggled in unison and said, "Nooo, we're stylists and bloggers, *The Gallivanter Girls*!"

Erica and Adelaide could easily pass for sisters as they were both thin, nearly the same height, and shared that effortless downtown grunge chic look. Adelaide, the slightly shorter, darker blonde of the two, pointed to my water bottle filled with lemons, mint and cucumbers.

"Your water looks so fancy—like spa water."

"Oh, yeah. It makes the workout more tolerable and helps glamorize hangovers," I winked. "I really love your blog!" I exclaimed, while doing the best I could to adjust my sweaty sequined tank. "I actually pull a lot of inspiration images from it for work! I'm Bex—I'm the Creative Director and VP of Design for Playboy. We should talk," I added before we were shushed loudly by the instructor.

When we left the class fifty minutes later, I handed them my business card. I was always looking for new stylists, and we arranged to meet up the following Tuesday. I hired them for a shoot and we quickly became friends. They later confided that they initially thought I was asking them to pose for Playboy since the famous lifestyle and entertainment magazine is known more for nude pictorials than for articles. My role though, was overseeing design and development of all branded products— basically anything with the little rabbit head logo on it. Much to their relief, I had only wanted their help in styling a fashion shoot for our Asian market, which required no nudity.

Before being promoted to Creative Director, I was initially hired as Lingerie Director: the ultimate dream job for someone who not only loved fashion and beautiful women, but was also the daughter of a former Playboy Bunny. During my initial interview, I used the surprising anecdote that I grew up with the brand's logoed product before the licensing department even existed. My mom was thrilled to visit my office and have access to photos of her and her old friends from the 70's, stored in the Playboy archives. My dad wore head-to-toe Playboy swag, from rabbit head logo golf clubs to swim trunks. They loved bragging about what a cool job I had. My friends clamored to be invited to fashion week parties and star-studded Playboy events. The doormen in my building were extra nice, being the recipients of gifts of Playboy Zippo lighters and boxers. Everyone started to introduce me as "Bex, the Creative Director of Playboy." My identity became just as tied to the rabbit head logo I covered myself in, as to being a New Yorker. The job made me cool and kept me worthy. As a result of that, I vowed to do everything I could to keep it. I worked nights and weekends and slept with my work phone under my pillow. Emails from Asian and Australian partners were answered at all hours of the night, much to Amanda's dismay. In the heart of the recession when they closed the New York office, I moved my entire life to Chicago for six months to build a new department there with only half the budget and headcount of the New York team. Erica and Adelaide ended up styling several shoots at Playboy and were my only friends that got a peek inside my world. It *was* glamorous having a corner office that overlooked 5th Avenue, but it felt more like a luxury branding agency and less like the Playboy Mansion after dark, despite most people's expectations. Erica and Adelaide were still undeniably impressed the first time I walked them down the Warhol-lined hallways, asking if I reported to "Uncle Hef."

Typically, I did not report to Hugh Hefner, though I did have to get his approval on some high level bunny costume-related projects. Instead, I reported to a young Midwestern dude named Mark. I was in a meeting with the CEO one day regarding my promotion to VP when he informed me that I would now be reporting to a new boss. Mark walked in as if on cue, looking barely twenty five and straight out of a fraternity. *This is my new boss? Oh Holy Madonna, no.* We ended up bonding over the fact that age and appearances can be deceiving. Mark achieved impressive success in the tech industry right after college. He was a Virgo and consequently, incredibly ambitious and entrepreneurial. He was also as chivalrous as I was. We fought over opening doors for the models and playmates coming in and out of the office as well as for each other. Mark turned out to be the kindest and most dynamic boss I had at Playboy—and he was a good friend. He was also the one who had to solemnly break the news to me, two months before Amanda asked for a divorce, that Playboy was doing away with remote work from New York and Chicago. As a result my options were to move to Los Angeles to stay with the company or be let go.

"As in, immediately?" I asked, knowing the answer, trying not to let my voice break.

After all the late nights, moving my entire life to Chicago and back, having to let go of good people: kids I hired and trained out of college—and prioritizing the "Creative Director of Playboy" identity over everything—including my marriage—this seemed impossible.

"Unfortunately, yes… assuming you are unable to move to L.A.," he answered.

This would be the first of many ego deaths; a mere appetizer to my Saturn Return. I hung up the phone, looked in the fridge, and saw a pitcher of spa water and two bottles of Sancerre. I chose the Sancerre. Pouring myself a half bottle into the largest wine glass I could find, I began packing the equipment and supplies that needed to be returned to Playboy. Then I piled up all of the rabbit head logo items from my closet, down to the very last bunny bra, and marched them down the hallway to the trash shoot. When some people are hurt they hold onto things for a really long time. On the other end of the spectrum, when an unhealed Sagittarius is hurt, they will burn that shit or throw it down a garbage shoot. The only evidence allowed to remain of my career was a rabbit head shaped wine opener, my friendship with Mark, and the once Playboy consulting stylists, Erica and Adelaide.

I was still scrambling to grab my phone from the table on the third ring.

"Finally!" Addy sighed when I managed to answer. "Where *were* you last night? You missed a killer Oscars-themed party at the Hudson Hotel! You could've *totally* worn that sexy Marlene Dietrich ensemble. The one with—"

"The veiled hat and low cut satin tuxedo shirt!" I finished Adelaide's thought with sincere disappointment over missing an opportunity to sport a top hat on a weeknight.

"I'm so sorry, I completely forgot! I ended up at a book signing with Gia and Andy."

"How was that?"

"Interesting… I may or may not have hooked up with Gia's 'straight' friend."

"Oh my god, ERICA, come here!" Addy switched her phone to speaker mode so they both could hear the story.

"Yeah, that's not gonna be messy AT all," truth-bombed Erica after I'd recounted my exploits from the night before.

26

"It's gonna be FINE," Addy said reassuringly. "Just DON'T catch THE FEELS."

I knew that Adelaide and Erica probably weren't the best source of any kind of sound advice on relationship matters since they were several years younger and a hell of a lot crazier than I was. Yet their encouragement of my recent messiness was not only comforting, but convenient since all I was looking for was a green light.

"Anyway," Erica went on, always the more business-minded of the two, "We wanted to ask if we could pull some of the leather corsets from your line for a shoot on Thursday."

"Yeah, of course! I'll have apps and spa water waiting... pop by whenever."

I hung up the phone, grateful that the Gallivanter Girls didn't criticize my recent misadventures filled with blue martinis and rogue hair extensions. I mean, it was pretty convoluted. Melissa was almost two decades older than me, adamantly "straight," and Gia's best friend to boot. But I loved that Addy and Erica never judged me. After the hellacious couple of months I had been through, I wanted to hear from the easy judge on the panel. It was also immensely appreciated that they were giving me a pass to go to the next level, no matter how messy it might be.

Rejuvenating Spa Water

For after workouts or other calorie-burning misadventures.

- **6 cups still mineral water**
- 1/2 medium cucumber sliced
  + *Medicinally: aids hydration*
  * *Magically: enhances beauty and prolongs youth*

- **6 thin lemon slices**
  + *Medicinally: vitamin C, antibacterial, antioxidant*
  * *Magically: clarity, happiness, solar plexus boosting*

- **4 medium sprigs of mint**
  + *Medicinally: anti-inflammatory, antibacterial, aids digestion*
  * *Magically: healing, prosperity*

- **2 medium sprigs of rosemary**
  + *Medicinally: digestion aid*
  * *Magically: youthfulness, protection*

Combine all ingredients in a large pitcher and serve by the glass or pour into reusable water bottles on the go.

CHAPTER IV

THE FIVE OF PENTACLES
RED FLAGS AND TRUTH SERUM

Five of Pentacles: Adversity, Disgrace, Financial Struggle

The problem with my "bedroom noir" color palette for the season was that it was impossible to locate specific fabric swatches in the sea of black and dark burgundy. After impatiently *Where's Waldo-ing* through piles of satin and lace I finally located a small scarlet mesh swatch. I pinned it to the corresponding bra sample and began unpacking boxes of lace panties when my phone rang.

"Ok, so I'm officially embarrassed that you not only know I have a weave, but that you woke up to it in your bed," Melissa squealed with embarrassment.

"It takes a weave connoisseur to know one, sweetie," I laughed.

"Well, I guess that's the benefit of being with a woman," she added.

"Oh, there are many," I assured her.

"I'm beginning to realize that. I love my panties by the way... and yes to Friday night. I'm looking forward to it."

With those words, anxiety coursed through me—a perfect cocktail of nervousness and excitement. There was so much potential there between us, but I could also see a multitude of barriers firmly set in place. The situation felt taboo yet incredibly alluring at the same time.

I'd made a reservation at Bell Book & Candle in the West Village for Friday night. It was a quaint, farm-to-table restaurant with a secret, rosy-pink private room complete with 1960s, Pucci-esque printed wallpaper of naked ladies. As a result, the elusive Pink Room—or "Naked Lady Room" as those in the know referred to it—was nearly always booked. Thanks to my Playboy connections, I managed to snag it for my dinner with Melissa who showed up nearly an hour late. But once she arrived, we couldn't keep our eyes—or hands—off each other. She told me about her business and her two daughters, and how her dedication to work and family had prevented her from having a real relationship in years. I asked if she had ever been with a woman before, and she revealed that she'd hooked up with several women. Melissa explained that in the 90s, long before dating apps or even Craigslist existed, she would answer ads in the Village Voice for girl-on-girl encounters. But she had never fallen in love.

As I listened to her talk, I couldn't help but register that the torment and shame she felt around her attraction to women was completely foreign to me. Every relationship I'd ever been in had been completely transparent. I was beginning to truly recognize how grateful I was for the rights and respect that my generation was given. Until I met Melissa, I had been beautifully sheltered without ever realizing it.

"I don't know though... this feels... different. I can't stop thinking about you," Melissa admitted, a blush coloring her face. And immediately, I heard Addy's voice in my head... *Just DON'T catch THE FEELS!*

It was time to pull back before things spiraled out of control. I gently told her that I felt the same way but that I also knew myself; I couldn't date someone exclusively who wasn't out of the closet.

"I guess I shouldn't fall in love with you then," she said, batting her eyelashes at me flirtatiously.

"Probably not," I agreed, doing my best to stay firm but unable to hide my smile at her confession.

"Well... I guess I'll just stay in deep-like with you, then," she sighed.

The check came and I immediately grabbed it. Melissa made a weak attempt to reach into her purse and eventually fished out a credit card from the depths of her bag. I glanced over at it, stopping dead when I realized the name Mona Vargas was printed on it.

Was Mona her real first name? I wondered as I looked at the card more closely.

I pushed her card away with a smile and said, "No, I asked you. It's my treat."

The next morning I met up with Andy around the corner from his apartment, at the Starbucks on 23rd Street. I recounted the play-by-play of the night before as we waited for our coffees to shoot across the wooden counter.

"Andy, Bess..." the barista shouted out her list of completed orders.

I shook my head, annoyed, "Every time! It's not that hard... It's just sex with a B!"

Andy then launched into his complete review of my date without even taking a breath until he paused to sip his iced latte.

"Ok, for starters, there's NO way she's 'staying in deep-like' with you, Bex. You're a fucking lesbian unicorn. You're hot, immaculately dressed, have a sexy job, and spoil the women you love more than Christian Grey would. Hell, I'M more than 'in deep-like' with you. Also, who the fuck is Mona? That is NOT her first name. She's a public figure and highly Googleable."

"I don't know. She always pays for things in cash and that's the only card I've ever seen her use."

Andy briefly lost focus as he checked out a handsome, salt-and-pepper daddy type who was headed into the David Barton Gym: a luxury, boutique ninety percent male gym—aka a prime gay hook-up spot in the heart of Chelsea.

"He's not hot enough for you," I said flatly, as a way of strategically bringing Andy's focus back to me and my problems.

"Ha! You're right. Listen, I'm on the case. Since I'm doing her makeup this afternoon, I'll suggest we have lunch after AND make sure that we at least split the check."

After coffee, I headed back home and powered through three fit sessions in a row. When I finally finished, sweaty and starving, I reached for my phone to order an early dinner and I saw there were two missed calls from Andy plus a text that said:

"Call me asap re: Mona
Mattress Money."

"Andy!" I said the moment he picked up, "What happened???"

"So, I did her makeup at her apartment..." he paused dramatically.

32

"And??!" I demanded, accidentally dropping a handful of pins from my samples on the floor as I clutched the phone tighter in suspense.

"And afterward, she reached into her purse and pulled out some cash. But when she realized it wasn't enough, she excused herself. I pretended to compliment her bedroom rug so I could follow her and ask where she found it. Then, get this: she reached UNDER HER MATTRESS for a few more twenties! I didn't say anything about it but asked if she had time to do a late lunch, and we went to this place around the corner. I ordered some margaritas, aka truth serum, and then, she tried to pay with the fucking Mona credit card! So naturally, I fully called her out."

"No you didn't!" I gasped, both shocked and impressed by Andy's sleuthing skills, not to mention his unapologetic bluntness.

"I said, 'Who's Mona? Is that your alter ego or something?' She just looked at me all confused and said that she must have accidentally grabbed her mother's card by mistake. Honestly, a menopausal woman paying with wads of cash OR her mom's card is a hot mess either way. Bex, what the fuck?"

The closest thing to high crimes and misdemeanors I had experienced in a relationship up until this point were occasional PG-13 texts. Amanda wouldn't send any form of explicit messages due to her concern that "the U.S. Government has access to all phone records!"

"I think it's kinda sexy and mysterious," I smirked, equal parts intrigued and anxious.

"Said everyone who ever got murdered by the mob," finished Andy.

"I mean, it's not a reason to END things. Anyway, I'm supposed to go out with Melissa and Gia tonight. Wanna come?"

"Right... because the closeted 'straight' thing isn't reason enough. But, yeah, sure. I'll come. I obviously need to keep an eye on your whereabouts!"

Andy and I showed up at Up&Down, a club in the West Village, around 10:30 p.m. The dimly lit nightclub was a popular spot for aspiring DJs, D-list celebrities, and trust fund babies. When we arrived, we immediately spotted Gia frolicking between two male admirers in the center of the dance floor in a silk, cobalt-blue dress, just low cut enough to be simultaneously sexy AND tasteful. As soon as she caught sight of us, she waved giddily and directed us to a nearby table.

"Where's Mona Mattress-Money?" Andy whispered, excitedly looking around the room for the main character of tonight's drama to enter the scene.

"Shhh! Oh my God! That is NOT a thing. Do not make that a thing!" I scolded him, rolling my eyes in exasperation.

"Bex and Mona Mattress-Money, sittin' in a tree," he laughed obnoxiously.

I mustered all my willpower to fight the urge to either slap him or, more effectively, swipe his cocktail.

As if on cue, Melissa walked over from the bar with a giant margarita, lighting up the moment she saw us.

"Bex! Don't you LOVE Andy's work?" she gushed, tilting her face towards me to show off her makeup.

"I do… and it looks especially flawless on you, beautiful," I smiled.

Melissa was only on her second Patron margarita but already her hand was slowly slipping down my spine.

"I like the back of your dress," she giggled.

"You mean the lack thereof?" I asked, thanking myself for choosing the backless, black halter dress I was wearing that evening.

Andy sat down and might as well have grabbed a bucket of popcorn to munch on, given the amusement with which he was watching this scene play out.

"Well, haven't you two gotten CLOSE?" Gia observed with a hint of jealousy.

"I think I have a tiny girl crush on Bex," giggled Melissa, tracing little hearts on my back.

"Oh, is *that* what they're calling it?" asked Andy.

I shot him a dirty look as Gia complisulted Melissa's dress.

"Wow, your dress is…" Gia took a sip of her drink before continuing, "that's such a bright color for you."

"I like it," affirmed Andy. "It almost looks like it's made of… a bunch of red flags all sewn together," he said as he smiled diabolically at me.

Andy's Spicy Truth Serum
For when you need a little help in coercing confessions.

- **2 ounces Patron Silver tequila**
  (sub with Ritual Zero Proof Tequila for non-alcoholic)

- **1/2 ounce orange juice**
  + *Medicinally: vitamin C, antioxidants, potassium*
  * *Magically: clarity, divination*

- **1 ounce fresh lime juice and 1 wedge of lime**
  + *Medicinally: heart health, magnesium, potassium*
  * *Magically: cleansing, awakening, healing*

- **2 jalapeño coins**
  (slices of jalapeño pepper with the seeds removed)
  + *Medicinally: vitamin A, vitamin C, and antioxidants*
  * *Magically: removes negative energies and deception*

- **1/2 ounce agave syrup**
  + *Medicinally: antiseptic, anti-inflammatory*
  * *Magically: helps to release blocks, increases trust*

- **salt**
  + *Medicinally: anti-inflammatory*
  * *Magically: purification*

Rub the rim of a rocks glass with a lime wedge, dip in salt to coat, and set aside.

Add the jalapeño coins into a shaker and gently muddle.

Add remaining ingredients and ice and shake until well-chilled.

Strain into prepared glass over fresh ice.

Garnish with a sliced jalapeño coin.

PART TWO

THE MOON

The Moon: Revelations, Duality, Illusions

"But the stars that marked our starting fall away.
We must go deeper into greater pain,
for it is not permitted that we stay."

— Dante Alighieri, Inferno

CHAPTER V

THE THREE OF SWORDS
LOVE, LOSS, AND HEART-HEALING HOT CHOCOLATE

Three of Swords: Heartbreak, Loss, Grief

Friedrich Nietzsche (or was it Deepak Chopra?) once said, "What starts in chaos ends in chaos." There couldn't be a more perfect description of my relationship with Melissa.

It started as a perfect, sexy, post-divorce distraction but somehow turned into a full on—albeit closeted—relationship. Melissa's free spirit was a breath of fresh air and a beautiful escape from my divorce, my grief over Justin's death, and the upheaval of my career. It was the reckless, beautiful, and raw teenage love affair that I had never experienced. Our chemistry was addictive and it was impossible to refrain from physical contact: at the beach, in her Hamptons house, on the long car rides back to the city... even once in Gia's walk-in closet.

We would stay up all night talking and sharing stories. We'd lay in bed, our limbs hopelessly tangled, while she'd describe the apartment she wanted to build for us in West Chelsea and the exotic vacations we would take together. We became best friends and collaborators. I contributed to the growth of the creative side of her business and she advised me on the operations side of mine. But when it became undeniable that we had both unintentionally "caught feelings" as Addy would say, it got complicated.

I admitted to Addy, Erica, and Andy that my fling with Melissa had somehow become an actual relationship. I even introduced her as my girlfriend to my mom and sister. Melissa, on the other hand, would only kiss me behind closed doors. She would hold my hand, but only if we were below 23rd Street, where she was far less likely to run into her friends. Initially we always stayed the night at my place but when I was finally invited to hers, it was only when her daughter was with her dad. Her rules were always changing and impossible to keep up with. I was constantly left questioning, failing, and walking on eggshells in thick, platform Louboutins.

A few months after we started dating, Melissa decided that she wanted me to meet her younger daughter, Blaire. Her eldest was away at George Washington in her sophomore year of college. I was incredibly nervous about this scenario. One of the reasons my marriage ended was because I didn't want children. I also had never lied about being in a relationship with anyone. And as a Sagittarius, I have zero poker face. I finally agreed to come over to her place for dinner, but asked if I could bring Addy and Erica as my back up.

The girls met me at my apartment to prep. They loved a crazy themed mission and, after much discussion, we decided this dinner was *Basic-Instinct*-inspired since I needed to successfully pass the teenage equivalent of a lie detector test.

"You need a white dress," Addy noted.

"Yeah, innocent and chic," Erica agreed.

I walked out of my bedroom in a form-fitting white mock neck dress and heels.

"Like this?" I asked, reaching to pull up the center back zipper.

"Oh my God—the full Sharon Stone!" Erica gasped in appreciation.

"Yessss! I mean, do the full updo and everything. You should carry an ice pick and scarf! The kid is too young to get it, but it's funny as fuck for the rest of us!" Addy laughed.

I swapped the ice pick for two .5 mg pills of Xanax and headed uptown with my blonde squad in tow.

"Are you kidding me? What are you wearing?" Melissa exclaimed breathily as she opened the door.

"Well, it helped Sharon Stone's character pass a lie detector test when she was a hundred percent guilty so…"

I was aware that I was starting to mumble; the Xanax had just begun to kick in. I felt a little foggy as a result, so I couldn't tell if Melissa was turned on or angry, but it numbed me enough not to care either way.

"How am I supposed to keep my hands off you in that dress?" she whispered in my ear.

"Oh, you will…" I replied. "It's a thousand percent necessary, given the fact I'm meeting your daughter as your new *friend*." I pecked her on the cheek icily as her daughter Blaire walked out of her bedroom to greet us.

Blaire had long, thick hair like her mother, but light green eyes that I assumed were inherited from her dad's side of the family. She was very soft-spoken and far less intimidating than I had anticipated. I said hello nervously and quickly introduced

Erica and Adelaide in order to draw attention away from me and divert it to my cool, younger friends with the fashion blog.

As I hoped, they served as the perfect distraction for a teenage girl. Blaire had heard of their blog, and Erica and Addy happily regaled her with their own ridiculous high school stories. They even broke into a full cheerleading routine from their glory days while Melissa and I sipped champagne at the dining room table. Blaire didn't stay long before coolly peacing-out to meet up with some friends downtown, demonstrating that *Gossip Girl* was actually pretty factual: Manhattan high schoolers really did act more like twenty-somethings than teenagers.

Addy and Erica left shortly afterward, and Melissa immediately snuck up behind me, wrapping her arms around my waist as I cleared the table.

"Seems like the dress worked. Blaire loved all three of you, especially you."

I pulled back and turned to face her. "I mean, I'm glad, but I feel weird lying to someone that's such an important part of your life."

"It's not lying... we're just not... telling her everything yet."

My stomach sank with the concession of being someone's dirty little secret while my head raced through an onslaught of anxiety-ridden questions: *When will you stop feeling ashamed to admit you're dating me? A few more months? Years? Ever?*

Melissa grabbed my hand and pulled me into her bedroom. With one glance she took complete control of my heart. Her gaze held me with intense passion and connection, as if we were seeing each other for the first time and couldn't believe we had found one another. In the chakra system version of the rock, paper, scissors game, heart ALWAYS trumped third eye and solar plexus.

Another six months passed, and Melissa still hadn't told her teenage daughter anything more about us, let alone, the true nature of our relationship.

I began to feel increasingly uncomfortable around Blaire, who was sixteen and far from stupid. To make it worse, over the months I'd been with Melissa, Blaire and I had become close. Eventually she became suspicious of our Bert and Ernie "friend" sleepovers and went hunting in her mom's laptop for evidence, successfully uncovering the emails and messages Melissa and I had sent back and forth to one another. But when Blaire confronted her mom, Melissa remained stone-faced and in complete denial.

"Sometimes best friends kiss and say I love you," Melissa explained, as Blaire looked at her, incredulous. Blaire then angrily stomped into her room and slammed the door, clearly exasperated with her mom's weak attempt at a cover-up.

I mean, I never once kissed Andy on the lips… and I doubt her daughter bought this explanation either, but that didn't stop Melissa from continuing to hide behind her fabricated reality. It became obvious that the longer she defended her secret, the more jealous and possessive she became of me, my female-centric world as a lingerie designer, and my highly "out" nature. At one point, she even publicly picked a fight with one of my models in a Donald Trump-esque Twitter exchange.

But the irrational fights were always counterbalanced by the intensity of our connection. I woke up the following morning, a little nervous that I might somehow still be in trouble for Twitter-Gate. Not wanting to wake Melissa, I tiptoed to the kitchen to make coffee and breakfast before we both had to begin work. She soon came out of her bedroom enticed by the aromas and plopped down across from me on the breakfast bar stool. Sleepily, she re-tied the sash to a satin and lace purple robe I had designed especially for her to put in last season's line.

Our eyes met and she smiled sheepishly and said, "I just… I just love you so much."

I instantly melted and leaned across the marble sink to kiss her.

"Babe!!! You got my favorite almond milk! Zabar's was out! Where did you find it??" she stared at me excitedly and all my wariness temporarily subsided.

I wish I could bottle the way Melissa looked at me, like I was pure magic. She nicknamed me Tinkerbell because—aside from the obvious petite blonde physical similarities—she said I managed to create things effortlessly as if by sorcery. She oohed and ahhed over the simple breakfast of avocado toast and scrambled eggs I'd prepared for us.

"OH MY GOD, BABE! You need to open a restaurant!"

I sat down beside her, kissing her cheek softly before taking a sip of my latte. I loved our mornings. This was the place that we could just be, without the perceived threat of lingerie models or running into her Uptown friends who she had to hide me away from. I wanted to live with her in this morning place forever.

But outside of our private bubble, I struggled to navigate the rules. The constant need to tread lightly sent my recently diagnosed Generalized Anxiety Disorder into overdrive. I was consuming more Xanax than water and I'd experienced eleven panic attacks in the year and a half of dating Melissa—two of which I was hospitalized for. I knew this situation wasn't healthy for me, and probably equally unhealthy for Melissa, due to her visceral and deep-rooted shame around dating a woman. Yet every time I got close to leaving, the Universe—and Saturn-the-asshole—would rip another layer of security out from under me, pushing me to cling to any remaining familiar (even if unpredictable) areas of my life.

Over the next couple of months, there had been far less time spent in the morning place and a lot more time mourning the loss of anything resembling a real relationship. One chilly Monday, I woke up three times before my alarm went off. I L-O-V-E sleep, so the only culprit could have been extreme anxiety. I wasn't even sure why it was happening. Nothing dire or even out of the ordinary had occurred in months.

The previous night we'd gone out with my friend Chloe, an effortlessly suave tech entrepreneur. She also happened to be my only female friend that Melissa actually got along with because Chloe was just THAT cool. She was the only CEO I've ever met that rocked a Joan Jett haircut, forearm tattoos, and a leather jacket, and could get away with regularly inhaling a vape pen like a 1950s ad executive during board meetings. We'd briefly dated in our early twenties, a fact that enraged Melissa before they met, but Chloe's magnetic personality and charisma managed to cut through Melissa's jealous skepticism. Chloe was also a serial monogamist, which added another layer of assurance. I couldn't help but envy Chloe's current relationship. She and her new girlfriend had been dating less than two months and were already throwing around "we" more times than drunk white girls post #RoséAllDay for Memorial Day Weekend on Instagram.

I started to climb out of Melissa's California King bed, trying not to covet Chloe's relationship too much, when I realized Melissa was already awake and on a work call in the living room.

"FUCK! FUCK! FUCK! No!!" she yelled as she walked into her bedroom. She was staring at her relic of an iPhone 5 that she insisted on using with all of her Taurus stubbornness.

"What? What's wrong??" I said, rushing over to comfort her.

"They are going to print my real fucking age!" she explained, looking disheveled and distraught.

I blinked. I literally thought a relative had been hospitalized, when instead, accurate journalism was the cause of this outburst.

"That means they're printing it, right? The New York

Magazine feature? This is AWESOME!" I smiled excitedly, trying to get her to look on the bright side.

"I have to sit down. I would rather it not even go to print if this is the case," she shook her head solemnly.

I sat across from her, trying to wrap my head around what she was telling me. She was about to be featured in New York Magazine for the success of the business she single-handedly built as a female entrepreneur, but she was completely devastated that they would print her age as part of the story. Heaven forbid the media portrayed women over the age of forty in any kind of inspiring light.

Melissa attempted to decipher whether the age reveal meant this article would do more harm or good to her career, as all of her business accolades would now be inseparable from her factual biography. At the same time, I was perplexed by the two Melissas. There was the determined, beautiful entrepreneur who lit up the room with her contagious, bubbly, Betty Boop playfulness, as well as her captivating ability to remain alluringly present. But there was also the Melissa who was paralyzed with the all-consuming denial of the things that made her... well, her: her age, her height, her sexual orientation—and anything else she deemed as less than ideal to societal norms. But I also knew that I couldn't have one without the other.

"Why are you sitting there silently staring like that?" Melissa asked.

"It's just... Well, I think this article is amazing. I'm so proud of you. I don't really see a downside here. I guess it just makes me sad that you are so ashamed of your age," I explained, thinking back to the first time I'd discovered her secret.

I'd seen her driver's license on my nightstand and thought it was odd that the five year deduction was something she so adamantly upheld. Not wanting to start a fight, I never brought it up until I got the incredible opportunity to address it when the customs agent in Paris accidentally mixed up our passports on a vacation I'd booked for us.

"Babe!" I said dramatically, "I think the U.S. Government got your birthdate wrong!" I looked at her with wide eyes as I held out her passport.

"No! No! No!" she yelled, wanting to block out the undeniable reveal of her actual age.

"Don't get mad at me for this one. Nope! No way I can be blamed here. Plus, I already knew," I said as I kissed her on the forehead while en route to the airport bar. I ordered a glass of champagne for each of us to celebrate this new level of transparency, and to calm Melissa's nerves which had just officially aged five more years in the last five minutes.

Still clutching her phone and staring at the digital text of the article, she opened her mouth slowly to explain:

"Babe. It's the only thing I'm not honest about. Just let me have this one thing," she said exhaustedly.

"It's just the *one* thing?" I asked rhetorically.

"Obviously!" she confirmed.

The morning magazine drama had made me late to a meeting, but I kissed her on the head before speeding out the door. I knew I needed to end things when the familiar What-Ifs kicked in before I climbed into my Uber: *If this was her reaction to seeing her real age in print… what would her reaction be if people found out she was dating me? Would she need to sit down again? Would she feel sick with shame?* Before I allowed myself to face the obvious truth, my phone rang and snapped me back to the present.

It was Jean-Claude's assistant.

Her voice was shaky as she started to explain her reason for reaching out, "I just wanted to contact you before this hits Page Six tomorrow. Jean-Claude passed away last night."

"But he… he just called me yesterday! I couldn't talk for long because I was going into a meeting. But I just spoke to him. Yesterday," I said with a stubborn certainty, believing in some way that the conversation's existence was proof that he was still with us.

"I'm so sorry, Bex. I know he loved you very much. I'm emailing you all the details for the service now."

Jean-Claude was the adopted son of iconic Parisian performer, Josephine Baker. The original Chez Josephine was a chic bistro in Paris owned by his adopted mother. When Jean-Claude moved to NYC, he opened a French restaurant of the same name in midtown, where he'd fed me copious amounts of free foie gras and encouragement while I was a young, struggling designer in my early twenties. In return, I accompanied him to doctor's visits and made him custom leather kimono tops to greet his adoring fans at Chez Josephine. More recently, he'd gently encouraged me to start working on my lingerie line and he'd called me every day for a month after my divorce to ask "Mon chéri, how is your heart today?" He was the eccentric New York uncle I always wanted. We'd bonded over the fact that we were both extroverts who struggled with depression, and on that brisk winter night, his got the best of him.

My first call after receiving the news was to Amanda. She also loved him dearly and I wasn't sure if Jean-Claude's assistant knew we were divorced or would even think to call her. Amanda and I hadn't spoken in nearly a year and when she picked up, she sounded a bit confused, as if she'd been wondering if maybe it was a butt dial.

I was so relieved to hear her voice, but I couldn't speak. I just sobbed into the phone.

"B! Are you okay?"

"It's Jean-Claude... He... died by suicide last night."

"I'm coming over," she said and hung up the phone.

Amanda showed up looking solemn but perfectly put together in her wool pea coat, J Crew button-down, and blue jeans. As soon as I hugged her, I burst into tears all over again. We both did. For Jean-Claude, for the loss of us, and out of gratitude to see each other again. I missed my best friend over this past year. It felt so good to be in her presence, like I was safe again even if just for a short moment.

"He called me yesterday, Amanda. I should have kept talking. I rushed off the call to go into a fucking manufacturing meeting," I repeated in disbelief, feeling terrible that I hadn't spoken to him longer, and that I hadn't called back immediately after the meeting ended.

"We both know this is not your fault. He was struggling with this for a long time, maybe his whole life."

She put her arms around me in a comforting hug.

"Oh fuck!" I said, pulling back and wiping my face with my hands. "I got mascara all over your shirt. I'm so sorry."

Amanda looked down at her crisp white button-down, now smeared with YSL Black Fog.

"Yeah, my dry cleaning costs a lot less these days," she said with a smirk.

Amanda always had a knack for saying the right thing at the right time: the comforting thing, the inappropriately funny thing, the thing that would snap you out of the most intense pain, if only for a second. I missed that so much over the past year. After we rehashed all our favorite Jean-Claude stories, we decided to grab dinner around the corner and catch up. Apparently, Amanda had moved to the Upper West Side and, after a rocky few months post-

THE SATURN DIARIES

divorce, she landed a great new job, found a fabulous apartment, and met a woman that she'd started dating shortly after I'd met Melissa.

"I can't believe it's been a year since I've seen you."

"Um, I can," Amanda noted, clearly referring to my stubbornness, which is legendary.

"I think, I… I mean we, we both just needed some time to heal, but I'm so happy to see you. And I'm glad you're doing so well," I said sincerely.

"What about you?"

"I mean, I probably did exactly what you expected. I showed my line at fashion week. I partied in the Hamptons and on yachts with D-list celebrities. I hosted lots of dinner parties. I started dating Gia's 'straight' friend…" I said, realizing that the rebellious, glamorous "dream" life I thought I wanted so badly now felt more like I had just consumed a shitload of spiritually empty calories. My chest tightened with embarrassment.

"Well, *are* you happy?" Amanda asked, raising an eyebrow as if she already knew the answer.

"I was… at first. I felt like when you first go to college after living with strict parents; I could do anything I wanted. And for a while, that was really freeing. But now… I mean… I don't know. I know we did the right thing in getting divorced. But I don't know what my life is supposed to look like anymore, and I always knew what my life was supposed to look like," I admitted.

"That's where I was when I first moved out. I think you tried to dodge that part for a while, Bec, but that's where the healing happens. You're gonna be great, I just know it," Amanda said, smiling reassuringly.

From anyone else, this may have sounded trite. But Amanda said it with the enthusiasm of a proud mom coaching her eight-year-old to get back in the game after they dove for the ball, missed the goal, and skinned their knee. She was going to be an incredible mother, and I felt nothing but gratitude for the fact that I didn't take that chance away from her.

I excused myself to the bathroom and when I returned, Amanda had already paid the check and ordered my favorite dessert: white chocolate mousse. There was a single candle stuck in the center of the mousse and a cup of what looked like thick, decadent hot chocolate sat steaming alongside it.

"Happy belated birthday, B. Here's to a year of true healing," she smiled, adjusting her long dark hair behind her shoulders, her crystal blue eyes sparkling. "Make a wish," she grinned.

I took a sip of the hot chocolate and it tasted different than I expected, not quite as sweet with a little hint of spice.

"I love this! What is it?" I asked after the first swallow.

"It's called Mayan Spiced Cacao. It's like hot chocolate but with fewer calories… so I thought you'd like it," Amanda winked. "It's made from raw cacao beans and prepared without milk. I think the spice is cayenne. It's a heart-opener and healer. I just learned about it from my friend Kayla—she had it at some big healing retreat last fall. I hope it helps."

"Me too," I smiled weakly.

I blew out the candle and thought of how sorry I was for the shitty wife I turned out to be. Amanda was beautiful, intelligent, kind, generous, and above all that, she was always confidently herself. She was truly one of the best humans I had ever met and she deserved so much. I really hoped that she had found everything she wanted in her new relationship. As I took a sip of the spiced cacao, I thought of all the things I regretted. Like all the times she was tired from working for an abusive boss and wanted to go home from group dinners before midnight.

Instead of looking out for her, I insolently called her boring, threw my AMEX down, and ordered more drinks for the table so I could numb my worries—while being perceived as the fun ringleader of the group. I cringed when I remembered how, especially towards the end of our marriage, I gave far more attention and affection to Andy and Gia than to my own spouse. I thought of the times Amanda came home from work to find us tipsy in the living room, finishing off all our rosé, and smoking cigarettes while fully knowing how much Amanda disliked when we smoked indoors. I thought of how sorry I was for all of it, and how I wanted to disclose the million other things that I wished for her, but all I managed to say was:

"I'll see you at JC's service this weekend, right?"

As Amanda walked out of the restaurant that evening, I knew I had to change something... and that something was most likely my relationship with Melissa. But as I did a quick inventory of my life, she was all I seemed to have left.

- Hot shot corporate VP job: GONE
- Marriage: GONE
- Best friend and mentor: GONE
- Adopted New York uncle: GONE
- Financial savings: (almost) GONE
- Friends: (mostly) GONE due to my instability, flakiness, and avoidant behavior
- Relationship with Girlfriend: extremely unhealthy but still HERE

It was too much for me to face in real time. So the minute I got home that night, I poured myself a giant vodka martini to blur the reflection of my current situation for just a few ounces longer.

Heart-Healing Hot Chocolate (aka Cacao)

For heart-opening and healing.

- **Natural sweetener of your choice:**
  such as honey, agave syrup, cane sugar, etc.
  This is optional. It is not necessary to sweeten the cacao
  drink to benefit from the cacao, but most people will find
  the drink more enjoyable this way. Use to taste.

- **8 ounces of water**
  (or 4 ounces of water, 4 ounces non-dairy milk if you
  want it creamier)

- **2 ounces (about 6 tablespoons) cacao**
  (I recommend DrCacaos)
  *+ Medicinally: improves heart-health, antidepressant,
  lowers blood pressure*
  * Magically: heart-opening, heart-healing

- **Pinch of salt**
  + Medicinally: cleanses, antiseptic
  * Magically: protection/purification

- **Pinch of ground cayenne pepper**
  *+ Medicinally: improves heart-health and blood
  circulation*
  * Magically: speeds things up

- **1/2 teaspoon of cinnamon**
  + Medically: blood sugar stabilizer/digestion aid
  * Magically: increases intuition

- **1 tablespoon of rose petals**
  *+ Medicinally: polyphenols in rose petals reduce risk of
  heart disease*
  * Magically: increases openness to love

- **1 teaspoon of wildflower honey**
  + *Medicinally: antiseptic, antibacterial*
  * *Magically: love, beauty, abundance*

Boil the 8 ounces of water.

Add a pinch of salt to purify and protect. Salt, like sage, is one of the cornerstones of cooking and elixir-making for cleansing purposes.

Then add the cacao, stirring clockwise* until the mixture becomes a consistent, dark, chocolatey blend. Bring the temperature down to a medium setting.

Stir in the other herbs and honey/sweetener continuing in a clockwise motion.

Add non-dairy milk as desired.

Can be served right away as hot cacao or chilled/shaken over ice. I love this chilled in a martini glass, served with extra rose petals on top as a garnish.

It is beneficial to stir clockwise while focusing on the intentions of the ingredients and the elixir being created when you are manifesting something into your life. When releasing, the same focus and intention should be given while stirring counterclockwise.

CHAPTER VI

THE KING OF SWORDS
MESSAGES FROM THE RADIO GUIDES

King of Swords: Mental Clarity, Intellect, Truth

A few months passed after the funeral and I continued to avoid friends (and my own intuition) at all costs. Bills continued to pile up for my lingerie line while less and less money was coming in. My biggest role, even above chasing retailers for unpaid invoices, became projecting the perfect life while I Duct-taped together what was left of mine behind the scenes. After a manufacturing partnership went south, I charged nearly all business AND personal expenses onto an ever-expanding array of credit cards. Simultaneously, I plastered my social media with pictures of my line featured at Lady Gaga's *Art Pop* performance, as well as photos of Beyoncé's dancers and Paris Hilton wearing BEXnyc. Alone, behind closed doors, I ate sad cheap meals from neighborhood delis while I saved what little credit I had left to attempt to buy Melissa's love. She had been going through a particularly tough bankruptcy and jokingly referred to me as her "younger sugar momma." This only solidified my fear that I was only loveable when I was doing the giving.

The night before we were scheduled to leave for the Hamptons for the 4th of July weekend, Melissa closed a big deal. To celebrate, I messengered her a Zadig & Voltaire dress and a pair of heels she had been eyeing with a note that said, "Congratulations, my gorgeous rock star. Meet me at Lincoln at eight for dinner."

Despite my undeniable internal unrest, I was still trying to keep Melissa happy and hoped that in doing so, I would feel loved.

That night, Melissa showed up in the white, iridescent dress looking radiant. Her dark, gorgeous locks were perfectly blown out and her pouty, glossed lips curved in a sexy smile as soon as we made eye contact.

"Hey Babe!" she exclaimed breathily.

No matter how bad I knew this dynamic was for me, it never failed to take my breath away when she entered a room. I loved that feeling and I was scared that if I walked away from her—from this—that I'd never feel that kind of giddiness again.

I greeted her with a cautious and casual kiss on the cheek. We were uptown after all, and I knew how touchy she could be about overt, public displays of affection.

"Have you been here before?" I asked.

I had chosen the restaurant not only for its Michelin stars and gorgeous view, but because more than anything, Melissa loved a scene.

"No…" Melissa said, focused completely on her phone. "Ugh, Lisette is in St. Barths… I want to be in St. Barths! Like WHO is in the city this time of year?" she asked, annoyed and clearly dissatisfied with her current location.

I sighed as I took a sip of water from the full goblets on the table in front of us. I hoped the wine list would come soon. It seemed like the harder I tried to surprise her with fancy dresses and dinners, the more apparent it became that I couldn't compete with her friends, whose aging billionaire husbands were flying them around on private jets to much more exotic locations than 5 Star Manhattan restaurants. But before Melissa embarked on a full-on pity party, I attempted to change the subject.

"So, are you excited for Gia's party tomorrow?" I asked, hoping she'd take the bait.

"Yeah! Maybe I'll wear my new dress!" Melissa exclaimed, her mood brightening with thoughts of the upcoming Hampton's clambake.

I was less than excited about the event—not that she asked or even noticed. I gratefully reached for my glass of Chardonnay from the waiter as Melissa continued envy-diving back down the rabbit hole of Lisette's posh Instagram account. I perused the menu, silently dreading the weekend that lay before us. In the Hamptons, I became even more invisible than in Manhattan. At least Manhattan had pockets of safety we could exist in openly— mostly downtown—where we could hold hands in public, and share the company of my friends who knew the true nature of our relationship. But in the Hamptons, outside the safe walls of Melissa's house, we assumed a very strict platonic Bert and Ernie existence. I realized though, as challenges continued to mount in the relationship, that it may be my last clambake playing the role of Bert, so I might as well make the best of it.

Melissa and I arrived in the Hamptons the next day and headed to Le Biblioquet, a large French restaurant with table options both inside as well as on the gorgeous dock outside, overlooking the bay. We chose to sit inside the restaurant which was outfitted in white with cozy accents of natural wood. East Hampton was nothing if not the capital of luxurious minimalist interiors.

As we waited for Melissa's friends to join us, I silently asked the Universe for a sign. In response, my body acutely tuned in to the music playing from the restaurant's speakers. I focused on the Whitney Houston song in the background and cringed and thought of a harsh truth bomb Andy had recently thrown at me when I tried to elicit sympathy over one of the countless times I'd gotten in trouble for doing something wrong in my relationship.

"I'm gonna stop ya right there, my friend. Do you wanna be a Robyn or a Portia?"

"Who the hell is Robyn?" I asked.

"Exactly—almost NO ONE knows who Robyn is. There have been recent articles and I think a book about it. She was Whitney Houston's secret girlfriend who Whitney slept with, lived with, traveled with, employed, but always introduced as a friend... Oh wait, does this sound familiar? And on the other hand, there's Portia. And ya know what? No one asks who Portia is, and not just because of her acting career, but also because Ellen has basically created billboards of their love story for the world to see... Listen, I gotta run, but you're a Portia. Remember that."

I focused back into the song quietly playing over the restaurant's sound system.

"Is that Whitney?" I asked Melissa, looking up quizzically.

"Babe. She died. Like years ago," Melissa answered distractedly as she dug through her overflowing purse for her phone.

"No, I know. Not in the restaurant. I meant the song… Wasn't that… Anyway, did you know she had a girlfriend?"

"No. She was straight. There's no way," Melissa said matter-of-factly.

"Yeah. That's probably what she would have said, too…"

Ok, I hear you. Thank you. I'll keep listening. I acknowledged the Universe's messages for the first time in a very long while.

We were quickly joined by Melissa's friends, Frank and Al, an immaculately dressed couple who'd brought their friend, Ted, with them. I shook hands all around while I attempted to decipher the dynamic between the group. Initially, I'd thought that perhaps Frank and Al were in an open relationship that Ted was also a part of. Ted seemed much younger than his companions. He was Abercrombie handsome with sun-kissed blond hair and a surfers tan. Turns out, there was no clandestine threesome to speak of. Ted was merely renting their pool house as his bachelor pad for the summer.

As I moved cutlery around and shifted the calla lily centerpiece over to the side of the table to make the appropriate amount of space for the five of us, Frank asked how Melissa and I met.

"Melissa told us all about you!" he exclaimed. "She showed us what a little hottie you were. I follow you on Instagram now!"

Al giggled as he interjected, "Oh my God! Melllll! You were so lit at that dinner! But you did spill some good stories!"

This was undeniably a bit of progress, but still far from ideal. Melissa, once in a great while, told her gay male friends about me, but only after she'd had several cocktails.

"Oh, well, we met at a book signing party in the city," I smiled warmly, grateful for the acknowledgement.

"Aren't you two just the cuuuutest little lezzie couple," Al exclaimed with a whistle.

"I'm NOT a lesbian!" Melissa declared and quickly began talking about how she loved cute cowboys and made a show of checking out the ass of a male waiter. She quickly ordered a third bottle of Domaine Ott Rosé for her friends.

Just then, two women came by to say hello to Melissa. I watched in disbelief as she introduced Frank and Al by name but didn't bother to include me. When the waiter finally brought the check, Melissa dramatically rifled through her purse, coming up empty handed.

"Babe, I forgot my wallet," she whispered. "I wanted to get this one but can you pick it up?"

"Sure," I replied weakly, as I scrambled for the card that would hopefully cover the pricey Rosé-filled brunch for five.

I handed it over to the waiter. I was sure I heard the card scream, "Owwwwwwww," from halfway across the restaurant as it was swiped through the reader.

When we arrived at Gia's party twenty minutes later, Frank and Al began talking about how they didn't believe in hearts and flowers or other kinds of romantic bullshit, including monogamy.

"I do," Ted spoke up after being silent for most of brunch.

"Me too," I said, smiling softly at him.

"That's because you two are young," Melissa retorted, laughing and rolling her eyes.

I felt Ted's eyes on me as I looked down, pretending to inspect my manicure. His gaze was still focused on me when I tugged at the neckline of my silk top to hide the red, splotchy anxiety hives that were making their way north to my chin. I wanted to leave, as I had in so many similar scenarios with Melissa. She was still laughing loudly at her own response though, completely oblivious to my feelings. But I was sans-car in the middle of the Hamptons. I should have felt trapped but this time was different. This time someone else saw me. I mean, I had been seen before, usually by other homosexuals who were familiar with being jammed into closets themselves: there was Juan the doorman who always gave me a pitying nod, and Chuck, the videographer. Chuck and I met on set for a photoshoot I styled and art-directed for Melissa. I ended up having a horrible stomach flu that day but I still showed up, wanting to make sure everything went as planned for her and the shoot. Melissa swiftly tucked me away into her daughter's room before I could say a word and told the crew "her *friend* wasn't feeling well", while checking on me between takes.

Chuck popped his head in and said, "The outfits came out great, honey. Oh, and by the way, I know you're more than friends. It's ok, we've all been there."

At the time, not fully certain if the nausea was from his words or my stomach bug, I thought, *Is this really ok? Had we all been there?*

"Hey, Bex," Ted said nonchalantly, "Gia mentioned earlier that she needs more rosé and I offered to do a quick run. You wanna keep me company?"

"Yes!" I said, way too excitedly, standing up and grabbing my bag, then scampering towards the door without looking back.

As I fastened myself into Ted's Lexus, he adjusted his mirror and said, "Bex, I know it's none of my business, but I can tell that you're a good person…"

He turned to check his rear window and his deep blue eyes caught mine as he smiled gently.

"I see how well you treat her, the way you look at her, and how much you must care about her to not only sit through, but then pay for that fucking brunch. You deserve better. You deserve the real deal."

All at once, I broke. Maybe it was the fact that he'd seen through the act, or maybe it was just that he'd seen *me* when no one else had—not even Melissa. But when I heard his words, the tears began rolling down my cheeks and I was suddenly powerless to stop them.

"Ok, we're gonna go for a little drive," he said, putting the car into gear. "Fuck it... a long drive if that's what you need."

He reached into his middle console and pulled out a wad of tissues.

"I'm so sorry, I know we just met," I said, grabbing the tissues and wiping my nose.

"Nothing to apologize for. I've been there," he said reassuringly, patting my hand as we pulled out of the parking lot.

"Damn, I wish you were a lady," I laughed, using more tissues to blot my smeared eyeliner back into place as much as I possibly could.

"Hahaha, likewise, my dear—except I wish you were a ripped dude," he retorted.

"Ugh, the Universe is cruel," I concluded.

"Nah. The Universe knows what she's doing. This is all part of the ride."

He took his palm off the top of my hand to turn the volume up and announced, "We're gonna listen to some Britney Spears until you feel better. And if that's hours... well then, I guess every liquor store in the Hamptons was out of rosé!"

Thanks to our ride, I too was feeling *Stronger*, and right then and there I decided I was going to break up with Melissa the morning after the party. Apparently, Ted also dreaded these events and didn't know many people aside from Al and Frank, so we devised a survival plan. We did a quick check-in with Gia, took a stroll through the kitchen, then spent most of the time chatting in a dimly lit corner of the backyard.

I learned that Ted was a singer-songwriter, who was also studying biochemistry. He was trying to decide which of the two paths to pursue, or determine if he was capable of juggling both. He grew up on Long Island and had met Al and Frank through friends. They gave him a good deal on the pool house in exchange for some manual labor around the yard—and, undoubtedly, the free eye candy he provided when cleaning the pool shirtless. We discovered we both loved Madonna—all Madonna—but especially *Sex* book era Madonna. And both of us were seeking a monogamous, out and proud, over the top, "You're my person," rom-com kind of love.

After the fireworks over the water concluded, Melissa annoyedly walked over and asked, "Where were you all night?"

"Oh, just chatting with Ted. I didn't even realize how late it was!" I lied. "He offered to give us a ride back if you don't want to wait for Frank and Al."

Fortunately, she obliged.

When he dropped us off, Ted got out to say goodbye to both of us and gave me the warmest bear hug before whispering, "Good luck tomorrow, sweetheart. You got this. Stay in touch, ok?"

That night, I barely slept, thinking about how this was the last night I'd fall asleep in the same bed as Melissa, the last time I would wake up to her sweet, sleepy smile in the morning. It was likely the last time anyone would ever be insanely excited over my almond milk lattes. I couldn't help questioning, if I exited Melissa's life, would Blaire hate me? We'd become so close over the past year—like family. As I tossed and turned, I thought about all the times I'd made Blaire dinner, and how the two of us would settle in to watch movies on nights Melissa was working late. I loved how Blaire sent me funny memes when she was supposed to be studying for the SATs. I remembered the little Ziploc bags of snacks and the custom good luck pencils with her Instagram handle I packed for her to take to the exam. *Was I doing the right thing?* I had no idea. All I knew was that something needed to change.

After lying in bed for what seemed like hours, I finally got up at 7:45 and snuck downstairs to grab the necessities for a much needed escape to the local coffee shop. I opened my purse to deposit the house keys from the counter and saw that I had a few singles inside. Knowing I needed to end things with Melissa later, but still feeling immensely conflicted, I concocted an energetic "Insurance Spell" in case I was making the wrong choice. I grabbed a Sharpie marker out of the kitchen drawer and quickly drew a black outline of Tinkerbell on one of the dollar bills to symbolize the nickname that Melissa gave me. In place of her signature fairy dust, I drew an asymmetrical heart-shaped B being blown like a kiss. My signature was placed just under her right wing.

The air was unusually cool for summer but felt soothing in my lungs. I walked slowly and methodically to the small shop tucked in South Hampton between Bellacure Nails and the Doggie Day Spa. Usually packed with Hamptons moms rushing for their caffeine fix before their weekend workout, today the interior was eerily quiet aside from the humming sound of the espresso machine. Only one slender man in running gear and a baseball cap was in front of me in line. I actually wished I had more time before releasing my little fairy into the world. I knew the odds would be stacked in favor of finding it, as this was the coffee shop that Melissa—who always paid cash—frequented weekly. I was also not-so-secretly hoping to have Tink captured again. I ordered two iced coffees with almond milk, possibly the last I would ever buy for Melissa. As I handed over eight singles with my spell hidden in the middle of the pile, I gave the dollar its directive: *OK Tinkerbell, if you're circulated back into Captain Hook's hand, then our story isn't over. Otherwise, may you enjoy your journey. Do what you gotta do, girl.*

I snuck into the house and checked upstairs. Melissa was still sleeping and I gently placed her iced coffee on her nightstand. The gravity of ending the relationship began to kick in, and I lost my fight to hold back tears. Ducking into the bathroom, I caught a glimpse of myself in the mirror above the double sink and immediately began to cry, like UGLY cry. It was almost as if Ted's kindness and ability to truly see me after feeling invisible for so long, acted as an emotional laxative. And for the first time that I could remember in the past two years, I wasn't hungover. I was afraid of losing the clarity I gained through my connection with Ted on our ride, so I'd only had one cocktail at the party.

"Babe? Is everything ok?" Melissa asked timidly.

She'd undoubtedly heard me crying and knocked on the door to check on me.

"Uh… yeah, I'll be out in a minute," I said as I wiped my eyes, frantically digging through my makeup bag for eye drops to mitigate the redness.

I pulled my tear-soaked hair back into a messy French twist that I secured with an eyeliner pencil and headed back to the bedroom.

As I walked into the room, Melissa smiled at me and touched the pencil holding my locks in place. I moved my head to the side. The eyeliner was barely holding my hair together and just one little nudge would cause the entangled strands to collapse into a big mess.

"Oooh, Sexy Librarian vibes. I like," she said coquettishly.

I couldn't help but smile back.

Am I doing the right thing? I wondered again. *Maybe I need just one more sign.*

And then Melissa's phone pinged, and we both looked down at the screen.

OKC: Cute N Sexy - You have 3 Messages.

"Are you fucking kidding me? Still? You could at least hide the OkCupid notifications. It's just insulting at this point."

In spite of all my other issues, jealousy was never one. I'd never cheated nor been cheated on (that I know of), so I never felt the need to keep tabs on my partner. But in spite of that fact, the notifications had always irked me. It just seemed so insensitive.

"Babe!!" she exclaimed innocently, her eyes wide and guileless, "I told you, I haven't used it since we met! I don't even know how to deactivate it to turn off these annoying notifications."

Looking at her face, I actually believed her, but also believed this was the sign I was looking for. Yet somehow, I was still uncertain that I was making the right decision.

"So, let me get this straight," I began slowly, pinching the bridge of my nose trying to compose myself. "You get angry at me if my ex-wife texts to ask for our old chiropractor's info. You stopped talking to me for a whole evening when one of my models made a comment on a photo in my Tweet. But it's perfectly okay that you are still active on a dating app?"

I sunk down the wall I was leaning against, hugging my knees to my chest feeling heavier by the second.

"I'm so stupid. I cannot believe how dumb I am," I said quietly, more to myself than to Melissa.

My anxiety was back in full effect, and my chest felt tight—as if I were on the brink of an asthma attack. I closed my eyes and tried to take a deep breath in.

"I'll get rid of it! I'll delete it right now!" Melissa yelled as she started pulling up screens on her phone.

"No," I said slowly. "Don't bother."

"What?" Melissa asked, looking up, her face full of confusion.

"You know what. Please keep it. Please go out with whomever just messaged you. Since you feel the need to declare your heterosexuality daily, please go date lots of men—and women—and figure it out. I hope you find whatever you're looking for. I really do. Clearly it isn't me. I can't do this anymore."

"What… what? Is that why you were crying in the bathroom? No! No! I just want you! I'm deleting the app!!"

"I'm sorry. I love you so much. Honestly, I clearly love you more than I've loved myself this whole time. I just can't do this anymore. I know myself… or at least I used to… and I know that this…" I said, motioning back and forth between the two of us, "this isn't good for me, and I don't think it's good for you either. It's just constant shame and lying. Don't you want to be with someone you are proud to introduce to your friends? Someone you can brag about and show off? You deserve that too," I said, wiping my tears aside, feeling pain as my chest seized tighter.

"I AM proud of you. This isn't about you at all. It's about… that I was one way my whole life, and now I'm supposed to be this whole other way."

I grabbed her hand.

"I don't want you to be any way but yourself. And when it's just me and you, we feel real, but when we're in the world I feel your fear, your embarrassment and anxiety. It hurts me too. It shouldn't hurt like this. Have you ever dated someone who hid their relationship with you?"

"Yes! I have! When I was dating a married man. And I was okay with it! I understood!" She brightened, feeling confident that she had answered the riddle: I was the one who needed to be more understanding.

"Ok… and why did you understand and feel ok about being hidden?" I asked, already knowing the answer.

"Because he was cheating on his wife!" she answered.

"And that's something you felt morally was wrong?" I said, asking yet another rhetorical question.

"Well, yeah," Melissa admitted.

"Do you feel that being single and engaging in a consensual relationship with another single woman is also wrong?" I asked, genuinely wanting to hear her answer this time.

"Well… It's complicated. I'm just not used to this. And my *friends* aren't used to me like this. So I need to get comfortable and get them comfortable," Melissa responded, grappling for words.

"I'm sorry," I said quietly after a long pause. "We're just in really different places. It's not complicated for me. And it hurts me that you find shame in our relationship, and how much weight you give to your friends' opinions. Do you think there aren't friends of mine who think it's crazy I'm dating someone who is almost twenty years older than me and identifies as straight when my ex-wife and the majority of girlfriends before were all lesbians my age? But I don't care. Because I love YOU. And this is OUR relationship."

"Who has a problem with my age?" Melissa asked heatedly, crossing her arms tightly.

"That's not the… It doesn't matter. What matters is that this isn't working." I said.

"You're not perfect either! What about the drinking? And the blacking out and all the Xanax?" she shot back.

"I know. I don't want to hurt you either, and you're right, I'm obviously not okay. We're hurting each other too much trying to stay together. Sometimes, love just isn't enough to make it work."

I offered to take the Jitney back to the city, but she insisted on driving me home which was even more awkward because we had to pick Blaire up on the way. I didn't want Blaire to see my puffy eyes, but luckily it was sunny, so I was able to hide behind a pair of oversized Chanel shades. Melissa teared up on and off for at least two and a half hours of the three-hour trip, blaming pollen. When we arrived at Melissa and Blaire's condo, I started opening the car door with the intention of getting an Uber to head downtown, but before I could even get one foot onto the pavement, Melissa put her hand on my leg to stop me. She said she would drive me home. I popped out quickly to give Blaire a hug, fearing it might be our last.

She squeezed me way tighter than her usual cool girl hug and whispered, "You guys okay?"

"It's complicated," I said, patting Blaire's back and trying not to cry again.

"It always is," she said with a sarcastic smile. "See ya later."

I jumped back in the car and counted the blocks downtown until we arrived in Chelsea. The normally seamless ride down 7th Avenue moved at a glacial pace. I fidgeted in my seat and my chest contracted with every red light we hit. We finally pulled up to my building, but as soon as I started to unbuckle my seatbelt, Melissa held her hand up and made no attempt to unlock the doors.

As I opened my mouth to say goodbye, she hunched over the wheel and continued sobbing with muddy mascara tears running down her neck. I leaned over and embraced her as she shook in my arms, remembering all the times she'd also held me: when Jean-Claude died, when I was terrified of the outcome of losing money in my business, when she sang *Like A Prayer* off key to comfort me during my panic attacks.

Suddenly, she pulled back from me and said defiantly, "I know this is hard. I know. But you don't know what I'm capable of!"

She sat up straight with a sudden surge of confidence that our relationship wasn't really over.

It sounded almost ominous.

"Babe, I love you," I said, gently smoothing her tousled hair behind her back, "But you're right, I don't think YOU even know what you're capable and incapable of right now. I know you don't like therapy… but what about finding someone you feel comfortable enough to talk to about all of this with? I know it felt like a lot to me when I was just eighteen, and I had help from a big support system of LBGTQ friends. I can't imagine at—" I stopped myself. I knew without the words ever leaving my lips that the age card plus the sexuality card was too heavy a hand to deal right now.

"I don't know," I said, cutting myself off, "Talking about it can really help."

"Wait, I just..." Melissa looked up at me innocently, and seemed so lost. "I just can't imagine my life without you in it."

"I know," I said, one hand on the door handle, "me neither... and maybe one day we'll be friends, like me and Chloe. But I think we need some time."

I smiled weakly, trying my best to offer her some bit of comfort.

A surprisingly sharp tap from the passenger side window forced me to jump in my seat. I turned to see one of my overly perky neighbors standing on the other side of the glass.

"Bex! Happy 4th! I thought that was you!" She smiled, waiting for me to respond.

This is my moment, I thought.

I felt like a hostage who happened upon a third party. I wiped my face again, popped the lock and opened the door, but before I got out of the car, I turned to Melissa.

"I DO love you," I said softly, my voice breaking as I spoke, "so much. We both know this isn't working. But I also know you're going to be ok—you're so much stronger than you're feeling right now."

Before she could respond, I tugged my duffel bag out of the back seat and stepped out of the car, heading inside my building without looking back.

"Thank YOU!!" I said genuinely to Perky Neighbor.

Three weeks later, drenched in sweat from walking less than four blocks in the height of the August heat, I stopped for an iced coffee on the way home from a PR meeting. As I put my key in the door, I realized it was unlocked. Though my skirt was still sticking to my legs from the eighty-nine degree afternoon, I suddenly felt my temperature drop. I had a few interns working for me that were frequently coming and going from the apartment, but they were always good about locking up. I held my breath, opened the door hesitantly, and walked into the living room.

Suddenly, I heard Melissa's voice.

"Babe?" she called softly.

I walked down the hallway into my bedroom where she was sitting on my bed. Her hair was blown out with a full face of makeup as usual, wearing a black corset under a blazer with wax-coated black jeans. She looked like she had lost at least ten pounds on her already small frame since I had last seen her.

"Hello?" I said, trying to find my words.

"Hi, Babe!" she said looking up half-heartedly. "Do you like this top? I popped into this vintage shop in the East Village after I had brunch with a friend on Sunday and I saw this corset. I asked the sales girl, 'Does this look like something Madonna would wear? Because my girlfriend loves her, so that's what I'm trying to go for.'"

She stated this as if this was just a normal day rather than the first time we had seen each other in the past several weeks after our breakup.

"Wait, what? Melissa... you've lost weight. Are you ok? What... What are you DOING HERE?"

"Well," she said, taking a deep breath, "I've been going to therapy, and today I said, 'I need to see her. She is my person. I am going to marry her.' My therapist told me to give it some more time, but my legs just... well, they just took me right here."

She looked at me with her signature kryptonite combo of wide-eyed optimism and unwavering confidence that consistently disarmed me without fail.

"But... how did you get in?" *And why do I pay for a doorman building?*

"Oh, Ella... or Elsa, you know, the sweet French intern, she let me in. I told her I had something for you and I would just wait."

I missed her so much and just wanted to hold her and hear her say all the right things: the things that would mean we could be together, openly as equals. But those dreams were overpowered by my genuine concern.

"Uh.. Ok.. are you ok? Have you been eating?" I said as I slowly sat down on the bed next to her.

"No, not really. I mean, barely since you broke up with me anyway. I've been so sad. Everything reminds me of you. You know how you've always wanted a teacup Pomeranian? Well, I saw one on Park Avenue this weekend!"

I smiled and was about to say "Aww" when she excitedly continued the story.

"And I said to the owner, 'I will give you $1,000 cash right now for your dog! That is the exact dog my girlfriend has always wanted and it might help me get her back.'"

I stared at her, stunned. I was partially impressed at the lengths Melissa would go to for a grand gesture, but was also very disturbed for the dog's owner.

"What did the owner say?" I said, still in shock.

"Well, I didn't show up with a puppy, did I? No, she wasn't impressed. She scooped her dog up into her purse like I was a serial killer and crossed the street."

I couldn't help but laugh. She did the most bat-shit crazy things, but always with the best intentions.

"So, no teacup Pomeranian, but it's ok because we are going to be together regardless. We're going to Saint Tropez next week, and I'm going to marry you!"

Her face lit up with visions of us bikini clad, frolicking along the French Riviera.

My heart fluttered as I fought a smile. Of course, I wanted to live in that world. I wished more than anything for that reality to be possible. But I also knew that while Melissa was fiercely feeling these things in that exact moment, it wasn't sustainable once the reality of her Upper West Side life clicked in. So, I decided to do the hard thing, the thing that would burst this French coastal fantasy for both of us, and ask the realistic questions.

"How did this all come about? Let's go to the living room and talk for a minute, ok?" I said, trying to negotiate. "I mean, what's going on? Has therapy been helpful? Are you feeling that you are making steps towards a place where you can be open and honest about being in a relationship with a woman?"

"I mean... eventually... maybe... I don't know... I think it will just happen," she smiled, trying to reassure both of us. "Anyway, we have to go! I had my travel agent get us tickets."

"Ok, well, it sounds like not a whole lot has changed. I'm sorry, but you'll need to call her and cancel," I stated firmly. "This can't... this ISN'T going to happen."

I knew this would be her answer, but there was still that small piece inside of me that was hoping the dream was possible. I pictured my mom's facial expression every time her lottery ticket revealed she had not, in fact, won the mega-millions jackpot.

"Just think about it. You don't have to decide right now. Just don't say no yet," Melissa negotiated, as she moved closer, reached out, and clung to me.

As I embraced her, it was clear neither one of us wanted to let go. I loved the way that we were almost the same height and how perfectly she fit into my arms. Deeply inhaling her perfume, I thought back to the first time I smelled it on my pillowcase. I had asked her the name: Passage d'Enfer, which is the French term for "highway to hell." That fact had never been revealed to Andy, knowing it lent too easily to a punchline. And with that realization, I snapped back to the present moment, remembering that Andy and Chloe were coming over for dinner in less than an hour.

"Ok... I'll think about it," I said, stepping back and grabbing her hands. "Are you ok to get home? Do you want me to call you an Uber?"

"I'm so much better now, just seeing you. So, we'll start planning the trip tomorrow then?" she asked rhetorically, still confident that we were back together and going to France.

"I will speak to you tomorrow. Please let me know you got home ok," I said as I walked her to the front door.

I closed the door slowly, looked at my phone and sighed heavily, realizing rent was due tomorrow. *FUCK.* I quickly checked my bank balance and saw that it had now officially dipped from five digits to four, the lowest since I was straight out of college. The bleak total at the bottom of my screen also reminded me I had enough for maybe two months rent left. I needed a new source of income... like yesterday. But since Chloe and Andy were already likely en route, I decided to pour myself a giant glass of wine and obsess over plating appetizers from Trader Joe's instead. I was really good at making cheap shit look expensive. This one talent alone left many people oblivious to just how poor I was becoming.

"Wait, back up a second. She BROKE IN?" Andy nearly did a champagne spit-take onto the elaborate cheese plate and charcuterie board.

He dramatically dabbed his mouth and his fitted Tom Ford button-down with his napkin.

"In fairness, my doorman let her up and my intern let her in…" I explained with a shrug, as though it was no big deal, even though it had been one of the most confusing and emotionally taxing afternoons in recent history.

"But also, when did she leave and how did you do all this?" Andy motioned to the full spread of appetizers, champagne flutes and crystal candle sticks on the table.

"Oh, that's how Bex processes anxiety: cleaning and prepping," Chloe answered on my behalf. "I used to call her Monica Gellar from *Friends* when we dated years ago."

Chloe then added, "Call me a hopeless romantic, but two things are problematic here: one, a proposal should involve a *question,* not a statement, as in 'Will you marry me?' versus 'I'm going to marry you.' And second, it should never involve breaking and entering. Even if you wanted to say yes, this one calls for a do-over."

"No, no do-over," I said, exasperated. I raised my champagne flute, which Andy took as a cue to refill my glass.

"I love her, I do. But nothing has changed. Knowing her, she'd give me a ring only intended to be worn around the house," I said, intending to make Andy and Chloe laugh, but instantly felt pangs of sadness from the truth behind that statement.

"You're not somebody's maybe. You're someone's absofuckinglutely. This hasn't been good for you, boo. You know that." Andy lovingly put a hand on my shoulder.

"I mean, we both weren't good for each other. She wasn't always great to me, but she's right in that I did drink a lot. I did black out. So there's blame to share." I admitted.

"Like that time she said you were flirting with Gia? Didn't

she refuse to let you in when you both got home to her place, so you had to sleep in the hall of her building?" Andy reminded me.

"Yeah. That was bad, guys... really, really bad. Maybe I deserved that. I couldn't defend myself because I honestly don't remember what happened. I often felt the anger, the silent treatments, and the punishments were all warranted because of what a mess I was." I could feel the cycle of addiction and codependency actually start to unravel as I admitted that out loud.

"You think you *deserved* to sleep in a hallway?" Chloe asked, concerned. "Where was I?"

"I don't know guys. I barely knew where *I* was." I said, putting my head in my hands.

"For the record, I've observed you drunk more times than anyone, and from what I've seen, you mostly just like to eat an excessive amount of carbs and dance... and sometimes buy plane tickets." Andy noted.

I smiled at his attempt to comfort me. "At the end of the day, we were both hurting each other. So I think ending it was the kindest thing I could do. But I don't know..." I said, second guessing myself. Andy, noting my hesitation, sat up straighter as he prepared to serve a big dose of tough love.

"It feels like you stayed as long as you did because you don't fully love yourself right now. So I'm going to ask you: what do you love more than you? With all your heart and soul?"

I sat there, racking my brain for the right answer. "My lingerie line?" I answered like I was guessing at a math problem. I thought that answer would satisfy my two most successful entrepreneur friends.

"Ok, I get that..." He said patiently, "but let's go a little deeper here... WHO or what person do you love like that?"

"Sabrina." I said immediately, feeling my heart expand as I

pictured by my eight year old niece.

"Right." I saw the wheels turning behind Andy's crystal blue eyes. "Disclaimer: I'm going to give you a dark hypothetical scenario but I think you need it."

"Ok..." I said both hesitant and morbidly curious.

"Bam. Your sister and brother-in-law have just died in a car crash. You are now Sabrina's caregiver. It's your job to show her what being a strong, loving, powerful woman in this world looks like. So I ask you, Bex, is your relationship with Melissa what you'd want Sabrina to believe a partnership should be? Would you want to show her that it's ok to not be valued, not to have space made for you? Would you want to teach, 'Hey Sabrina, this is acceptable and you'll probably grow up to find a relationship just like it because this is what you've been shown repeatedly by my example?'"

"Oh my God. NO!" I blurted out, immediately horrified. I felt the oh-so-familiar anxiety hives moving up my chest to my neck as I held back tears at the thought of my favorite little human ever being treated the way I treated myself by remaining in this relationship.

"I know... so maybe... try to start loving yourself the way you love your niece. I love *you* like that.

"I love you like that, too." Chloe added.

"Right. So, what's the plan moving forward?" Andy asked as he reached for the brie.

He always needed a strategy for success, which is how he'd built his multi-million dollar business by his mid-twenties.

"I guess tomorrow, I'll call and tell Melissa I'm not going to France. I think that's really all I can do, right?" I asked as I reached for the champagne bottle yet again. I was not yet ready to quit my favorite numbing elixir. Despite the undeniable damage it did to my romantic relationships, it also helped me to anesthetize the pain of knowing that no matter how much we loved each other, Melissa and I were not meant to be together.

"Maybe I should get a Pomeranian," I pondered. I recounted the Park Ave Pom story to switch the conversation to a lighter note after the sweet relief of the champagne began to hit.

"Definitely!! Dogs are the best," Chloe encouraged.

"That is probably a terrible idea with all that you're dealing with right now, but still, better than getting back with Melissa!" Andy noted.

"Cheers to Bex getting a Pomeranian! And maybe a Nest Cam?" Chloe added, thoughtfully.

"And some sage," Andy chimed in as he raised his glass warily.

Radio Guides/Alexa Divination Spell

For those leaning towards clairaudience
(hearing audible messages, signs and synchronicities).

1. When in a public place with music playing, simply ask your Higher Self/the Universe/your Spirit Guides: "Play a song to help provide clarity around this issue." (like I did in the restaurant)

2. When driving or working with a radio, ask the same question and turn on a random station.

3. With Alexa/Siri just ask: "Play me a song to provide clarity around X issue."

CHAPTER VII

THE FIVE OF SWORDS
UNDER COVER CRYSTALS

Five of Swords: Conflict, Loss, Settling

Ipeeled back my black satin eye mask the following morning to silence my 8:30 alarm and noticed two missed texts from Melissa. Before responding, I decided a quick hit of caffeine would be necessary. I downed a shot of espresso and opened the dishwasher to deposit my empty coffee cup but was presented instead with the self-inflicted game of dishwasher Jenga. I was doing my best to shuffle last night's champagne flutes around in order to fit the dirty demitasse into the tray when my buzzer sounded. My heart leapt into my throat with the assumption that it was Melissa, impatiently seeking an answer from yesterday.

Luckily, it was Chloe chipperly singing, "Starbucks Delivery!"

She was on the way to a meeting around the corner, and thoughtfully brought me an iced almond milk latte to ease the pain (and champagne headache) from yesterday. As I hugged her, my phone rang; I took a deep breath, again assuming it was Melissa. The screen informed me that it was actually Pierre Poiret, the owner and namesake of a lingerie wholesaler I had been in talks with to replace my previous manufacturer. I jammed the door closed and answered the phone hurriedly.

"Hello!"

"Hey, Bex, good news! I think we have a way we can work together. I'll need you to iron out the details with my second in command, Foxy, but can you swing by Thursday around ten?"

"Absolutely! Thanks, Pierre! See you then." *Did he just call me Foxy? Or is his "second in command" named Foxy?*

I really didn't care which it turned out to be; either way it was good news. I smiled as I hung up, pressing the phone gratefully against my chest. Money had been really tight in general since the deal with my previous manufacturer fell apart, and also because of everything I had foolishly paid for in my endeavor to buy Melissa's love. All of my credit cards had been maxed out except one, so a potential agreement with Pierre was the first hint of anything resembling financial progress in a long time. Before I could explain the good news to Chloe, my phone buzzed in my hand—this time it *was* Melissa. Fueled with renewed optimism around Thursday's upcoming meeting, I answered confidently.

"Good morning."

"Morning Babe! Excited for France?" she asked eagerly.

"Yeah, I wanted to talk about that. Listen, it was so good to see you last night. It was. And I'm glad we spoke, but I think we both know Saint Tropez isn't a good idea. I don't think that anything has really changed, and I still feel we did the right thing in breaking up..." I paused, trying to find the right words that were both kind and firm.

Melissa did not like to be told no. I loved that about her, until I didn't. At this point, I had run out of words—even for me. Melissa began to sob.

"I was looking at rings for you today," she said through audible tears.

"One sec," I mouthed apologetically to Chloe.

"The thing is…" I started.

"The thing is we love each other!" she stated emphatically.

"The thing is…" I paused, pinching the bridge of my nose as I tip-toed into the other room not wanting Chloe to hear the next part of the conversation.

Apparently I wasn't as stealthy as I'd hoped because Chloe, visibly confused, looked up from the screen of her phone while Melissa yelled loudly through the receiver, "It's not that you're in the way!"

There was a long pause followed by, "Oh… So I guess that's that. You've already decided," Melissa stated defensively.

I felt a stab of guilt in my stomach. As a Sagittarius-Aries rising, I'm incredibly decisive and I process quickly. And once I've hit a pain threshold, I can't go backward. Thinking back to being called "icy" by Lindsay, Amanda, and even Chloe at points in the past, I took a deep breath and tried to soften.

"I'm sorry, I just… Things have become clearer over the past few weeks. Like I said, *I Will Always Love You*, and all I want is for you to be happy; I don't think you were happy in this either. But I think it's really good you are going to therapy. I hope you keep going because sometimes I worry…"

"No need to worry about me," Melissa interrupted.

Before I could respond she fired out, "Good luck with your life and all your dreams," and then the phone clicked.

Her adolescent habit of hanging up the phone anytime she heard something she didn't like was something that had infuriated me throughout our relationship. I often wondered if she did that to business associates—it wouldn't surprise me if she did.

Chloe stared at me with disbelief.

"Um, hold up. Did you... just plagiarize Whitney Houston... in your breakup speech?" She asked, fully calling me out for my unoriginal concluding thoughts.

"Ok, for starters, we already broke up. Many, many times. I just... I have had this conversation repeatedly. I'm on like three hours of sleep. I don't know. I feel like my own words weren't landing at all."

"And she didn't NOTICE that?" Chloe shook her head. She gave me a quick hug and took a step towards the door. "Ok, I'm gonna head out. I know you have a million things to do, love you!"

She turned around before closing it and said, "Oh and... don't worry. It's not right, but it's ok."

"I love you so much," I smiled.

I tried to hold on to the warmth that Chloe's coffee and morning drop-in brought, but I was still clutching the phone against me. There was a dull pain in my chest, like a wound that had begun to heal but was unexpectedly struck in the exact spot where the initial trauma had occurred. I knew it was over. All the signs were there: the freedom I felt in my decision, Pierre's offer arriving immediately after the break up, and now being hung up on. I knew I was doing the right thing, but part of me had hoped that maybe she would come to terms with who she really was and what she really wanted. And if that happened, we'd magically come back together in rom-com style. For now, I had to employ my Elsa Ice Queen secret weapon and at least pretend to *Let It Go* while I prepped for my meeting with Pierre.

In addition to pulling line sheets and wholesale totals for my best-selling lingerie pieces, Lindsay recommended that I wear some citrine crystals to the meeting to manifest abundance. I had no idea how this worked, but I was pretty desperate for anything that might attract money so I purchased a tiny citrine crystal for $3.99 at a metaphysical shop five blocks south of me. Then I looked for my most padded bra. I grabbed my sewing scissors and hacked a big slit into the foam cup and jammed the citrine crystal into the padding with all of my maniforcing abilities.

Two days later, I arrived for my appointment at the thirty-eight story office building in the heart of the garment district in midtown Manhattan.

"Here's the woman of the hour!" Pierre declared as I walked into his office at 10 a.m. on the dot. His light blue eyes glistened as he smoothed his white mustache with his thumb and index fingers.

I adjusted my black leather pencil skirt before extending my right hand.

"So good to see you again, Pierre."

"What do you think of the new showroom area?" he asked proudly. Pierre gestured for me to take a seat in the chair facing his extravagant cherry wood desk which was piled high with papers, at least twelve framed photos of children and grandchildren, and various hardcover Hebrew books.

"The showroom looks great! The lighting fixtures are striking. I'd love to also see the design area while I'm here," I said. Throughout my years in the industry, I learned to always ask to see where the designers work, as the spaces were normally more depressing than the basement of a dollar store, and definitely not conducive to being productive or creative.

"Yes, yes, we'll get to all that, but I want you to meet with Foxy first to work out the agreement."

Ok, there IS someone named Foxy. He didn't inappropriately call me that. Good.

A middle-aged woman with many apparent facial surgeries and overly processed platinum-on-the-road-to-being-white hair, walked in as if on cue.

"You must be Bex. I'm Foxy," she said sharply, adjusting her glasses.

I reached out to shake her hand, but she sat instead with pursed lips and a severe expression.

"You will be my special projects director. We'll be able to help you out with manufacturing in exchange for your services on some of our existing lines and your retail connections. I heard you sell your line to Bloomingdales and Bendel's."

"Yes, I'm in my second season with Henri Bendel, but…"

"Good. Let's have you start Monday then. Our hours are nine to five," she interrupted, and dramatically stood up as if to punctuate the end of our exchange.

"Um ok, I still will need time to meet with my retailers and work with press appointments, but I'm sure we can work the hours and schedule out. Would I be able to see the design area before I leave?"

Foxy turned around sharply, seemingly annoyed by my request, but motioned for me to follow her. I thanked Pierre and walked hurriedly to keep up.

"You want to see design, here is design," she motioned somberly across a stark, dimly lit sea of gray cubicles and stained commercial carpeting. There was no apparent air circulation, let alone windows.

"So, would I… be working from here when I'm in?" I asked hesitantly, fearing the answer.

"Yes. I'll put you right near my office. Come," she confirmed as she wiped her Chanel glasses with the edge of a Celine scarf. I knew the designers of each piece because nearly every item she was wearing was very loudly logoed.

Foxy pointed to a bleak empty cubicle and said, "For you," and then waved me into her office.

By contrast, the office was large and bright with a window overlooking 38th Street. In place of artwork or framed photos were multiple stacks of papers, technical packs for garments, and piles of sad, cheap samples. The only personal item in the entire space was a Swarovski-crystal-adorned whip.

I pointed to it and smiled.

"Great accessory," I complimented.

Foxy almost cracked a smile and said, "It was a birthday gift."

She picked it up and cracked it on the desk and continued, "Because I'm the boss."

"Indeed," I said cautiously, unable to tell if she was joking.

She slid a one-page outline across the desk to me. The offer was a salary of less than half of what I made at Playboy with the addition of the ability to utilize their manufacturing capabilities at a slight discount in exchange for aiding with the company's existing lines as a fashion director. I knew it was a terrible deal, but it was the only offer that had been on the table in nearly a year. And because I had not been a salaried employee for some time, and had only sporadic tiny bits of earnings trickle in from my line, unemployment wasn't even a potential income source. It was literally *this* or nothing.

As I walked out of Foxy's office and down the gloomy hallway hidden away from the front showroom, I looked up at a creased Xeroxed photo masquerading as art. It was a black and white image of Marilyn Monroe leaning forward over a balcony, looking down at Fifth Avenue. I thought back to the iconic Marilyn

Monroe cover of Playboy and the *actual* Warhols and Vargas that decorated the hallway leading into my former corner office that overlooked Fifth Avenue between 57th and 56th Streets. Of course, that was before everything in my life fell apart.

I chastised myself for taking those hallways for granted and simultaneously felt a stab of guilt in my chest. I knew I should be grateful for this offer, maybe this was what I deserved after the mess I had made of my life since my divorce. This was better than nothing, and I kept trying to convince myself that it was also better than my previous manufacturer. Even in the beginning, before the deal fell through, there were countless problems with that partnership. I rolled my eyes thinking about the *Women's Wear Daily* article that came out after I signed the deal, "Eastern Apparel Acquires BEXnyc." Congratulatory texts and emails had flooded my in-box because everybody loves a winner. But they didn't know that I was making less than I did in my first job out of college. While their contract promised me my own office and showroom, in reality, it delivered a tiny, dark mildew-infested storage closet with no windows.

I looked back down at the offer letter Foxy had given to me one more time before heading into the elevator. I guess this was limbo between Warhols on Fifth Avenue and working from a janitor's closet.

This is fine, I told myself, *it will be fine.*

As I adjusted my jacket, I felt a little jab in my breast, reminding me that the citrine was still in my bra. Sometimes, maniforcing abundance just hurts.

Undercover Crystals Talisman

For hidden protection when neccessary.

In your left pocket (or bra cup lining), place crystals intended for the energies you wish to attract.

Left is associated with divine feminine and receiving/calling in.

In your right pocket (or bra cup lining), place crystals intended for the energies you put out into the situation.

Right is associated with divine masculine and sending/putting out.

Some of my go-tos are:

- **Citrine**: abundance
- **Rose Quartz**: love
- **Tiger's Eye**: confidence, strength and resilience
- **Smoky Quartz**: anxiety relief, clarity
- **Onyx**: protection
- **Amethyst**: intuition
- **Malachite**: transformation
- **Jade**: balance and harmony
- **Carnelian**: motivation and stamina

CHAPTER VIII

THE MOON (WATER)
INSTAGRAM VERSUS REALITY

The Moon: Revelations, Duality, Illusions

Several months later, completely beaten down by my new day job, I found myself in the middle of an especially frigid New York winter. I was single for the first time in almost a decade, but not completely alone. Chloe and Andy's advice had been wisely taken and I invested in several bundles of sage and a Nest cam. I also adopted a teacup Pomeranian even though my mom, Amanda, and almost everyone aside from my two besties agreed that I had no business becoming a pet owner at this particular point in my life. Despite recently winning a Design Entrepreneur of the Year award from F.I.T., my lingerie line was still hemorrhaging money. My "agreement" with Pierre Poiret's company was little more than an underpaid employment agreement for which I sold a big piece of my soul. Working for Foxy (who I learned was actually named

Nancy Lyon, but insisted everyone call her Foxy because that's what her husband, "Big Papi Lyon," called her) beat any sense of hope I had left out of my system. Every morning, she sent her assistant to take attendance at nine sharp. If you weren't at your desk, you received demerits, and demerits resulted in cuts from your paycheck. There was also a strict dress code, which until now I thought did not exist in the fashion industry. I had already been "written up" for violating it due to a keyhole back DVF blouse. There was also an unspoken rule of not being allowed to fraternize with coworkers. I would have to strategically plan to leave a few minutes apart from the few women I was friendly with for our break, so we could meet up on a nearby street corner if we wanted to grab our sad to-go salads together. Due to my diminishing finances, I usually went for the walk (slash escape) claiming that I preferred to bring my own lunch, and would covertly eat my Tupperware serving of rice and canned tuna back at my desk.

Lindsay, also a fashion industry hostage, became my lifeline.

"Hey, Mofo," I answered the phone flatly, despite being happy to see her number on my call display.

"Hey, Mo," she said. "You don't sound so great... hold on."

I heard her move the phone away and say to her husband, "Oh my God, no it's not a homophobic slur to call her 'Mo.' It's short for mofo, *not* homo. Geez!"

"Mofo, you still there?" she said to me.

She always knew how to cheer me up even when it was subconsciously guided.

"That's priceless! I'm dying. Austin is the sweetest. You married a good one."

"Like I would actually fuckin' call you Homo! Who does that? Anyway, how's your prison camp treating you?" she asked empathetically.

"Well, I only received two demerits this week, one for dress code violation and one because I got to my desk on Wednesday at 9:05, so, ya know, whatever that equates to on a scale from 'demoralizing to mental breakdown.' How was yours?" I volleyed back to her.

"Well, today I had to try on bikinis for the entire team in a fit meeting because they are too cheap to hire a proper fit model and they decided 'Lindsay is sample size,'" she grimaced.

"Oh my God! That is not okay! Is that even legal?" I asked in horror.

"I don't know, Mofo. Is it legal to dock your pay because the subway ran late? Or because of something you wore? Maybe not, but what are we going to do? We're not exactly trust fund babies or trophy wives," Lindsay said with a hint of bitterness.

Lindsay and I often bonded over the fact that we were both granddaughters of Polish immigrants and, as a result, were taught to work hard, put our heads down, and just be grateful for what was offered from our employers. We came from humble backgrounds where things like trust funds and spouses who fund your every whim felt like an urban legend. The difference between Lindsay and I occurred in my post-college adult life. I elbowed my way into a front row seat to view how Manhattan's elite lived and discovered that, even with all the wealth they had at their disposal, they weren't any happier than the rest of us.

"Yeah, but a lot of the trophy wives and trust fund kids are pretty miserable too. I don't think that's the answer either," I said gloomily.

"I don't know what the answer is, Mofo. I just know that we don't have a lot of options other than to deal with these dreadful environments right now."

I opened my pink Valley of the Dolls pill case and popped a Xanax. Switching my phone to speaker, I freed up both hands to open the bottle of $6.99 chardonnay I bought at the local deli. My skimpy rations for the week only included the wine, white rice, Bumble Bee tuna, and one chicken breast, yet I continued to watch my bank account diminish. I was grateful for Lindsay's genuine understanding of the underbelly of the fashion industry: the verbal abuse, the poor office conditions, the thinly-veiled threats of losing your income if you didn't sign over all of your waking—and often non-waking—hours to your employer. I couldn't help but wonder if the way that we normalized it, like two members of the same cult, was only causing us to acquiesce longer.

As both my savings and self-respect dwindled, I yearned for any semblance of optimism or unconditional love, much like a woman deciding to have children during a crisis point in her marriage. Instead, I used my debit card and two nearly maxed out credit cards to purchase a one pound, sable-colored Pomeranian puppy. Though nothing else in my life was anywhere close to stable or safe, the amount of love I felt for this tiny redheaded ball of fur that looked up at me with her big brown eyes, made me feel a little less afraid and a lot less alone in the world. My next thought was, *Dear God, she's so small! I hope I don't accidentally kill her!*

Erica and Adelaide showed up two hours later in matching Commes Des Garçon draped, woven tops.

"We come bearing gifts for the child," Addy said dramatically in a mock procession, handing me a little teddy bear dog toy and a bottle of vodka.

"They were out of frankincense," she said with a grin.

"Oh my God! She's soooo tiny!" Erica exclaimed, adjusting her wise man-inspired shawl while beginning to stage a whole puppy photoshoot as Lola ran around in circles on the couch.

"So, how did you come up with her name?" Addy asked while taking snaps of the tiny Tasmanian devil for her Instagram Story.

"Well, I named her after Madonna's oldest daughter, obviously. I figured, when we meet, I can feign surprise that our kids are both named Lola! Plus, I think @LolaTheDomPom is a catchy Instagram handle. 'Lola: The Dominatrix Pomeranian.'"

"Perfeeection!" squealed Erica.

"Are you looking for an apartment?" Adelaide asked, pointing to my laptop screen which was open to StreetEasy.com.

"Uh, yeah," I said, caught off guard and slightly embarrassed.

My lease renewal came through earlier that week for nearly $800 more a month than what I was currently paying, which sadly wasn't that uncommon in Manhattan apartments that weren't rent stabilized. I could barely afford my apartment as it was. Despite the splashy pictures of Beyonce's Billboard Awards performance and Lady Gaga hiring me for custom lingerie pieces for her ArtPop launch, actual sales on my lingerie line had continued to be dismal. For months, I had been sliding further and further into debt and hemorrhaging money from my company in a way that not even a super-plus tampon of a business plan could mitigate.

"I just think... It's time for a new start, you know? A lot of bad shit happened here," I motioned around the living room, as if to telepathically depict images of my divorce, the fights with Melissa, the panic attacks, and the phone calls to alert me that Justin and then Jean-Claude had died.

"Yes, absolutely! We can help!" Adelaide grinned broadly as Lola chewed on her fingers.

"When are you looking to move," asked Erica.

"April 1st. So, I have some time."

Weeks flew by and I still hadn't found an apartment that I could afford or that even seemed close to livable, especially considering how much I'd loved living in my current home. And now, I had a fur-baby to care for as well!

Lola was a headstrong Gemini who had the temperament of a honey badger. She thwarted my attempts at crate training her by defecating and tap dancing through her own poop each time I placed her in the crate. I decided to set up a baby gate in my bathroom, where at least the tile floors were easy to clean, but within twenty-four hours, she'd learned to scale that damn gate like a fluffy, obstinate monkey. But, every time I was at my wits end, she would strike a pose with one little back leg out and smile up at me: my most effective teacher in presence and forgiveness.

I wasn't sure if it was the exhaustion from my attempts to train my puppy, my continued nightly cocktail routine, or the ever-mounting financial and work stress, but I uncharacteristically decided to take an extremely tiny ground floor apartment on Prince Street in a decrepit building in SoHo. This "one bedroom" that totaled 380 square feet, was actually a studio that the agent claimed was a one bedroom due to a thin wall separating the living room from the grim, closet-sized room that fit a twin size bed. Though it was nearly a third of the size of my current home, in a terrible, pre-war, walk-up building with no natural light, dishwasher, or full-sized appliances, it was also half the rent of my current apartment. And since I feared my credit might not check out much longer, and I'd been approved for the unit, the decision was made, seemingly for me.

I didn't show anyone the apartment before I signed—I didn't want to have to face the reality of how terrible it was. I was just so grateful it was available within the time I needed to move, was a price I could afford, and was still in a desirable zip code. My ego justified that if I could tell people I moved to a chic neighborhood and they never SAW my home, it wasn't necessarily a massive downgrade. They didn't need to know it was actually more SoHo-close-to-Chinatown than SoHo.

My move-in day was spent Instagramming artsy shots of the desirable parts of my neighborhood. I was careful to offer up zero photographic evidence of my actual apartment, except for very closely cropped photos of Lola on the hardwood floors. In this day and age, perception is reality, right?

As I unpacked boxes next to the rusty, loud, inconsistent radiator, I found the silver dry erase plaque that hung on the back of my door in my previous apartment. The last checklist I had written myself was still etched in fading marker:

- Get Rich
- Get Famous
- Get Almond Milk

I smiled weakly. *At least I could still (barely) afford almond milk*, I thought as I looked out of the apartment's only two-by-two foot window covered by wrought iron bars.

That night, I didn't sleep well, partially because of the drug deals going on in the alley just outside my window. I now completely understood why the iron bars were there. I wasn't sure if it was the voices outside or my chilling nightmare that had woken me. I dreamt that I was in the apartment in the dark all alone, even Lola wasn't there. A shadowy figure was slowly coming towards me and there was nowhere to run. At first I felt panicked, but then a somber certainty that there was no point in trying to escape took over: *If you don't get out of here, you're going to die, alone in the darkness...*

I sat up and wiped the sweat off my forehead. The voice

that had sounded strangely like my own, ominously faded into the din in the alleyway. *Get out of what?* I wondered. My hair was drenched. This was a common side effect to always drinking before bed. I often woke up hot and dehydrated. Even my regularly appearing alter ego, Blackout Sally, managed to fill a bottle of tap water each night knowing my liver would need it in a few hours. The sweating wasn't the weird part, it was remembering the dreams. I used to have vivid dreams growing up, and once in a while, genuinely jarring dreams that came true. The last time it had happened, I was seventeen. I had a horrific dream that my high school friend Evelyn had been surrounded by four shadowy figures that were pinning down her wrists and ankles. I woke up at three in the morning and, in a time before texting existed, I snuck to our family's computer room and emailed her to tell her I had a scary dream and hoped she was okay. She called me back early the following morning saying she was drugged at a party and raped by four men. She only told me and her sister and informed me she never wanted to speak about it again. I couldn't imagine what Evelyn was experiencing. I protested, asking lots of questions to which she would not—or could not—answer. In order to support her and provide what she was asking for, I reluctantly agreed to honor her request.

That moment had been traumatizing for me as well. I never wanted to know terrible things again, especially those that I couldn't stop from happening. I first began drinking socially in college, then more in my mid-twenties, and it peaked around my early thirties with the end of my Saturn Return. The alcohol took a massive toll on my physical and mental health, creating horrible anxiety and depression, but it blocked the dreams. It also eliminated having to sense and know things that other people didn't. Alcohol took away the voice and I was grateful for that. But, somehow, my perceptions were breaking through again.

I wasn't dead, so maybe this wasn't true. Maybe if I just ignored it, like the credit card balances, the headaches, the empty Xanax, and the spent wine bottles piling up in the trash cans, maybe, it would go away. I suddenly felt a tiny little tongue licking my ankle and looked down at Lola. She had no idea how shitty this place was. She was just happy that we were in it together. *Maybe if we had each other,* I thought, reaching down to pet her little head, *then maybe I could be okay here, too.* And just like the day that Evelyn and I never spoke of, I never told anyone about the dream of me dying in that apartment.

A few days after I'd settled in, I invited Amanda over. She had always been great with interiors and had decorated all the apartments we'd ever lived in throughout our marriage. As she looked around, taking in the cramped, practically windowless space, I sensed she was trying her best to hide the horror she felt at my living in such squalor. I could see how bad it really was through her stalled commentary. Amanda was never at a loss for words, and as she pasted a bright smile on her face, I noticed that she'd stopped talking entirely.

"I mean… It's a little bit… Harry Potter's cupboard under the stairs. But maybe we can work with that… as a theme," she said, trying her best to sound optimistic.

"Ugh. I know. It's awful. I've already seen eight cockroaches. One was nearly the size of Lola, so I keep the door to the 'bedroom'—if you can call it that— shut, and jam a towel under the crack. I also discovered a hole after being here a week that I was hoping led to *Fraggle Rock*, but a large rat hole seems more likely. I plugged it with tin foil and towels and have just been taking Lola with me whenever I can as a precaution," I said, as

I walked the two feet from the couch to the kitchen to wash my pathetic confession down with a glass of cheap Chardonnay.

I did my best to make the rental as homey as possible, painting a large Madonna mural in the hallway. Andy helped by perfecting her brows and makeup. Nearly all my furniture from the Chelsea apartment had been sold, mostly because I desperately needed the money, but also because most of it didn't fit into the Cupboard Under the Stairs. I managed to find a used tiny table and three stools that someone threw out onto the street and that miraculously fit in the hallway/kitchen so I could still cook meals for Addy, Erica, and myself. I only ever allowed the girls, Andy, and Amanda to come inside. With everyone else, I just stuck to my "I moved to SoHo" story. I would meet friends at their apartments, or at bars and events with complimentary cocktails. And before leaving the apartment, I'd made it a ritual to prepare a bottle of water, which I stored between the bars in the window to keep cool, for when my future self would inevitably wake up dehydrated with alcohol tremors.

One morning, a chipper neighbor wearing striped linen pants and Birkenstocks was walking her dog in the drug deal alley next to my unit. She waved, and asked in a tone that was far too perky for 7:45 a.m., "You making Moon Water?" while pointing to the bottle jammed between the metal bars.

"Um no... just stays cooler out here and tastes better. Also, I have literally no space for a shelf or nightstand," I answered matter-of-factly.

"Probably tastes better because it's being charged by the moon," she said confidently.

"Cool, thanks," I said as I rushed to get ready for work.

I hurried into the office, claiming I had come from a retail deskside meeting to account for my past-9 a.m. roll call arrival. Waiting for me at my dim little cubicle was an email from Amelia, Foxy's assistant, attendance taker, and rule-enforcer extraordinaire. I assumed this was about receiving demerits for something—I still didn't know exactly how demerits worked aside from resulting in an arbitrary amount of financial loss and degradation. But, this time, she asked me to meet with her. Apparently, Amelia played the role of HR as well.

As I sat down in the vacant office she led me into, she scooted a manila folder across the empty desk and said, "Unfortunately, your position here won't be needed moving forward. We are offering two weeks severance. Foxy couldn't be here today, but if you have any questions, you can wait to sign."

Despite the seemingly sudden randomness of this decision, I had no questions except, "So, if I sign now, I receive the severance immediately, correct?" I was almost giddy that I never had to step foot in this place again.

"Yes. Uh, right here," Amelia pointed, confused at my enthusiastic response.

I didn't have many personal items because I loathed being in the space, so I just grabbed a few lingerie samples from my desk. I waved happily to a couple of women I'd befriended. I knew I needed to be concerned about money, but for now, I just wanted to enjoy the gratitude I felt for the alleviation of the daily mental and spiritual abuse I'd been subjecting myself to over the past eight months. I pulled up my bank statement on my phone and winced. *Ok, I still have two weeks of pay to figure out next steps. This is fine,* I thought to myself, somehow more optimistically than when I had accepted the job.

Those two weeks flew by and inevitably money became tighter and tighter. I wanted to be home with my new roach and rat roommates less and less, so I decided to try to rent my apartment on Airbnb. It was a shithole, but it was in an alluring zip code so I took a few very "artistic" shots of the interior and many photos of the surrounding neighborhood and listed:

*Dream Artist Pied-À-Terre One Bedroom
Apartment in the Heart of SoHo*

Steps from the best restaurants and shopping the city has to offer. Runway hall entrance leads way to a master bedroom and living room complete with sofa sleeper couch, allowing the apartment to comfortably sleep up to four guests. Complete with Apple TV and Espresso maker for your convenience.

And the crazy thing? People actually rented it.

Only one woman walked in, said "Oh my God NO!" and turned around and demanded a refund from Airbnb.

In retrospect, I applaud her standards and she remains one of my idols to this day. But all the others actually paid to sleep in the Cupboard. New York is funny like that—it's the city where the hustle was born. Whenever my apartment was booked, I was always just so grateful to be out of the space and be able to put some money towards rent. By this point, all other sources of income had ground to a halt. I had already cashed out my 401k from Playboy and sold any stocks I had to help keep my line in business and to mitigate my debts. There were no more parachutes left.

When my apartment was occupied, I would stay on friends' couches and walk their dogs, cook for them, or buy them dinner in return. When I couldn't find a place to crash, I sometimes booked hotels that were priced around the same amount my apartment was renting for—just to get the hell out of there. Even the Canal Street Holiday Inn in Chinatown was a palace compared to my place: no visible insects, no bars on the windows, consistent heat and plumbing. They rated five stars in my book.

But there would always be evenings that Lola and I were forced back into that shitty apartment at 161 Prince Street. I spent a lot of nights out with Andy or Addy and Erica, at parties and events where free cocktails were flowing and where we could call passed appetizers our dinner. And on the rare occasion that I did come home in some form of lucid state, as soon as I had to crawl over someone passed out in the hallway, or saw a cockroach scamper by the bed, or heard drug deals in the back alley behind the barred walls of my little window, I popped a couple more Xanax and poured a glass of cheap wine—or three. I did anything I could to not have to acknowledge the fear and sadness of my new life anymore.

Moon Water

You can create Moon Water by leaving water outdoors to charge under the moonlight. The Moon affects the ocean's tides, demonstrating the energetic connection between the element of water and the Moon. Key moon phases, especially full moons, can activate our water.

1. Find a bottle or jar, ideally glass.

2. Fill it with water, preferably natural, spring water, etc.

3. Set your intentions (abundance, love, gratitude, etc.).

4. Hold the bottle in your hands in front of your heart, meditating on your intentions.

5. Set the bottle in an area that is in the view of moonlight, either outside or near a window with exposure.

6. Optional: surround the jar with any crystals you would like to work with (for more guidance on selecting crystals, see Chapter VII: Undercover Crystals).

7. Leave overnight.

8. Retrieve before sunrise.

9. Seal the bottle and sip, spritz, or use in ritual work as desired.

Timing:

Waxing moons to full moons are best for infusing water to call energy in (e.g. abundance water, self-love, etc.).

Waning moons are best for releasing energy water, i.e negativity clearing, heartache release.

Full moons are the most potent time for creating moonwater.

CHAPTER IX

DEATH
EMPTY BOTTLES AND GRATITUDE JARS

Death: Transformation, Transition, Endings, New Beginnings

I woke up shaking and dizzy on the floor of a massive, vacant apartment. From the view of the balcony doorway, it appeared to be a penthouse. The floor-to-ceiling windows overlooked the entirety of Central Park with a north-facing view of the city skyline. Even without furnishings, the rich mahogany flooring in the empty apartment confirmed that I managed to somehow find my way to luxury, like dying pet turtles who instinctively head towards the familiar comfort of running water.

I looked at my watch; it was apparently 7:14 on Saturday morning. *Whose building was this?* I wondered, as I tried to get my eyes to focus, blinking rapidly while fumbling for my bag and phone. It was a morning routine I had become accustomed to: waking up in a rush of panic, not knowing how I got home or even where my purse was. Having no idea where I was, added a whole new and inconvenient bullet point to this routine.

The smell of fresh paint surrounding me was especially nauseating in this state. By some miracle, my quilted Chanel bag—the one nice thing I hadn't managed to sell over the past two years in my desperate attempts to stay afloat—was lying on the dark hardwood floor a few feet away from the front door. I opened it and held my breath. Somehow my phone, keys, and wallet were all still safely tucked inside.

"Thank you, Coco," I sighed, clutching the bag to my chest as another wave of dizziness washed over me.

My phone showed six missed calls and eight angry texts from Amanda, most of which were commentaries about my irresponsibility and apparent propensity for "partying with twenty-five year olds." *Ugh, whatever!*

I rolled my bloodshot eyes, annoyed. My ex-wife knew damn well that Addy and Erica were twenty-SEVEN. I shook my head, as though those two extra years somehow made all the difference.

It took me a few minutes of racking my brain to determine if I might have somehow consciously planned to sleep in this empty penthouse. The idea wasn't completely out of the question since I had been forced to live a somewhat nomadic existence recently, changing locations weekly, or even nightly. I'd sold any remaining sense of security or consistency in my life to Airbnb in exchange for the bare minimum amount of cash I needed to pay my rent and phone bill every month.

I stood up shakily, teetering on my stiletto boots which were still on from the night before, and opened the door to see if the hallway held any further clues regarding my whereabouts. The instant I saw the dark geometric patterned carpeting and the Restoration Hardware-esque light fixtures, I closed my eyes in horror.

How in the actual fuck did I get here? I wondered, a little frightened and still very sick to my stomach as I frantically texted Adelaide and Erica.

> Ladies, how did I end up
> in a vacant penthouse in
> MELISSA'S building?

Saturn, the mean teacher of the planetary system, was now resting firmly in my sun sign of Sagittarius—the partying free-thinker of the zodiac. If my Saturn Return in Scorpio was supposed to be the dark night of the soul, it had been one big messy VIP party compared to my life with Saturn in Sagittarius. Like trying to quiet a screaming two-year-old with candy, I partied, drank, and Xanaxed my way through most of it. But this morning was an all-time low, even for me.

Addy called me back instantly.

"Oh shit, Bex! It's my fault. We were all pretty drunk last night at the Boom Boom Room and because you said you were staying at Amanda's place while she's in LA, we just assumed the first uptown address in your Uber account was Amanda's. So... I ordered you a car to that address."

Fuck. My. Life.

I looked around at the bleak, sterile, freshly-painted eggshell walls void of lighting fixtures, and the large gaps where the electronic appliances would eventually be placed. It was a perfect metaphor for my life—empty, cold, and devoid of any stability or warmth. When I glanced in the bathroom mirror, I barely recognized myself. My smeared black eyeliner and disheveled hair looked like what Erica and Adelaide idolized as "heroin chic" but I couldn't even believe that convenient lie anymore. My once-toned petite frame was still thin, but it had morphed into the unhealthy, bloated type of skinny that was the result of surviving on a diet of coffee and alcohol, with an occasional piece of deli chicken breast thrown in for good measure. My shoulder-length blonde hair was frail and breaking off at the ends, and my once spirited green eyes just looked dull and hopeless.

Enough. Enough of the blackouts and the anxiety-ridden morning afters. Enough of the Instagram posts of the "glamorous" evenings out that I didn't remember when I woke up in my dark, dingy, rat-infested apartment. Enough pretending I was fine when I was really just a useless, unlovable shell of who I used to be.

Enough, I mouthed at the girl in the glass, a face I barely recognized anymore.

Enough.

I scrolled through the multiple raging texts from Amanda, and then, angrily texted back:

> Fine, your fat ass can
> fucking delete me then.

I had never called Amanda fat. Ever. I didn't even think she was fat. I did, however, know this was her biggest insecurity, and in all of my self-loathing and destruction, I fired the lowest shot I had. I instantly felt a pang of shame in my stomach, but I quickly dismissed it to focus on where I would be sleeping tonight.

Amanda was in LA this week, so I originally thought I would continue to crash at her place, as I had rented mine on Airbnb to try to make rent. But since she'd just kicked me out of her life via text, I was fairly certain that also included any further use of her apartment.

I headed back to Amanda's to feed Lola. Even throughout the scarcity of the past six months, I made sure that Lola was always taken care of. Some days, I would strategically buy cheap deli sandwiches with chicken, pulling apart enough for the both of us to eat for the day. Yesterday, I splurged on Wellness dog food, thanks to the Airbnb money coming in by staying at Amanda's place.

"I'm so sorry Lola. I'm failing both of us so badly," I said, kissing her on the head as tears started to swell in the corners of my eyes. "I don't see how things are going to get better for me. But I know they will for you. I KNOW they will. I love you SO much."

As Lola ate her very delayed dinner-slash-breakfast, I unpacked my cosmetics case and pulled out all of my many prescriptions. I had just refilled them a couple of days earlier thanks to Obamacare. Carefully, I counted them; I had twenty-one Xanax, twenty-seven Prozac and twenty-seven Lexapro in my possession. In the icy depths of Amanda's freezer, a full bottle of Tito's vodka and Casamigos tequila waited for me. I smiled and thought of how much I loved her thoughtfulness and generosity. She wasn't a big drinker, but always had nearly everything in her home to make her guests feel welcome.

I grabbed the massive bottles and lined them up next to the pills, pushing the capsules into strategic, perfect piles arranged in an ombre display from white to light blue to darker blue. *Why were all of the meds for anxiety and depression colored almost exclusively in various shades of blue?* I wondered, as I moved the pills around on the counter. It seemed counterintuitive. If I were in charge of designing them, I'd make them resemble bright, happy Skittles with little hearts and rainbows printed on them. *Maybe a career for another lifetime*, I thought.

I walked away from the meticulously arranged piles of drugs and Googled "How many Xanax, Prozac, and Lexapro would be fatal?" I mean the only thing worse than my current life would've been ending up living the rest of my life as a burden to my parents, spending my days practically comatose in my childhood bed.

I sorted through ads for suicide hotlines and eventually found some links to articles about the fatality of overdosing. I roughly calculated that I had more than enough drugs to peace the fuck out of my misery. The only monkey wrench in this plan, and a representation of just how bleak my life had become, was that I had no real job to show up to and I lived in one of the shittiest buildings in Manhattan. This meant that, with no one noticing me missing for a while, Lola would undoubtedly be left alone for a significant period of time, and could starve to death. Amanda really loved Lola, almost as much as I did. She'd become close to her as we'd navigated our way into a newfound post-divorce friendship. She even joked she was glad I got Lola *after* we split up, because she would have fought me for custody. I knew she would take her if I asked. I took a deep breath and dialed her number, which I was absolutely not looking forward to as I recalled the horrible text I'd sent earlier.

"Hello," Amanda said solemnly, and my mouth suddenly went dry with fear.

She normally greeted me with a chipper, "Hey B, What's Up?"

"Hey. Look, I didn't mean that. I'm just… I'm not ok."

"I KNOW YOU'RE NOT FUCKING OK! YOU NEED TO GO TO REHAB OR THERAPY. OR BOTH!"

"You think I can afford that?" I actually laughed out loud at the thought.

I currently had $253 in my checking account.

"YOU NEED TO FIGURE IT OUT! I DON'T CARE WHAT IT TAKES! BUT IF I EVEN HEAR ABOUT YOU HAVING SO MUCH AS A SIP OF WINE, I WILL NEVER SPEAK TO YOU AGAIN."

At this point, I was sobbing. I just wanted to die. Quickly. But I needed to know that Lola would be taken care of. And Amanda was flying home soon.

"Amanda… I'm sorry. I am. I just want to ask. If anything were to happen to me. You would take care of Lola? Right?"

"WHAT ARE YOU SAYING? ARE YOU ACTUALLY GOING TO KILL YOURSELF IN MY APARTMENT? THAT'S WHAT I AM GOING TO COME HOME TO?!" and she hung up.

I sank to the floor shaking and crying, pulling myself into a ball. I couldn't even find the strength to stand and consume my pretty piles of pills. All I could concentrate on was trying to catch my breath as my chest heaved with sobs.

I don't know exactly how long I lay there for, but at some point, my ringing phone jolted me back to the present. I hoped it was Amanda calling back so I could breathe easier knowing Lola would be okay and that our horrible screaming match wouldn't be our last conversation. I didn't want her to remember me like that.

Are there memories or does it just go black when you die? I think it feels like sleep, I told myself. *Sleeping was the only thing that felt ok these days.*

I looked at the screen; it was mom calling. I don't quite know what pulled me to answer, but I did.

"Hello."

She was crying and softly said, "Rebecca? Are you okay? I've been calling non-stop."

"No… I'm not ok at all," I sobbed. "I haven't been ok in a very long time. A *very* long time. I'm so sorry."

Amanda had hung up and immediately called my mom, crying into the phone, begging my parents to help me. My parents love me very much, but in those dark Saturn years, I think they were afraid to question anything. They believed that if they trusted me when I lied to them and said everything was fine, then eventually, somehow, everything would be.

My mom's voice steadied, relieved that I had finally answered.

"Whatever you need, we'll help you. We'll help you with money for therapy. And I can look at apartments with you. You need to get out of that place as soon as possible! I would offer for you to come back here for a while, but I know that would only make you feel worse. It's going to be okay, I promise. Please just don't give up."

I cried, but this time they were tears of relief.

"Ok?" she asked.

"Yes. Ok," I gasped.

Despite knowing that AA probably wasn't the most aligned modality for me, it was the only form of free therapy I could find until the check arrived from my parents. So, once I got off the phone with my mom that night, I located a meeting for the next day and vowed to attend.

The meeting was held in a cold church basement in Midtown. Plastic schoolroom chairs had been deliberately arranged in a circle; everyone took a seat and introduced themselves.

"Hi, I'm Bill. I'm an alcoholic."

"Hi, I'm Sophie. I'm an alcoholic and cocaine addict."

And then, it was my turn.

"Hi, I'm Rebecca. This is my first meeting. I've been struggling with abusing alcohol and Xanax for the past couple years."

There was a longer pause than usual after my introduction. Then a few more people introduced themselves and the group leader began the lecture for the evening. Afterward, as I was gathering my things, a curly-haired, middle-aged woman with a warm voice came up to me and introduced herself.

"Hi, I'm Peggy. No jokes about my name," She laughed heartily at this.

"I don't even know any," I said honestly.

"Oh, you know Peggy Sue... Peggy Lee, all the Peggy songs... Well, you might be too young for that," she laughed again. "So, it's your first meeting, huh?"

"Hi, Peggy. I'm Rebecca. I have admittedly terrible taste in music so I apologize for not getting the reference. Love the name regardless, and yeah, this was my first meeting," I smiled at her kindness.

"You know, I used to struggle with admitting that I'm an alcoholic, too. But until you do, you'll just keep going back on the booze rollercoaster," she said while making a dramatic undulating motion with her hand along with a whistling noise ending in a crash sound. "So, the quicker you embrace the fact you're an alcoholic, the faster you're outta harm's way."

This reminded me of my first Holy Confession when I was eight years old in rural Pennsylvania.

In our second-grade CCD church group, we were told we needed to start confessing our sins once we committed them. We had the option to sit behind a screened door or in a chair, face-to-face, as we recounted our unholy acts to the priest. When my turn came, I popped right into the chair because, well, I had nothing to hide.

"Hi, Father. Oops, I meant, Bless Me Father," I smiled, wide-eyed.

"Hello, my child, what would you like to confess today?"

"Oh, I didn't commit any sins, Father. But Mrs. Marley said that I'm supposed to sit here, so here I am."

"We all have sins. You have nothing to share? Did you fight with a brother or sister, perhaps? Did you disobey your parents this week?"

"Nope," I said proudly.

I swung my legs back and forth under the chair, waiting until I could be dismissed. The hyper-vigilant achiever in me assumed I would get a prize for a sin-free week. It turned out there was no gold star or lollypop, but rather a call to my parents letting them know that I refused to confess.

My older sister sat me down and said, "Listen, next time if you haven't done anything, just make something up, and then they tell you to do a couple Hail Mary's and you're done. That way they won't call mom and dad."

"But, if I don't feel like I did anything wrong, why would I say I did just to not get in trouble?"

This confused the hell out of my eight-year-old brain.

And this is exactly how I felt again at age thirty-four when Peggy told me to take on a permanent title that I didn't believe accurately described me.

"It was so nice meeting you," I said to Peggy and nearly sprinted to the door.

"You should really get a sponsor!" She called after me.

I genuinely respect that twelve-step programs help a lot of people. Chloe had started NA in her early twenties and hasn't touched a drug since. But the idea that this one period in my life would define me forever just didn't sit well with me. I certainly didn't intend to go forth for eternity declaring: *I'm Rebecca and I'm a divorcée,* any more than I wanted the past few years of abusing substances to become my identity for the rest of my life.

The next morning I Googled "NON-twelve-step recovery" as if capitalizing the NON would remove all the factors that I felt were alienating about the previous night's experience. After being bombarded with pop-ups for super pricey California-based options, I finally managed to find one that was much more affordable. It was a month-long, three-days-a-week outpatient program, and it was almost the exact amount of money my parents were able to send me for therapy.

I called the number and signed up immediately. It wasn't possible to start for another week, but I felt hopeful that I at least had a scheduled plan for some sort of help. I had no desire to go back to AA, but in my current state, waiting an entire week felt like an ice age. So, I looked into therapy that I might be able to afford on a sliding scale till then.

I had done therapy in my past when I still had money to fund it. I saw a psychiatrist who prescribed mountains of SSRIs, a psychoanalyst, a CBT therapist, an EMDR therapist, and one who practiced hypnosis. Aspects of each were helpful at different points, but basically it was a super-expensive version of dating. I had to spend a lot of time, money, and repetitive conversations with a multitude of people trying to find the right fit. And honestly, I still had yet to experience that "magic connection."

Two days later, I headed into a depressing office building in the garment district for an appointment with a social worker who offered therapy on a sliding scale. I sat on a metal folding chair in a hallway/makeshift waiting room. After a few minutes, a woman with the demeanor of a disgruntled DMV clerk popped out briskly and shoved a clipboard full of paperwork at me. I filled it out and handed it back to her for the "intake" session. She flipped through the paperwork and zeroed in on the "employer" section.

"Oh, this is a problem. You have NO income?"

"That's kinda why I'm here," I said, looking around.

My old shrink's office looked like the Four Seasons compared to this place, I thought smugly to myself.

"Well, the sliding scale depends on income. I'm going to have to figure that out after our intake session, which will be $70."

"SEVENTY?! I thought the intake was complementary to see if it's a good fit?"

"No," she said and stared up at me from the pile of paperwork with a condescending expression. It was as if I had just asked her if living in NYC was inexpensive.

"Intake is $70," she repeated.

"Oh... okay."

She proceeded to ask what brought me to her, my history with therapy, and current medication and substances I was using. I shared the CliffsNotes version of my recent trajectory with her.

"Well... our time is almost up, but it sounds like you are quite resilient," she said flatly.

"Will that be debit or credit?"

I felt my chest seize up as I handed over a quarter of my current net worth to her.

"MOTHERFUCKER!" I heard my debit card scream.

"I know. I'm sorry," I said softly to my TD Visa.

"Excuse me?" shot back the disgruntled caseworker.

"Oh, I mean, yes, I know. I'm sorry I misunderstood the intake fee."

The last thing I needed was to be misdiagnosed as schizophrenic. God knows how much THAT would've cost me.

I decided not to spend any more money on therapy or healing, but to take advantage of free online resources until I actually had incoming funds and a stable bank balance. I watched a lot of videos on YouTube and listened to free guided meditations. I found a young, handsome, incredibly powerful spiritual teacher and thought leader named Eli Vate. His bright blue eyes lit up as he explained energetic shifts and healing in mindful yet relatable ways. I watched his videos daily. I started a gratitude list in the mornings. A self-help blog I read said to try to start with at least three things to be grateful for. Another one suggested writing the list each day, folding it, and placing it into a gratitude jar, which you could empty on either New Year's Eve or whenever you needed a reminder of all the energetic abundance you already had received. I like accessories so I went with the jar. I cleaned out a used Snapple bottle and tore 8.5 x 11 notebook paper into quarters. I'm not gonna lie, my deposits weren't very impressive at first. Sometimes, it consisted of no more than:

Today I am grateful that:

1. I'm alive
2. I got out of bed.
3. I brushed my teeth this morning.

I wasn't great at the meditations at first either. Especially one which specifically called for gratitude for your current home.

Begin by thanking your stove for heating your nourishing food.

"Yeah—my gas no longer works so that one doesn't apply... Next," I spoke to the narrator like she was Siri.

Now, thank your stable walls that form the foundation of your home.

"I mean, thanks to a couple of them, but not sure how sturdy that one with that massive rat hole is... Do I still thank it?"

Give thanks to your running water and toilet. Even ancient Kings and Queens didn't have such advanced waste removal systems.

"Yeah... Well, call me an ancient Queen because mine has

been overflowing for two weeks and I've been using the bathroom at the coffee shop next door."

I finally stopped using that specific track and decided to save it for future use. But still, somehow, these little exercises along with Eli's messages were much more helpful for me than the AA meeting or the $70 therapy session I attended. I started incorporating guided meditations and other small modalities daily, which made the wait for my first counseling session a bit less painful. I started to notice a shift—albeit a small one—towards hope.

The following week, I finally walked into my first NON-twelve-step counseling session feeling optimistic but cautious, given my recent track record with therapy. As I exited the elevator into the therapy center located in a cool WeWork space with a hip and friendly vibe, I exhaled in relief. The counselor, Keith, who didn't appear to be much older than I was, shook my hand and walked me to his office. I sat down and noticed a Madonna coffee table book on his desk.

"Cool book," I said, offering up a compliment to break the ice.

"Oh yeah. She's the best," Keith laughed.

You're in the right place.

This was the first time I acknowledged a sign from the Universe in a long time, and the first time I heard "the voice" since trying to ignore that horrible dream. *Was this what my Higher Self sounds like?* I always thought Source/the Universe/my Higher Self would sound like a firm British lady or maybe Morgan Freeman. But this just sounded like a calmer and more confident version of myself. Maybe that's why it was so hard to hear, let alone trust, when I hadn't felt calm or confident in a really long time.

Keith proceeded to do the opposite of every therapist I had encountered up until this point; he opened up about himself. He vulnerably shared his transformation from heroin addict to a successful artist in a loving relationship with a condo in Hell's Kitchen. He admitted that he had tried twelve-step programs multiple times and they just didn't work for him. So he developed his own program based on a combination of scientific research on addiction and the methods that helped him to turn his life around. Keith explained that, at the core, his program stressed that we were all actually power*ful*, and that, at the end of the day, we always had the power of choice in every situation.

"I believe that both connection, and that power, is within us. Not outside of us."

"Kinda like the Strength card in Tarot," I mused out loud... thinking of the Eighth Major Arcana card that represented how true strength came gently from within.

"Is that a Tarot thing? Yeah maybe... I actually don't know Tarot that well. My boyfriend's a big astrology fan though," he smiled.

I felt myself relax into the chair as I realized this might not be as hellacious or impossible as I feared. I'd struggled with the ideology of powerlessness; I'm sure that for some people it was freeing. But I had already felt so incredibly powerless over the past few years, and it was that exact feeling that had led me to self-soothe with gallons of vodka and copious amounts of Xanax.

"One thing I have found helpful in this process is the fact that most of us have already walked away from negative habits or people in our life at some point, and when we give attention to that, it reminds us we can do it again. Have you ever successfully quit something before?" he asked, leaning back in his chair.

"I quit smoking a few months ago!" I remembered excitedly. "I mean, I used those little vape pens for a month or so which probably poisoned my insides more than the two years of American Spirits, but yeah, I quit the vape pen, too."

"Awesome. See? You got this," Keith said, smiling reassuringly.

"Oh!—and I broke up with an ex that was really hard to leave… even though I knew it wasn't a healthy relationship, I teetered back and forth for a while… so that probably doesn't count."

Fuck! Am I gonna go back on this, too?

As if Keith read my mind, he calmly responded, "And honestly, you might drink again. You might have a Xanax in the future. And that's okay. Our work is to change your awareness around those activities and cause you to really pay attention to your choices, as opposed to operating on autopilot. And when you do that, chances are you're going to want to make different choices than you have in the past. So, if you're up for it, we'll meet three times a week, review the material for each module, share anything that's coming up, and basically, you'll take what works and leave the rest."

That would become one of my most powerful mottos for my own personal healing journey.

Keith looked up from his notepad. "Do you think you'd like to continue?"

"Hell yes!" I answered, maybe a bit too enthusiastically.

"I mean who wouldn't wanna hang out with you and Madonna three times a week?" I pointed out, smiling at the book on his desk.

Gratitude Jar Spell

To begin or end your day in a state of gratitude.

Tools:

- Jar or Container
- Paper and Pen

I recommend Post-it notes because they're a perfect size for this, but this is an exercise that can be done mentally or verbally if tools are unavailable. However, I have found the act of physically writing by hand activates the feeling of gratitude more deeply.

1. Label your paper with the date at the top and number lines 1. 2. and 3.

2. Choose a minimum of three things or experiences that you genuinely feel gratitude for and record them.

   Try to steer away from blanket statements like "my family members, my dog, etc." What do you actually, in that moment, feel thankful that you have or are experiencing? This exercise was tough for me in the beginning, but I was grateful for the days I was actually getting out of bed. The drive to shower or brush your teeth can feel monumentous. Start with what feels true. The cool thing is, when you empty the jar, I assure you, you will see an ever-expanding amount of experiences, people, and things come into your life that bring immense gratitude into your world.

3. Fold the paper and deposit it into the jar.

4. Empty the jar at a time you've chosen to review (New Year's Eve and Birthdays are great times for this.) and experience the gratitude that has come in. I have now transitioned this practice to a morning journal exercise, but visually seeing the papers of gratitude pile up and grow in volume in the jar really helped me in the early stages.

PART THREE

THE SUN

The Sun: Illumination, Enlightenment, Success

People always want to believe in overnight success stories. I think it gives us hope in those moments when we're in our own dark nights of the soul. Did you hear about J.K. Rowling? She was writing in a car and now—poof—she's a BILLIONAIRE and friends with Oprah! But I'm sure J.K. would be the first to tell you that there were a few more steps in between creating Neville Longbottom on a napkin in the back of her car and sipping lattes from twenty-four carat teacups with Momma O.

It seems like a lifetime ago that I laid on the floor of Amanda's apartment, preparing to die—maybe because so many people, practices, and shifts occurred since then in order to transform my life "overnight."

CHAPTER X

THE HANGED MAN
THREE'S COMPANY TELEPATHY

1

The Hanged Man: New Perspectives, Surrender, Sacrifice

My search for a new apartment took much longer than I had anticipated. It made sense; apartment hunting is quite a feat in New York, and I was being more selective than ever as I had to find a building that accepted both dogs and guarantors. For the first time since I was in college, there was no alternative but to ask my mother to co-sign for my apartment. My credit was completely ruined and I had closed all my credit cards and worked to settle them with a debt repayment plan. Moving would be overwhelming, but no matter where I landed, I knew it would be a step up from the gas leak and the rathole-enhanced Cupboard Under the Stairs. Plus, apartment hunting gave my anxious, unemployed, and newly-sober mind a focus in between therapy sessions.

One unseasonably warm April afternoon—the kind that could

make you fall back in love with New York *even after* it beat the shit out of you—I went to see an apartment in the East Village that was listed as having a bathtub and outdoor space, both rarities in my price range. When I arrived, the broker, who looked and smelled like he hadn't slept since a frat party the night before, hurried me into the dimly lit studio with aging appliances and a bathroom the size of a locker room shower. It did, in fact, have a bathtub, but that was about all that fit in there.

"Well?" he pressured, popping a second Listerine strip in his mouth. "I already have two applicants queued up for this one, so if you want to submit an application, I would do it now."

An application and background check fee in Manhattan in 2017 cost between $200 and $500. This was more than I had in my bank account and would have to ask my parents to borrow it, so I planned to apply only to one apartment—the one I intended to live in.

"Yeah, um, I don't know… Could you show me the outdoor space?"

Hungover Frat Bro made a dramatic gesture to open the door to the public city sidewalk and said, "It's right out your front door."

Luckily, Addy and Erica lived around the corner, and I needed a soft place to land before going back on to StreetEasy.com to look for more listings. Erica buzzed me up. When I reached the entryway, I positioned myself to heave the front door that always stuck because it was coated with the "New York Landlord Special," aka twenty-plus coats of paint to cover any damage instead of actually replacing the door.

Before I fully stepped inside, I heard Addy squeal from her bedroom, "Bexxxxx! Guess what?"

"You just received a massive job offer for you, me, AND Erica?" I collapsed on their worn blue velvet couch in defeat.

"No, but almost as good. Devin needs to stay in Florida for another month, so you can rent her room while you look for your new place!"

"Yesss! Hey, Roomie!" Erica said as she popped out of the bathroom with her long platinum blonde hair wrapped up in a bath towel rolled on top of her head.

"Yes! Great! Thank you!" I confirmed as I scooped up Lola in my arms, snuggling her close.

"*Three's Company*-themed party toniggggght," Erica called over the hum of her blow dryer.

"I assume I'm Jack?" I said with a giggle.

"Obvi!" They shouted in unison.

I headed home to pack up as much of my clothing and personal belongings as I could. The rest was already boxed up because I could not WAIT to move out. As I put my key in the scratched door of Apt 2B, I looked up to see an eviction notice. I'd almost missed it, the ripped slip of paper camouflaged among the peeling paint.

"Yes, please." I laughed. "Do me a favor."

I hadn't paid this month's rent yet. But, in fairness, I had requested that the gas leak be repaired and the water leak in the bathroom be fixed. My choice was between a carbon monoxide diffuser effect OR no gas to cook with, and the six-inch flood in the bathroom remained. On the upside, the water kept the cockroaches out of at least one room. I had documented these atrocities along with photos of the rat hole in my entryway and the homeless gentlemen who often slept in the building's hallway with no response from building management.

I tried to see the eviction as a blessing. It would allow me to save some money while I found my new apartment, and now I could actually afford to pay Devin for the use of her room this month.

I lugged my suitcase up the five-story walk-up to Erica and Adelaide's three-bedroom on Avenue C. Their building wasn't much nicer than mine, BUT it was carbon monoxide and rat free (as far as we knew). I began unpacking my things in Devin's room, which was painted a serene mint green, faintly smelled like sage, and had inspirational quotes scotch-taped to the walls. Devin also had the only TV in the place, so I had basically landed in the VIP suite of apartment 5F. Did I ever see myself living like a messy bohemian college kid in my early thirties? No. Absolutely not. But there was a lot of love here and that was exactly what I needed.

Our *Three's Company* dinner party, like all our "theme parties," consisted of Erica, Adelaide, and myself in themed outfits ordering takeout.

"These are actually really cute," I pointed to the 1970s-style velour track pants Erica had loaned me from their styling closet.

A major benefit of my stay at The Gallivanter Girls HQ was the piles of great clothes and accessories for styling, as well as countless beauty products that were regularly gifted to them. Home facials and DIY mani/pedis were a nightly occurrence. I looked up from painting my toenails aubergine—what Amanda used to call "pretentious for eggplant"—to notice Erica opening her laptop.

"Posting a blog?" I asked.

"Not now. Sunday night is the best time to look at the gigs section on Craigslist," she noted.

The Gallivanter Girls were amazing hustlers, a skill that was necessary to make it in New York.

"Oh, here's one for you, Bex! Experienced designer needed for the launch of a new lingerie line. Must have bra and corset construction knowledge, up to $6K for the entire project. God, I wish we had techy skills like you."

"OMG, that's more than I've made in months! Yes, please! Forward me the link," I said gratefully.

Adelaide scooted next to Erica and scanned the listings before narrowing in on one.

"Wait, what is a Grape Stomper? I feel like we could all stomp grapes... It says 'luxury fetish wine label seeks attractive women to stomp grapes barefoot. $200 per hour.'"

"Maybe if we all go together?" Erica said hesitantly.

"I mean, it's *$200 an hour*," Addy said, as though our answer should've been obvious from the beginning.

"Okay, okay," I said, caving.

Addy drafted a response with our profile photos and iPhone pics of our bare feet as requested, while I responded to the bra designer post.

The next morning, I fed Lola and headed to the kitchen to make a pot of coffee and scramble some eggs for all of us. I stopped in my tracks, pan in hand, when I realized that Addy and Erica were still asleep. Instead, I took my cup of coffee to the fire escape outside of Devin's window, from which you could just barely see the tip of the Empire State Building.

"Thank you," I said out loud to the Universe, to Erica and Addy, to Devin, and to the Empire State building, which was my favorite New York landmark.

I'd love to have a view of you in my next place, I thought as my eyes drifted over to Devin's closet, my gaze resting on one of the quotes taped up on the door.

Believe you deserve it, and the Universe will serve it.

As I finished my coffee and stepped inside to get a second cup, I noticed a deck of Tarot cards sitting on Devin's desk amongst some other oracle cards and piles of workout clothes. I remembered how I loved my first deck so much that I dressed up like the fortune teller on the box for my fourth-grade Halloween party.

I walked over and picked up the deck, shuffled, and pulled a card: The Hanged Man. *It's time to surrender.* I smiled. Since the night I pulled myself off of Amanda's floor and decided I was going to try, somehow, to tap back into this lifetime, I very much felt like I was hanging upside down and seeing life from a completely new perspective. It was hard and uncomfortable, but also humbling. Being forced to surrender also opened up a whole new realm of unknown possibilities.

"Maybe I will see you soon," I said to the Empire State Building before I headed back to the kitchen.

"OMG Bex's officially the BEST roommate! She made eggs, toast and coffee already!" Addy shouted in the direction of Erica's bedroom before walking over and planting a big kiss on my cheek.

We sat at the little kitchen table and carried out the millennial ritual of eating together while staring at our phones.

"Yesssss!!!"

"O-M-G!"

Addy and I squealed at our screens at the same time.

"The grape dude wants to hire us!!! $200 an hour, babbbbbby... Tonight!" she announced triumphantly.

"I mean if we all go together..." Erica reiterated again.

"Totes. We got this," I added.

It was probably the strangest job I'd ever agreed to, but I couldn't argue with the fact that the money would be incredibly useful.

"Wait, what were you OMG-ing about?" Addy asked, looking up from her phone.

"The lingerie post lady wants to interview me this afternoon!" I said wide-eyed, still stunned.

"Yessssss. Money manifesting Monday!!!!!" Addy sang in her best Biggie Smalls voice.

I entered a medical spa building later that afternoon, afraid I had the wrong address, when Vera, a stoic woman in her mid-forties with dark brown eyes and strawberry blonde hair, entered the waiting room using a walker. The ad explained that Vera was a former garment production Vice President who was now starting her own line.

"Rebecca? Hi, I'm Vera. This is my husband's office where I'm completing the interviews since we're based in Staten Island. You're Polish," she asked/stated.

"Yes. My grandparents spoke Polish, and my dad knows a little, but, unfortunately, I don't," I said trying to place her accent.

"That's okay. I only speak English and Russian. But I like Polish girls. They're the hardest workers," she nodded, mostly to herself.

I supposed that was true. I mean, I was currently willing to stomp grapes and take a job from Craigslist in Staten Island. Maybe it was in my blood. I thought of my grandmother, who worked as a housekeeper before marrying my grandfather. On our Disney World vacation, she would vigorously clean our Days Inn hotel room before the maid came each day. I find myself doing the same in hotels now, and I make sure to leave any spare cash I have for housekeeping, as an offering for my grandmother.

"I'm just gonna get down to it. Your background and portfolio of work is the best I've seen. Your communication is professional and efficient. And you're Polish. I'd like to offer you the job, but

I need you to start this Friday. I like to work straight through an entire day so you can come early in the morning and stay the night if needed. I expect the hand-off process to take a day and a half tops. The entire project will take four to six weeks max with two, maybe three, in-person reviews. The pay is $6,000 and I can issue fifty percent upfront. Any questions?"

"Yes!" I blurted out happily, feeling as if I'd just won the lottery.

"So? What is your question?" Vera asked.

"Oh, no. No questions. I mean, yes, I can start Friday."

As I climbed the Mount Everest of staircases to Addy and Erica's apartment, I began mentally preparing myself for the next gig, coming up in less than two hours. When I entered the apartment, the girls were already in the living room with piles of outfit options ready.

"I'm thinking latex. At least for the bottoms—easy to clean after if there's any grape juice on them," Erica said, picking up a pair of black latex leggings and eyeing them thoughtfully. They both paused to look at me in my super corporate pencil skirt and black button-down from my interview.

"Ok, let me go look to see what I have," I sighed.

How is this my life? This shit was cute in college maybe, but at this point? I put down my black tote bag with my laptop.

"Yeah, I hear ya on the latex, Erica, but I was thinking… more like… Italian Villa-inspired," Addy said, riffling through a mound of dresses.

Lola's head popped up from the pile like a whack-a-mole on cue. She always seemed to know when I needed a smile. I kissed her head and walked to the little green bedroom to change.

Nights like the one we were about to have were the hardest without drinking or Xanax. I had to actually feel all the discomfort of situations that I would have chosen to numb before. I looked in the mirror in the cramped little room and wondered how this was where I ended up. After successfully climbing nearly to the top of the corporate ladder in my twenties, I landed here—in my early thirties, living in a filthy fifth story walk-up, about to squash grapes in a warehouse for some foot fetish weirdo in order to pay my bills. A big part of me wanted to bail. Vera had just given me a check for $3,000 as a fifty percent deposit for the design project. This was more money than my starving little checking account had seen in a very long time. But I now knew trauma and fear of lack like never before, due to the inconsistency and sparsity of incoming funds over the past couple years. I had to go—I was afraid to say no to any opportunity.

God, I really, really wanted a drink. I knew the girls usually had free bottles of booze from blog sponsors in the freezer, but I also knew that would only make everything worse. I would let down my parents who were paying for my therapy. Amanda still hadn't spoken to me since *that* day, and she firmly vowed she never would if she ever found out that I drank or used drugs again. I couldn't afford to lose more than I had already lost. I looked back at the Hanged Man Tarot card flipped over on the cluttered dresser. *Surrender to new perspectives, alright. At least I wasn't having to do this alone.* My old best friends of Vodka and Xanax were replaced with Adelaide and Erica, a casting change that I became more and more grateful for each day.

I settled on a 1950s style black dress that reminded me of the *La Isla Bonita* music video. Addy wore a cap-sleeved black dress with a tiered skirt. Erica compromised and combined the latex pants with an off-the-shoulder shirt and pepper spray.

We arrived at an address just off the westside highway in Hudson Yards, half-picturing a serial killer's lair and half-hoping for the infamous grape squashing scene from *I Love Lucy*. We knocked on a steel gray door spray painted with the street address number 3115.

"Um. Hello?" Addy called out sheepishly.

"Hey y'all—right on time, come on in."

A large man in sweatpants and a t-shirt with several food stains creating an almost avant-garde-looking graphic down the front of his shirt introduced himself as Viper. He explained that he was the one Addy had been conversing with from the ad. He was a DJ by trade and, apparently, also the head of the warehouse "vineyard."

"So, uh, where are all the grapes?" Erica said with her hand firmly gripped on the pepper spray inside her purse.

"Oh yeah, come over here."

He walked us towards the center of the room where a green plastic tarp was already laid out.

"And this is where he rolls up the bodies," Addy whispered to me, only half-joking.

Before I could respond, Viper pulled out a plastic Gristedes grocery bag and produced two bunches of grapes.

He placed them on the green tarp and said, "If you wanna take your shoes off, I'll cue some music up," and headed back to the makeshift DJ booth.

"Ok... So, Erica, hands on the pepper spray at all times," I directed under my breath.

"Why do you think I wore long sleeves and the latex chastity belt pants? " she asked rhetorically, smiling proudly.

"Also, if this is in fact *not* a serial killer sitch, HOW do we make those two bunches last for an hour to get paid?" I whispered seriously, committing to making a minimum of $200 since we were already in this godforsaken warehouse.

"Squash slowwwwwly... Use mostly your little toe," murmured Addy.

Viper looked up from the speakers and said, "Dammmn, you girls do have some good grape stompin' feet."

He proceeded to put on Stevie Wonder followed by some other equally uncomfortable slow jams as we moseyed around the grapes, trying to count the amount of time by how many songs had passed.

After what felt like eternity and a day—and after there was nothing but a lukewarm puddle of translucent liquid with a bunch of flat grape peels—Erica finally caved.

"Uh Viper, I think we're done. We're happy to stomp some more, but we really macerated the heck out of these ones," she said.

He came over to examine our work and said, "Well, ladies, it's not quite the full hour, but if you could put on those heels," he said pointing to a pile of plastic shoes in the corner, "I will transfer the wine into bottles and you could present it."

"Is THIS the part where we die?" Addy whispered to us.

"I think I did die. I thought I didn't, but maybe I did and this is hell. Glad you guys are here with me," I answered.

"Do they not fit?" Viper asked, annoyed that we hadn't yet put on the seven-inch platform lucite sandals.

"I might die of a broken ankle," Erica whispered.

"Yeah, Viper, We're trying them on now," I finally chimed in after moving through most of the evening in a mute zombie-like state.

Once the three of us were all strapped into the clear pole dancing shoes, Viper brought us three recycled wine bottles, each partially filled with the grape goo from the plastic tarp.

"For the remaining fifteen minutes, why don't you present

the wine?" he requested as he played Def Leppard's *"Pour Some Sugar on Me."*

Viper was probably expecting a titillating *Coyote Ugly* dance routine of some sort. We locked eyes nervously and, as if by telepathy, we all got the mental cue of *Drop Dead Gorgeous*, the 1999 cult hit about a Midwestern beauty pageant—and simultaneously sprung into action. Instead of gyrating or pouring feet-juice wine seductively on one another, we did the most unsexy Miss America style pageant walk slowly in circles, holding our wine bottles up like trophies and doing circular hand waves at Viper.

After shaking his head and smirking, he just said, "All right, all right that's good. We'll cap it at one hour."

He pulled a wad of $100 dollar bills out of his wallet and made good on his word. We collected our pay before crawling into an Uber, trying respectfully not to get the driver's seats sticky from our grape-coated legs.

"Guys, how did you know to do the pageant wave?" Addy asked wide-eyed.

"I don't know. I just looked at you and I heard it. I heard *Don't Cry Out Loud,"* I explained, thinking of the hilarious performance number from the movie.

"You heard it? I saw it!" Erica exclaimed. "I saw Denise Richards doing the wave on the swan!"

"Power of Three! We are powerful witches, yo!" cheered Addy.

"I used to be able to do that as a kid… I never could when… when I was drinking though," I deciphered out loud.

After showering the grape goo off and hugging Erica and Addy goodnight, I crawled into bed with Lola and my laptop. I opened up my email and saw I had a response from Kevin Banks, who

I had met in my Playboy days and had done some branding and consulting work for in the past. The new agency he started had posted an ad that I had responded to a few days prior for a temporary role: their Fashion Director was going on maternity leave. He had emailed me and CC'd HR to set up an interview for next week. A chance at a REAL job again—albeit a temporary one.

I pulled out my little Snapple gratitude jar and began to write my list for the day. It was much more impressive than a few weeks back when I had started this exercise.

Today I am grateful:

- I get to live in a safe apartment this month with people who love me and who give me genuine hugs every day.
- I made $200 stomping grapes and did not get murdered.
- I got a gig designing lingerie in Staten Island and already received a deposit.
- I have an interview for a temporary job next week that I'm really excited about!

For the first time in a very long time, I wasn't able to fall asleep because of my excitement about opportunities, rather than anxiety keeping me up. I checked YouTube and Eli Vate had a new video up where he talked about living as a dot. He explained that he no longer made plans and just lived in each present moment fully and independently of any other moment, like a dot versus a line— very Hanged Man energy, really. This was hella uncomfortable for a maniforcer like me, but there was such a genuine peace and strength about Eli and his message. Coincidentally—or not—I had actually been living like a dot the past few weeks as these new opportunities seemed to appear, as if by magic, in my path.

Three's Company Telepathy Exercise

For more deeply connecting and/or when silent communication is necessary.

Honestly, at the time, I don't think any of us knew exactly how we were doing it, but Erica, Addy and I picked up on something with that cue to mimic *Drop Dead Gorgeous* for our sanity and safety. After learning more about psychic abilities and energies in the years since then, here's the best way I've found to tap into this.

1. **Roles:** Determine who is sending and who is receiving. If you are willingly practicing this, you can verbally assign roles. (Addy just stepped up as the sender in our case and Erica and I tapped into receiver mode.)

2. **Receivers:** Clear your mind as much as possible. It helps to picture a tunnel of white light that you are pulling the sender's message through. Pay attention to your most dominant sense. (You could hear cues, like the song I got in this chapter, or see visuals, like Erica saw the movie scene.)

3. **Senders:** Picture the image, ideally, one part of the image that is clear and crisp. Imagine pushing it through a tunnel of white light to the recipient. If possible, it helps to actually pull up the image as a photograph or video and look at it while sending it to the receiver. (For *Drop Dead Gorgeous*, Addy was sending us the pageant hand wave.)

4. **Keep practicing:** Take notes/record everything you're getting. You'll often get close or parts of the image/ symbol/word, but the more you practice the faster and easier this becomes. It is really helpful if you have others to practice with as well.

   * Helpful resources: *Mind Games* by Robert Masters and Jean Houston.

CHAPTER XI

THE EMPEROR
NEW BEGINNINGS AND PROTECTION SPELLS

The Emperor: New Foundations, Stability, Responsibility

The following Monday, I headed to the interview on Fifth Avenue and 57th Street for the temporary Fashion Director position at Nexxus Brands. Located near the Plaza Hotel and the Paris Theater, Nexxus was right in the middle of my favorite part of the city—the heart of old New York—surrounded by all the cheesy, romantic iconography I had always loved about Manhattan. Trying my best to utilize my newfound non-attachment and an openness to the Universe having my back, I took a deep breath and stepped into the elevator.

Whatever is meant to happen in my highest interest will. But please let it be that I get to work here.

The elevator opened to an outgoing, red-headed receptionist in cat-eye glasses and a warm smile. I instantly felt at peace inside, like there was kindness here. It was something I had no longer believed existed in the fashion industry.

Most design jobs are located in the Garment District, which is pretty much the armpit of midtown Manhattan. It's far too common that the company's receptionist desk and showrooms—where buyers and retailers meet and money is handed over—are posh, but design often sits on a separate floor or behind a creepy hallway with no windows, and feels more like prison labor. You have no hope of an office until you're a VP, and that's if you work for an established big brand. If you're on the licensee/manufacturing side of the business, you better get used to being jammed in a depressing, dark corner. I'd seen designers actually print 11 x 17 photos on office copy machines of the Manhattan skyline, or a beach, or of anything remotely resembling the outside world to give their bleak surroundings a small sense of hope.

Nexxus was nothing like this. The receptionist walked me through the whole office, taking me to meet Jessie, a tall, blue-eyed girl with her hair tied back neatly in a high ponytail. I would be potentially filling in for her while she was away on maternity leave.

"This is lovely," I said. "So, business and design all sit together?" I asked.

"Oh yeah, it's a small office, but it's cozy," Jessie smiled warmly. "If you want any snacks, cappuccino, or soda, it's in the kitchen."

I eyed the employee kitchen as we passed. All neatly lined up on the countertops were more snacks and sodas than I had been able to purchase in an entire month, triggering my survival instincts. I pursed my lips and internally scolded myself for having the urge to go into a full-on Little Orphan Annie, *"I Think I'm Gonna Like It Here,* a cappella solo.

Jessie walked me to the conference room. She was very pretty, soft-spoken, and smiled a lot. She was also incredibly detail-oriented and knowledgeable. Taylor, her counterpart, joined us. She oversaw the business side of the brand and had a Kate Winslet vibe, but with a sharper edge. She was very no-nonsense in a charming way. Jessie's role was a junior version of what I had done at Playboy.

"Thank you, Universe." I prayed silently, "I've got this."

I listened to Taylor and Jessie explain the nature of the brand, the licensing partners, and the day-to-day ins and outs.

Unexpectedly, an incredibly beautiful brunette quickly scampered in, looking undeniably frazzled, but impeccably polished at the same time. I would later discover she was a Gemini sun, Scorpio Rising, and therefore, a constant walking contradiction.

"Hey! I'm sorry I'm so late. I was on another call. I'm Myriam, the Senior Vice President of Merchandising."

"...Hi, I'm Rebecca," I managed to exhale after an uncomfortably long pause.

I have worked with countless lingerie models, actresses and celebrities... I mean, even Gia was pretty intimidatingly stunning in person, but Myriam was like... scripted TV gorgeous. She had this perfect La Mer commercial skin, seemingly effortless—but I'm sure super expensive—hair, and perfectly symmetrical features. She was also about my size, maybe smaller. I had an extreme weakness for powerful petite women: the Madonnas and RBGs of the world.

Taylor cleared her throat. She was trying to get through this interview as efficiently as possible and seemed slightly annoyed at the disruption.

"As I was saying," she continued, "Jessie will be here to

onboard whoever is hired for the first few weeks. After that, continue to CC me and Jessie on all emails…"

"And me!" Myriam added emphatically, "CC me on everything!"

"Yes!" I assured, a bit too energetically.

"So, you're in SoHo?" she asked, eyeing the address on my resume.

"Yes… but I'm moving," I said, trying to will that into being as quickly as possible.

"Oh, we live close to there: East Village, Avenue A," she said, running her hand through her hair in a way that flipped it into a perfect side part just slightly falling over her left eye.

"By *we*, she means her and her Pomeranian, Jade," Taylor said with a hint of mockery in her tone.

Pomeranian?! In the immensely twisted and creative theater inside my brain, I began to craft a music video of how Myriam would fall in love with me and steal the remnants of my heart that still belonged to the ghost of Melissa's past. It would all go down at an after-work karaoke team happy hour where she would sing a custom rendition of Taylor Swift's *You Belong With Me*.

She's in the Hamptons
I'm on Avenue A
She's on tv shows
And I take the subway…

Then, after the chorus, our Pomeranians would dance out as glitter confetti fell from the ceiling and we'd live happily ever after…

All of a sudden, Myriam looked at me quizzically. *Oh Shit. In my musical theater remake, I missed an interview question.*

"Yes?" I said hoping that she would repeat whatever I had just daydreamed over.

"What question did you have, then?"

"Right... Right..."

Luckily, I easily BS-ed a question about the difference in licensing partners in the US versus the UK, which the trio seemed satisfied with.

I was so flustered that I forgot to go find Kevin afterward. I shot him a thank you email to extend my gratitude for arranging the interview and congratulated him on the new office space. He had recently left his previous company and started Nexxus with his business partner.

Kevin was one of the kindest and most genuine humans I had ever met. A tall, blonde, handsome, adoring husband and father of three, Kevin was the type of guy you wanted your sister or your best friend to marry. Heck, I would want to marry a guy exactly like Kevin if I were into dudes. He really listened when people talked, and he saw the humans before and beyond the dollars and cents of the business, which was exactly what made him and his ventures successful. I worked on some smaller freelance projects for Kevin in the past, and from the moment I met him, I felt an admiration and connection to him that was extremely rare—like a brother from a past life.

As I headed home I could still feel the mindfulness and grace that radiated out of the halls of Nexxus like a rare, exceptionally good cologne. That was Kevin's soul signature.

Two days later, I was headed to a therapy session in an Uber ride I splurged on, thanks to my grape stomping and Staten Island lingerie line cash. I checked my phone and saw an email from Nexxus.

From: Jessie Trimmel <jtrimmel@nexxus.com>
Date: Wed, April 26, 2017 at 4:30 PM
Subject: Fashion Director Maternity Leave Role
To: Rebecca Szymczak

Rebecca,
It was a pleasure meeting with you on Monday. The team was very impressed with your background and would like to have you start the following week so we can work together for a couple weeks before I take my maternity leave.

-Jessie

I re-read that email three times, screenshot it, texted it to my mom, then texted it to Erica and Addy as I cried with gratitude. After the downward decline that had me working out of a sample closet at the horrible garment companies I had partnered with for my lingerie line, to taking random jobs from Craigslist so I could simply survive, I felt like I had just won a massive lottery. Being in a civilized office with kind, accomplished people would be enough to put me back on my feet. Even if the maternity leave were only a few short months, it would be a much-needed career rehab.

I looked up to realize that I was stopped in complete gridlock on 6th Avenue.

Shit! I'm gonna be so late, I thought as I grabbed my phone again to text Keith to apologize and confirm that I was en route for our therapy session.

After clicking send, and moving less than two feet in five minutes, I looked up to see the cross street to reference how far away I was. My eye was drawn to a sign that said, "Luxury rentals, No Fee, One Month Free." This building was nice, like *really* nice, and Chelsea was my favorite neighborhood. It was where I had lived almost the entire time I was in New York, with the exception of my death row stay in SoHo-close-to-Chinatown in the Cupboard Under the Stairs.

I instantly called the number on the sign and asked the cost of a studio.

"Wait—WHAT?!" I asked so aggressively into the phone that the driver turned around.

HOW was a studio in an elevator doorman building with a roof deck and gym basically the same cost as a windowless gas chamber?

New York real estate was insanely unpredictable like that, you never knew what you could find on either end of the spectrum.

"And there's no fee? At all? What is due upon signing?"

This was crucial because, at that time in New York, you could be required to pay an application fee of $200 to $500, first and last month's rent, a security deposit (often one month's rent), and a broker's fee of up to fifteen percent of the annual lease. So, in order to rent a small studio apartment in Manhattan, you could easily be required to hand over more than $10,000 up front.

"There's no broker fee, just a credit check fee of $50, first month's rent, and a security deposit of $750," the agent from the building's rental office reassured me.

"Can I see it now?" I asked excitedly.

"I'm about to head out for the day unless you can *literally* get here in the next five minutes," he scoffed.

"Yes. I *literally* can!" I exclaimed as I leapt out of the Uber, thanking the Universe for this rush hour gridlock.

I texted Keith an apology and asked if I could pretty please reschedule our appointment.

"No worries. See you next week," he shot back quickly, seemingly relieved to have the hour free.

The building was beautiful. High ceilings and marble floors. It smelled like Eucalyptus in the lobby. The doorman (yes, doorman!) directed me to the elevator up to the 12th floor for the leasing office. The agent took me to a 450 square-foot studio, which—unless you're a New Yorker—sounds teeny tiny and was undeniably smaller than the apartment I had shared with Amanda, but it was much bigger than the SoHo cupboard. It had a bathtub, marble countertops, stainless steel appliances, hardwood floors, and two walls of windows... with... a view of the Empire State Building!

"Where do I sign??" I asked the agent.

"Well, you have to fill out an application in the office," he said flatly.

I'm not gonna lie, I stepped out of surrender and back into maniforcer mode at that moment. I had a file folder on my phone of all the documents I needed to apply to apartments because I had been looking for weeks now. I called my mom excitedly and asked if she could help as a guarantor for this application. After hearing all my horror stories of looking at listings, she was thrilled I had found a nice and safe apartment that I wanted to live in.

"Yes, of course! It sounds amazing!" she said with so much love in her voice. "I can come and help you move in. This is great news! I love you so much!"

I was approved for the apartment two days later and my mom drove from Pennsylvania to help me move from the Cupboard Under the Stairs to my studio in the sky. We were both sweaty and covered in dust when we finally took a break from unpacking.

She wrapped her arms around me and said, "I'll do whatever I can to make sure you never have to live like that again. I promise."

I hugged her back tightly, trying not to cry. I didn't know where to even begin apologizing for what I must have put her heart through in those dark years. Instead, I just thanked her repeatedly, almost hourly, for co-signing the lease, helping me get into therapy, and ensuring I had a safe new home. I could feel her gratitude as well; gratitude that I was alive and much healthier due to my progress over the past month. She kept telling me how good my skin looked. Hydration happens more naturally, I guess, when your body doesn't need to process gallons of alcohol. I also felt her sorrow, for not knowing how dark things truly had been for me.

Together, we unpacked the entire apartment in forty-eight hours. In true Virgo fashion, my petite, sixty-four-year-old mom—whose love language is acts of service—drilled and hammered every piece of furniture and made sure every picture was hung so that I could wake up to go to work on Monday in a clean, peaceful, and organized new home.

That apartment inspired me, for the first time since childhood, to wake up early—as opposed to sleep-timing my alarm until the very last possible minute. I began waking just after sunrise so I could meditate on the roof and watch Eli Vate's newest videos before rushing into my day.

In his latest video, he shared, "Our life can change in an instant. We can quantum leap," with a reassuring grin.

As I closed my eyes to meditate that morning, I felt like I had quantum leapt right to this very roof-deck.

"Does it work?" a voice interrupted my morning meditation.

"The dog or the meditation?" I asked, slowly opening my eyes to see Lola curled next to me on the wooden bench, facing the eastern view of the city skyline.

"I meant the meditation. I see you here most mornings. But either, I guess?" the gardener smiled.

"Well, she doesn't work at all. Unless you count holding down the rug in my apartment. The meditation… It's a process, but it has been useful, yeah."

And it had. The free guided meditations and Eli's videos were the first healing tools that really helped me. Even before I found Keith and started therapy with him, meditating had drastically decreased my anxiety, and while it was still a very white-knuckled and often challenging effort not to drink, the meditations had allowed me to eventually wean off all my medications. It even helped me to be much more present and be able to hear the inner voice that I had blocked for so many years.

I waved to the gardener as I scooped up Lola to get ready for work.

The days at Nexxus—even the monotonous ones that were filled with emails and repetitive tasks—gave me a sense of purpose again. I was grateful to have a routine and a place to go where I made an impact. What made it even more enjoyable, were all the people that worked there, *especially* Myriam. That particular day, after a morning full of meetings, I planned to walk to the bank to deposit my paycheck. I did one quick scan of my inbox before heading out. An all-company email caught my eye:

From: Hannah Reese <hreese@nexxus.com>
Date: Mon, May 22, 2017 at 8:30 AM
Subject: Snack Room
To: All Employees

Dear Team,
We've recently noticed a shortage of supplies
in the kitchen. We encourage you all to enjoy
the complimentary beverages and snacks, but if
possible, we'd like to suggest two to three items per
person per work day. If anyone needs additional
assistance in any way, please come speak to HR.

Fuck! My stomach dropped as I looked below my desk into my tote, which had three Diet Cokes and two rolls of toilet paper from the office stowed away. I had never even taken paper clips from a job before, but I was still easing out of survival mode. While I was beginning to make a little bit of money from Nexxus, it still took a while for my paychecks to arrive, and I put everything I had so far into my new apartment. I cringed as I re-read the email. *They were so fucking kind about it, too.*

No one here knew how poor I was. I vowed to myself, *One day, I am going to be incredibly abundant again and I will send Kevin a case of Diet Coke and toilet paper with a thank you note.* I grabbed my jacket to head out to the bank, needing to deposit my check as quickly as possible.

I nearly body-checked Kevin, entering the elevator.

In my first few weeks at Nexxus, I had awkwardly managed to avoid Kevin. I was afraid he would see how broken I was and realize he made a mistake by hiring me. I was sure that at any moment, he would recognize that I didn't belong here with all these successful people who could easily afford their own soda and toilet paper.

"Sneaking out early?" he teased, stepping out of the elevator and into the hallway towards his office.

"Oh my God, no! I'm just running to the bank. On my lunch

break. It's on 57th. I'll literally be back in five minutes." I could feel myself turning red. *He knows I'm a TP thief! He's going to fire my ass, and then it's back to gas leaks and cockroaches!*

"I'm just kidding, Bex. Enjoy your lunch break," he smiled gently.

It's okay. You found a safe place to land.

That Saturday, I invited Chloe and our friend Sami over for brunch to celebrate my new carbon monoxide-free apartment and my employment at Nexxus.

"This is super cute, Bex. I mean, I never saw the other place, but I love this one," Sami said supportively.

Sami was a former model turned cardiology director who lived in suburban New Jersey, but came into the city often for medical conferences. We met through Chloe a year earlier when I was far too embarrassed to let a beautiful, successful doctor see the SoHo-close-to-Chinatown Cupboard.

"Well, all that matters is that we're here now," Chloe said warmly.

"So, what's new with Sexy Clippy?" she prodded as I set the small round table with three tiny stools for brunch.

"I mean, there was mostly just more work-appropriate touching, but I thought there was a breakthrough this week because she said 'my *lesbian sisters* and I are having dinner tonight.'"

"She has multiple lesbian sisters?" Chloe mused.

"I mean... yes. You got that right away? I naively thought she meant, 'Me and my lesbian peeps', because I'm also a lesbian... as in, I got all my *lesbian* sisters with me... Ugh. I'm such a loser."

"Wait... Back up, why do we call Myriam 'Sexy Clippy' again?" Sami perked up.

"Because she's a Gemini so she has that very flirtatious but scattered, frantic vibe. She's always sitting on top of my desk, playing with my hair or leaning over me while I work…"

"Like Clippy!" Chloe added excitedly.

"Huh?" Sami questioned.

"That cartoon paper clip, Clippy, from the OG version of Microsoft Word that would always pop up when you were working on a document asking if you needed help when you clearly did not," Chloe, the queen of 90s nostalgia, explained.

"Oh yeah… Wait, that paperclip was the worst! That sounds annoying AF," Sami concluded.

"I mean, yes, but she's really pretty. So, slightly less annoying than the paper clip," I added.

"That's why she's SEXY Clippy," reiterated Chloe.

"Ugh. The fact that I even CARE so much that Myriam is possibly gay is weird right?"

"In fairness, we spent just as much time playing the game of *Will Melissa Ever Come Out?* as now we do *Gay or Gemini?*" Chloe calculated thoughtfully.

"Ugh… I think the answers are: No and Gemini. I probably need to move on from this scenario as well."

"What do the cards say?" Sami asked, pointing to a well-worn deck sitting in a little glass case on my coffee table. She was one of my biggest supporters throughout my rediscovery of Tarot. The deck on display was the Hanson-Roberts deck that I got from Waldenbooks when I was eleven. I acquired several different decks over the years, but none of them quite worked with me the way that first deck did. I still felt drawn to its small card size and whimsical pixie-like artwork. Being guided back to Tarot recently while at Erica and Adelaide's, caused me to miss my OG deck.

My mom, in all of her Virgo organization and neatness, was still somewhat of an emotional hoarder. I often teased her about the containers of 35mm photos, Hallmark greeting cards, and my old high school art projects she had stashed away. But when I asked if she still had my childhood Tarot deck, she magically knew exactly which storage bin it was in and shipped it to me with a note that said:

Bet you're grateful for my hoarding now.
☺ Love you! Mom

I grabbed the Tarot deck off my coffee table and began to shuffle.

"I already know the answer to *Gay or Gemini?* so, how about I read for you?" I asked Sami.

"I mean, you know I'll never turn down a reading," she replied.

She and Chloe gathered around the small living room coffee table, my unofficial Tarot Parlor, and sat cross-legged on the floor.

As I flipped the first card over, I revealed the Eight of Wands Reversed coming through the recent past energies.

"Upside down! Is that bad?" Sami asked nervously.

"No, but were you supposed to hear about an increase or new level of responsibility at work that didn't come through yet?"

"Yes!!! Ugh, it should have been announced weeks ago."

I flipped the Star card next.

"It's coming. Just delayed. But there's a reason for the delay, so trust the timing," I explained.

"Do me! Do me!" Chloe chimed in.

I shuffled again and flipped over the Seven of Cups, Ace of Cups, and Knight of Cups. I began to giggle.

"What? What's funny?" Chloe demanded.

"It's just… Well, it looks like you might have too many Marys in the manger," I explained to the newly single and apparently *very popular* Chloe, pointing to the cards.

147

A few Christmases ago, Chloe's mom was setting up the annual holiday miniature nativity scene on an end table in the living room. She noticed that Joseph had somehow gone missing while unpacking and she made a DIY decision to replace him with another Virgin Mary figurine instead. Now, any time one of us has too many dating options (which is almost always Chloe) we reference the "Too Many Marys" Christmas.

"Chloe's manger is always rockin'," Sami added with a wink. "Ok, Your turn."

"Ok, just one for me," I complied. I shuffled again and flipped over the top card revealing The Lovers Reversed. I shook my head and we all laughed. The Lovers, ruled by Gemini, in the upside-down position was a clear "No" that even Tarot novices like Sami and Chloe understood.

That message got a bit easier to accept the longer I worked at Nexxus.

One morning, I walked in to hear Myriam complaining about a foul odor in one of the bathrooms.

"I mean, it is a *bathroom*," the receptionist stated factually.

"It's possible to train your bowels to go number two at the same exact time every day so there's no need to go in a public place. People just need to train themselves properly!" Myriam instructed.

"Oh hey, Bex!" Myriam smiled as she looked up from her digestion lecture. "I wanted to thank you again for watching Jade for me last week. I have something for you in my office," she said, referring to my dog-sitting the week prior. She motioned for me to follow her.

That was the thing about Myriam, just as I was ready to write off any potential for friendship between us due to her militant Mommy Dearest policing of the general public, she would surprise me with a heartfelt smile or laugh—or today, apparently, with a thank you gift.

As I stepped into her office, she handed me a shopping bag from ABC Home.

"Oh wow, I love this place," I said genuinely about the Flatiron home and gift shop that had been beyond my bank account for years now.

"It's just small—silly, really. You can return it if it's dumb. There's a gift receipt," Myriam said nervously, taking no breaths in between sentences.

Before even opening the tissue paper, I looked her in the eye and said, "I'm not returning it. I know I'm going to love it."

I reached into the bag and pulled out a beautiful navy linen box with gold etching of the Sun card beneath the words "The Illuminated Tarot."

"Oh my God! I love it! *How* did you know?" I asked, awestruck by her ability to find the perfect gift.

"I just know you're always talking about astrology and seem to be into witchy stuff, and it looked like you... But like I said, there's a gift receipt," she stammered.

I jumped up to hug her before heading to my desk. The funny thing was even though she didn't fully realize it, her Higher Self totally knew. But her human self seemed uncertain as to why she chose it, and equally confused as to how much I liked it. It was the first of many messages Myriam would deliver to me to help direct me on my path.

Taylor came over to ask my input about the hang tag designs on some men's t-shirt samples that had arrived the previous day. Usually very efficient and to the point, she uncharacteristically stopped mid-sentence and pointed to the Tarot deck on the corner of my desk.

"Do you know how to read Tarot?" she asked.

"Yeah. Kinda. I mean, I only do it for my close friends really, but, yeah," I answered, thrown off guard.

"Could you, I mean, would you maybe read for me? At lunch one day?" Taylor asked.

"Um, sure. I mean, I can today. We could go downstairs to Soleil," I said, referring to the little cafe right below our office.

"Wow, okay. Thank you!" Taylor smiled.

We quickly ordered iced coffees at the counter to justify occupying two seats during the lunchtime rush. We grabbed our drinks and headed further into the dimly lit cafe to one of the empty tables in the back. I pulled the cards out of my leather tote and began to shuffle.

"Is there anything you wanna look at specifically?" I asked.

"No. Well… Just a lot of changes coming up. So anything around that, really," she answered.

Great. That's not at all vague, I thought anxiously. I was really nervous because this was the first time I was reading for someone I didn't really know that well personally.

As I shuffled, I silently asked, *Please show me anything that is helpful, healing, and empowering for Taylor, and help me to translate the messages with clarity and ease for the highest good of all.*

I didn't know where that prayer/spell/intention came from, but I would continue to use that before every reading from that point on.

As I laid out the cards: The Empress, Nine of Cups, Wheel of Fortune, I affirmed, "Oh yeah, big changes for sure. Are you and your husband planning on having another child?" I asked.

"Oh my God, Yes! I'm pregnant! I haven't told anyone yet so please don't say anything," she said cautiously.

"No, of course not," I promised.

"But here," I pointed to the Wheel of Fortune "is there another change that this is inspiring? Another area of your life that you're wanting to reinvent? Like working in a different way maybe?"

"Yes. I mean, I'm still figuring it out," she answered cryptically, but I knew exactly what she meant.

"Well, it looks like you're being asked to lean into the potentially less secure, but more joyful feeling option, if that makes sense. You'll be rewarded for following that even if it feels a little scary," I assured her.

"Wow. Wow. Thank you! I didn't expect you to be this good," Taylor admitted. "Can I buy your lunch at least?"

"That would be incredible, thank you!" I looked down at my pitiful little sandwich in my tote bag. This meant I could save it for dinner—great success!

Thus, *Tarot Tea Time*—which was nearly every lunch hour— began. I went straight from trend presentation meetings to my unofficial seat at the cafe downstairs, and then back up to my cubicle again afterward. It didn't feel like working through lunch because it never felt like "work" the way tasks in the fashion industry did. I didn't have to prepare anything in advance and didn't have to double-check or memorize. After a session was over, there weren't any revision notes as homework, a need to change anything, or anxiety about getting it "right" in the future. I just had to show up and translate the information coming through, and when it was over, gently release the energy and reset. I was free to go about my day, or if I chose, I could open to another session and a separate delivery of information would come through to be shared.

I also felt really useful in a way I hadn't in years and was genuinely grateful to be able to help people. Unlike Sami and Chloe, I didn't know my colleagues well, if at all. This helped me to trust the information I was receiving when they confirmed things I would have no way of knowing otherwise. I learned that I was able to quite accurately see probable timelines for each of the people I was reading for. Every card has a number and an astrological association. Time frames are built into the four suits as well. Swords represent days, Wands represent weeks, Cups represent months, and Pentacles represent years. Seasons are also connected as Cups are associated with spring, Wands with summer, Swords with fall, and Pentacles with winter.

Word traveled rapidly, around both my friend group and the Nexxus office, of my accurate predictions of when new boyfriends arrived, pregnancies occurred, and even when deals closed.

I didn't really know how to charge. I finally started to accept dinners from friends in exchange for readings, but it wasn't exactly the kind of thing you could plug into a salary benchmarking website for analysis. Some people at the office bought me coffee, some paid for my lunch in return for a reading, others gave me cash or sent payment through Venmo or PayPal. I used the Tarot money as a "treat myself" fund to eat out and buy small luxuries like candles for my apartment, while I utilized my Nexxus paychecks towards rent and utilities. In the Emperor card of my life, Nexxus was the bedrock of the new foundation I was building, and Tarot was providing the tools I was using to expand upon it.

Divination Protection Spell

For Protection and Intention Used Before Reading Tarot or Using Other Divination Tools:

It's important to set a clear intention for the information coming through in a Tarot reading or other divination reading (e.g. pendulum, tea leaf readings, etc.). The spell/intention/prayer used can be as short or as lengthy as you like. I recommend including:

1. **What** you are asking to receive.

2. **Who** you wish to receive it for.

3. **How** you wish to translate it.

4. **Protection** for the reader and the individual receiving the reading.

Mine came to me that day in the cafe reading for my co-worker Taylor, and I have used a version of this ever since:

Please show me anything that is helpful, healing, and empowering for Taylor, and help me to translate the messages with clarity and ease for the highest good of all.

1. **What:** *Please show me anything that is helpful, healing, and empowering*

2. **Who:** *for Taylor*

3. **How:** *and help me to translate the messages with clarity and ease*

4. **Protection:** *for the highest good of all.*

CHAPTER XII

THE THREE OF WANDS
IN COSTA RICA, WE WEAR WHITE

The High Priestess: Journeys, Opportunities, Inspiration

I was in the middle of typing an email to one of Nexxus's licensing partners in Australia when I heard the familiar rhythm of heels clicking towards me. I looked up as Myriam perched herself on top of my desk.

"You know, I was thinking this weekend…" she began as she tossed her hair dramatically to the side.

Brace yourself, I thought, as I exhaled. That usually meant she wanted to scrap an entire presentation we spent weeks on because a new idea suddenly came to her.

"What's that…?" I asked.

"I was thinking, you would love this documentary my friend Miles produced," she said, adjusting her tortoise-shell glasses.

"Oh yeah? What's it called?" I asked, minimizing the window on the email I was writing before she could find any errors in it.

"I don't know… Something about Truth… and Ayahuasca," she answered.

It never ceased to amaze me how Myriam delivered these perfectly timed messages without any awareness of their contents, let alone potency.

"Wait, what?! I've been wanting to find a way to participate in an Ayahuasca ceremony, did I tell you that?" I swiveled around in my office chair, nearly knocking her nude Gucci pump right off her pretty little foot.

"No, I just know you're into all that stuff," she answered as she readjusted her shoe.

"Whose perspective is it told from? The medical field? The Shaman? The attendees?" I fired question after question.

"I don't know. I fell asleep. But you should watch it."

Kevin called her name from his office.

I frantically typed into my web browser bar, "Ayahuasca documentary Truth," based on the cryptic clues Myriam left me.

The Reality of Truth: Ram Dass, Deepak Chopra, Michelle Rodriguez came up with a link to a 2016 documentary. This sounded like my dream cast. I copied and pasted the link in an email to my personal account to watch later that night. I had been researching Ayahuasca for the past couple of months and had heard it worked miracles long-term with addiction. The reality of *my* truth was that outpatient therapy had been an important step, but it still felt like very intense white-knuckling. After six months of sobriety, I slipped a few times and had a couple of glasses of wine at events where no one knew I was not "supposed to" be drinking. I was always exceptionally careful when I was out. I still had the fear of Amanda popping out from around a corner and making good on her promise of never speaking to me again if I regressed. Because of that, I only ever had one to two glasses in public settings, but I had admittedly started to have wine at home again. There was always an inevitable, deep feeling of shame afterward, like a hideous wart that seemed to visually disappear but still lurked under the surface, threatening to pop up and create a big ugly mess all over again. I so badly wanted to cryofreeze the shit out of the root of this wart so that I wouldn't just battle the urge to drink, but eliminate it completely. From what I understood, Ayahuasca promised exactly that.

After watching the documentary, I knew, more than ever, that this was my chance at true and deep healing—the chance to obliterate the wart. The film shared the reactions and responses of a group of people that participated in plant medicine ceremonies and came from various walks of life. There were entrepreneurs and celebrities. There were people who had lost loved ones, and individuals that struggled with addiction. They all encountered life-altering experiences, but the most notable was the story of a man who had struggled with drug and alcohol addiction. As a result of his transformative experience with plant medicine, he decided to start his own center in Costa Rica that was comparable to a wellness resort, complete with western medical staff on site.

There were two things that previously held me back from my pursuit of Ayahuasca: 1) my bank account, and 2) I was more than a little nervous to travel solo as a 5'2", 105 lb female to the middle of the jungle in a foreign country in the hopes that I could find a legitimate Shaman who wouldn't take advantage of—or—kill me. However, thanks to my combined income from Nexxus and Tarot readings, the bank account situation had drastically improved. *And now there was the possibility of attending an Ayahuasca resort with medical staff and spa-like accommodations?* I could do that!

I flipped open my laptop and pulled up their website. The least expensive package was $2,800 for one week if you stayed with a roommate. I could afford that if I used nearly all my savings, but I would still need airfare to Costa Rica. I quickly searched flights while I held my breath, praying I could afford this. An economy flight from New York City to Liberia, Costa Rica was surprisingly less than I thought at around $300 roundtrip. *I'm doing this! I'm healing this for good!* I thought as I filled out the intake questionnaire.

I received an email the next day:

From: **Kelly Hechts <khechts@ lifeforceimprovementcenter.com>**
Date: Tues, March 10, 2018 at 11:11 AM
Subject: Awaken To Miracles
To: Rebecca Szymczak

Dear Rebecca,
Thank you so much for your interest in the LifeForce Improvement Center. We currently have a waitlist, but can add your name to the list. In the meantime, we would like to set you up for a call to confirm that LifeForce is aligned for your journey. Do you have availability this afternoon at 3 p.m. CST?

———

From: **Rebecca Szymczak**
Date: Tues, March 10, 2018 at 11:13 AM

Subject: Re: Awaken To Miracles
To: Kelly Hechts
Dear, Kelly,
Yes! 3 p.m. CST is perfect! Can you add my name
to the list now? And I will confirm again on our call.

Shit! Knee-jerk reaction! What if they screen for maniforcers?
I wondered after re-reading my sent response.

Kelly called at 5 p.m. EST on the dot. We talked through my intentions for coming and my medical history. She explained that she would send instructions for diet, preparation, and packing at least two weeks before arrival. I confirmed I wanted my name added to the waitlist and prayed that I would be called soon.

A couple of weeks later, I walked into ABC Kitchen to meet my friend Eden who was in town from Toronto. She looked exactly the same as she did at eighteen, a pint-sized Victoria's Secret Angel with perfectly blown-out dark caramel locks and a thoughtfully displayed six-pack beneath her long sleeve crop top. Squeezing her hello, I gave the girly-girl "mindful of the lip gloss" almost-cheek kiss. Then I sat down in the white chair at the ivory oak table, smiling at my love of the minimal decor that Lindsay called "insane asylum chic." As I adjusted my napkin, Eden's friend Rosanna, a gorgeous strawberry blonde with sparkling hazel eyes and Stevie Nicks' boho-babe style, sashayed up to the table with an enthusiastic open-mouth grin.

"BEX?????!!!!" she squealed.

"ROSANNA!!!" I answered.

"FINALLY!!" Eden cheered.

Rosanna and I had heard stories about each for over a decade, but we never actually met. It was a running joke throughout our college days in Toronto that, much like Clark Kent and Superman, we were actually the same person because, in spite of our undeniable similarities, we were never in the same place at the same time. We were both petite blondes with multiple jobs while in college. We were infamous for working hard and playing even harder. There were countless times I arrived at a party just as Rosanna left or vice versa. Tonight was the first time, after hearing about each other for fifteen years, that we were in the same room together.

We hugged each other tightly.

"Finally," I repeated Eden's sentiment softly as I looked into Rosanna's eyes and felt an instant connection.

"Rosanna, Bex. Bex, Rosanna. Yup, ya both exist, and apparently you both blew your lives the fuck up and now are on your path to becoming ascended masters. But can we get a group photo before diving into all that?" Eden said in her signature manner of cute quirkiness while assuming a selfie pose.

By the time our entrées arrived, I learned that Rosanna almost died in 2017 too—not by suicide, but by an accident onboard a ship in Nunavut that caused a near-death experience. Afterward, she got the clear message from her inner guidance system—whose voice, she also verified, did not sound like Morgan Freeman or a British Lady, but instead, a calmer version of herself—to stop drinking and partying.

After college, she climbed the ranks of one of the most powerful economic firms on Bay Street (Canada's Wall Street) to eventually become President and CEO. She also went through a divorce from her husband around the same time as my divorce, and was in the process of rebuilding her life.

"Wow. Even our dark nights of the soul happened…" I started,
"At the Exact. Same. Time," Rosanna finished.

"I mean, I don't think you guys were supposed to meet until
now," Eden said knowingly. "You probably would have ended up
in a gutter on Church Street, blacked out, stilettos criss-crossed,
while clutching your platinum credit cards in one hand and martini
glasses in the other."

"So true," Rosanna and I said in unison.

As we sipped our mocktails, I asked how she was finding not
drinking.

"I mean, it's been a year now, so I'm at a good place with it.
I'm still healing a lot of past trauma though," she said honestly.

"Yeah, it's been almost that long for me. I still struggle but
not anywhere as much as I used to. Occasionally I've caved, and
every time I do, the shame kicks in. I want to… not even want to
drink, for it not be a *thing*, if that makes sense. I'm on a waitlist for
this retreat in Costa Rica to do plant medicine and…"

"Ayahuasca?" Rosanna asked wide-eyed.

"Yes!! It's supposed to be amazing for addiction," I said.

"And trauma overall," she affirmed. "I am deeply interested
in this as well. Can you send me the link?" she asked, pulling her
phone out of her purse so we could exchange numbers.

I hugged Eden and Rosanna goodnight and hopped into my
Uber, feeling less fearful about my own future just by knowing
that Rosanna was in the world. It felt good to know I wasn't the
only one who silenced and ignored my inner guidance system
with Vodka and Xanax for years. Rosanna was healing, too, and it
felt reassuring to know I wasn't completely alone on this journey.

Two weeks later, I got a text from Rosanna:

I booked LifeForce for April 15-21!
I got a shared room for me and my
partner, Joel. Call now! There are
spaces from the waitlist opening!!!

I replied:

OMG Calling now! Thank
you!!!

April 15th would be exactly one year since *that day*. There was
also a new moon in Aries conjunct Uranus on the 15th, which was
supposed to be a window for making big and powerful changes. It
wasn't just *a* sign, it was *all* the signs.

As soon as I responded to Rosanna's text, I scanned my emails
for the office line to LifeForce.

Before I even got a chance to call, I received an email that I
was being offered a spot from the waitlist.

From: **Kelly Hechts**
<khechts@lifeforceimprovementcenter.com>
Date: Tues, March 29, 2018 at 11:23 AM
Subject: Opening Week of April 15
To: Rebecca Szymczak

Dear Rebecca,
Thank you so much for your interest in the LifeForce
Improvement Center. We have limited availability
for shared accommodations for the week of April
15 - April 21. Please respond as soon as possible
if you would like to confirm these dates. If you are

planning to attend, it is important that you begin the dieta attached right away as we are just days away from the fourteen-day preparation and detox plan. If you have any questions, do not hesitate to call my direct line. Looking forward to assisting you with your journey.

-Kelly

Attachment: MasterPlantDieta.pdf

I double-clicked to download the document.

MASTER PLANT DIETA

The participant must be in complete agreement to the following restrictions:

- **NO** prescription medications — Four (4) weeks/28 days before.
- **NO** cannabis — Two (2) weeks/14 days before.
- **NO** Alcohol whatsoever — One (1) week before but two (2) weeks ideally. One (1) week after.
- **NO** red or heavy meats (pork, beef, sheep, tuna, eel) — One (1) week before and after.
- **NO** dairy products (milk, cheese) — One (1) week before and after.
- **NO** hot food such as chilies, red pepper and black pepper — Two (2) days before.
- **NO** fermented food (pickles, herring, anchovies, old cheese) — One (1) day before and after.
- **NO** caffeine (coffee, black tea) — Two (2) days before.
- **NO** sexual activity — Minimum of one (1) week before.
- **NO** violent media (news, violent films, horror movies, etc.) — Three (3) days before.

Avoid/Consume Less:

- Avocados — Three (3) days before and after.
- Salt and Sugar/Honey — Three (3) days before and after.
- Tomatoes — Three (3) days before and after.
- Radishes — Three (3) days before and after.
- Onions and Leeks — Three (3) days before and after.
- Garlic — Three (3) days before and after.
- Citrus Fruit, Mangos, Pineapple — Three (3) days before and after.

You CAN and SHOULD eat lots of:

- Fresh or cooked vegetables.
- Legumes, beans, and peas.
- Rice, buckwheat, oats, barley, or other cereals.
- Fresh fruits and juices.
- Olive oil or ghee instead of other cooking oils, and avoid fried food altogether.

My party girl past-self would have bitch-slapped me for paying the price of more than one month's rent to deprive myself of everything on that list and go lay on a mat in the jungle for five days. Current me didn't even think twice about instantly replying yes to that email. I had surrendered so much already and something inside told me that this was the thing that would not just mask or repress my addiction, but might actually eradicate the root of the wart.

I had already verbally confirmed to the LifeForce reservation agent that, since we were within the twenty-eight day window, I was already off all medications, and I planned to follow everything else on the list to a degree that would make my top student self and Hermione Granger proud. I printed two copies:

one for my refrigerator and one for my desk at Nexxus. I also kept a screenshot of the list on my phone. Since the dates were a mix of anywhere from two days to fourteen, I decided I would apply the fourteen days to everything. In all of the blogs, articles, and YouTube videos I researched on Ayahuasca, it seemed the cleaner you were able to eat, the less you would experience the physical "purging" symptoms of vomiting or diarrhea in the ceremonies. I knew I could clear out the dietary stuff on my own. I needed to purge out soul trauma, not dairy products.

On March 31st, exactly fifteen days before I was scheduled to land in Costa Rica and one day before starting my very strict master plant dieta, I headed to dinner with Chloe and Sami. We sat down at The Smith in Nomad, Chloe's favorite restaurant. She could eat that damn kale and quinoa salad every day, and sometimes did. The waitress came around to take our order. Sami ordered the little gem caesar salad.

When Chloe's turn came up, Sami ordered on her behalf, "The kale and quinoa salad with chicken."

"And a side of truffle fries," I quipped.

"Heeey. What if I wanted something different tonight?" Chloe smirked.

The waitress paused.

"Nah, they're right," Chloe admitted, "and a glass of Sancerre."

"Bex, they have a vegan burger." Sami suggested, kindly looking out for my new Ayahuasca diet.

"I'll have... the filet mignon... and a Manhattan," I said, closing my menu dramatically.

Sami's eyes widened, not out of judgment, but out of sisterly concern.

"Day fifteen. The last supper," I said, exhaling deeply.

"Last supper! Go big or go home," Chloe patted me on the back.

"I still can't picture you in white," Sami said dramatically.

According to color therapy, black contains all colors, meaning it takes in everything. It's why a lot of witches wear black. It is believed to allow wearers access to all energies, with the theory that, in the absorption of everything, there is also greater access to knowledge and protection. White, on the other end of the spectrum, is the absence of all colors, representing purity, unity, and the ability to reflect rather than to absorb.

LifeForce's welcome materials encouraged us to pack white clothing for the ceremonies and I took that assignment just as seriously as the diet. I ordered a couple of inexpensive white sundresses, white cotton pants, and white linen tops online because, as a lowkey witch and a New Yorker, ninety percent of my whole wardrobe was black. I even ordered some new white underwear and socks.

"I didn't even wear all-white at my wedding!" I shook my head in response to Sami. "I'm actually a little worried that if my bag is searched at the airport I'll be detained and questioned about belonging to a cult. But in all seriousness, thank you guys so much. Thank you for watching Lola while I'm away and... just for everything. I couldn't... I don't know if I could do this without you." My eyes blurred with tears.

I had grown undeniably closer to both Chloe and Sami in the past year. There were so many stumbling blocks in shedding my former life as I tried to find my way into the new one. I often felt uncertain and vulnerable in ways that were raw and unfamiliar, like a lobster who had molted out of its old, too tight shell, and who hadn't quite settled into the new shell either. Chloe and Sami were so kind to me in that naked lobster stage. Not only had I shifted away from the numbing shield of alcoholism, but relationships were shifting, too. Four months earlier, Erica and

Adelaide moved to Tennessee as they had outgrown their bohemian Avenue C lifestyle and were focused on styling musician
clients in Nashville. Andy's business was booming and he now
had a successful product line in addition to all of his fashion week
and celebrity appointments. While we kept in touch via text, I
saw less and less of him now that I didn't live directly around the
corner. It's funny how, in Manhattan, a change of neighborhood
felt just as drastic as changing states.

After signing the checks, we shrugged on our coats to face the
chilly March evening.

Sami put her arm around me and said, "We know you've got
this, but it's ok to be nervous," as if she was offering a part of her
shell to my exposed little lobster tail.

"Ya know, it's not a fear of what I'll face, but I'm afraid to
stay," I smiled.

"You got this. You're ready to jump." Chloe said, knowingly.

It was true. My biggest fear wasn't that I would shit my pants
while hallucinating in the middle of the jungle. My biggest fear
was that—after just investing a huge chunk of my savings to go
on this journey—nothing would change.

"You got this, boo. Now go slay some demons. Next stop,
Costa Rica," Sami said with a smile.

Color Magic

From a metaphysical perspective, all colors have healing abilities. From a quantum physics perspective, all colors absorb or reflect energies. Black absorbs all colors, and therefore absorbs the most energy, whereas white reflects all colors, reflecting the most energy. A red dress contains a pigment which absorbs all the colors of visible light except for red. Since red is reflected to our eyes, the dress looks red. It's also why people wearing red are perceived as vibrant and lively because that is what is being reflected back to us when we view them, and we always remember how people make us feel.

Many in the spiritual world like to wear white for its reflection and purification properties. Though some would say always wearing black can be dangerous because you're always absorbing energy, I actually prefer it because it helps me to ground spiritual energy in the physical world. It helps me to deeply absorb, connect and understand energies in almost all situations.

Here is a list of colors and their properties to help you decide what might be most helpful for you in different scenarios:

White: Purity, Cleansing, Truth

Black: Power, Protection, Wisdom

Red: Passion, Energy, Vibrance

Pink: Love, Friendship, Nurture

Orange: Adventure, Success, Creativity

Yellow: Joy, Enthusiasm, Originality

Green: Vitality, Abundance, Growth

Blue: Tranquility, Trust, Peace

Purple: Intuition, Divination, Royalty

CHAPTER XIII

THE HIGH PRIESTESS
BROKEN BEADS

The High Priestess: Intuition, Sacred Knowledge, Divine Feminine

"**H**ey, are you going to LifeForce?" I asked timidly to a group of people at the shuttle stop exit of Liberia Airport.

"Yup. Let's get some miracles," a bearded man in a safari hat answered, taking a swig from a plastic water bottle.

"I like that shirt, kid. You seem like a 'Spiritual Gangster' to me," he said with a thumbs up.

"Thanks," I smiled, looking down at the block lettering on my sweatshirt.

"Are you… uh, doing the plant medicine?" a tall red-headed woman in Ray-Bans asked me.

Why would you come all this way NOT to? I wondered.

"Yes, what about you?" I asked.

"Oh, hell yeah," answered Safari Hat.

"I mean, I think so… I told my family I was going to a yoga

retreat. I haven't fully decided because you can just enjoy the resort and do yoga and meditate if you want," the redhead said, more to herself than to us.

"Yeah, I'm definitely here for the Ayahuasca, but I hear ya. I also told my parents it was a yoga retreat. I will tell them the whole story after, but I didn't want them to worry," I said.

As I hoisted my duffel bag into the shuttle bus, I thought about how weird it is that we feel the need to hide any form of non-traditional healing. I hadn't lied to my parents as much as I told them a partial truth. I explained that I was going to a meditation and yoga retreat with my good friend Rosanna from Toronto. There *would* be meditation and yoga, although Rosanna and I had only technically met for three hours a few weeks before, she would be there, and was from Toronto. I remained silent on the ride, nervously taking everything in. I double-checked my carry-on for my phone and Justin's scarf that I still brought with me everywhere. The wooly gray scarf was an odd juxtaposition to the tropical heat and palm trees that whirled past my window. I felt like I needed that security blanket now more than ever. I was hoping I could smuggle it into the ceremonies.

My small hands shook as I pulled out a journal that I bought especially for the trip. I opened it to revisit my written intentions. I believed the more I read them, the more likely they would happen.

1. Please heal my addiction.
2. Please heal my heart.
3. Please show me anything I need to know to become who I'm meant to be.

Forty-five minutes later, we pulled up to the LifeForce resort. I had already watched every video available from their site and YouTube, so the winding dirt road behind the entryway gate looked familiar. We were directed to the front desk to check in, which looked like the standard reception area of any tropical resort, except for a ticker-tape digital sign flashing 98.7% across the screen.

After spelling all the C's and Z's in my Polish last name, I asked, "What's the 98.7%?"

"That's the current average rate of miracles reported at check out," the concierge said, grinning.

"Just wait, you'll see," a slightly sunburned, but very blissful-looking man in his mid-thirties said to me.

"I want to be part of that," I said, giggling to the concierge.

But what if I'm the 1.3%?

You're not. You've got this.

The concierge informed me that the first thing I should do was check in at the medical facility for my intake. He then handed me a map of the property, my room key, and a flashlight keychain to navigate the grounds after dark. I had been told several times that the intake was just a standard check-up with some quick tests and diagnostics to ensure I was physically cleared to consume Ayahuasca. However, I was still nervous they would find a reason to reject me.

"Any medications?" the doctor asked.

"No, not for almost a year now," I felt the need to add, "I also followed the entire *dieta* for fourteen days. No alcohol, caffeine, totally vegan and mostly raw."

He smiled as I fidgeted with the Buddhist prayer bead necklace Justin's mom had sent me after he passed away. I had wrapped it around my left wrist like a bracelet. My hope was that Justin would show up in the ceremonies. I missed him so much; I packed all the physical reminders of him that I could.

The doctor took my blood pressure and heart rate. He then asked me to sign a form indicating whether I was choosing to take part in plant medicine ceremonies or opting out. I enthusiastically checked the yes box, signed my name, and went in search of my room.

The map of the property took me through a labyrinth of villas and past a beautiful temple where I assumed the ceremonies would take place. I pulled out my phone to take a photo, which reminded me to check if Rosanna's flight had landed yet. She was due to arrive a few hours after me. LifeForce encouraged us to arrive by Sunday afternoon to settle in as our first ceremony would take place at sundown on Monday evening. My phone showed multiple texts from Sami and Lindsay wishing me good luck, some photos of Chloe with Lola to remind me that she was in good hands, and one message from Rosanna.

All I could read from the first line of the display was: "Aaagh,"
Please let her still come! I thought. before feeling,
Either way, you've got this all on your own.

I clicked through to expand into the full text from Rosanna:

Aaagh! So our flight was delayed, and we are on the shuttle now. I hope the medical center doesn't close. Worst case, we can do the intake tomorrow. Can't wait to see you!

SO happy you're en route! Getting to my room now. The intake was fast, I think they're still open for another hour ☺

After pushing *Send*, I put the key in the door to my room to reveal a petite blonde with a pixie cut unpacking pastel pajamas into a nightstand drawer. I was taken aback by how much my roommate looked like my mom from behind. She turned around and had sparkling blue eyes, not unlike my mother's. She smiled warmly and walked towards me.

"Hi, I'm Cheryl," she said, reaching her hand out.

For some reason, I automatically wrapped my arms around her for a hug.

"Oh, you're a hugger!" Cheryl laughed kindly, embracing me back.

"I'm not usually," I answered, "It's just you… it's just that… I'm happy to be here," I said, trying not to appear any weirder than I probably already seemed.

My new roommate shared that she decided to experience LifeForce after enduring a stroke and massive health transitions over the past two years. She was seeking heart-healing as well. I shared that I was struggling with addiction.

"Oh my! You barely look old enough to drink," she said.

"I'm thirty-five, but you're officially my new best friend, Cheryl," I giggled.

I probably looked younger than usual because I had my hair in braided pigtails with no makeup, and was wearing a linen sundress from my newly purchased all-white, cult-couture wardrobe.

Cheryl and I walked to dinner together. The food was served buffet-style with abundant choices. After being on the limited *dieta* for fourteen days, I felt like Augustus Gloop, gorging himself on chocolate in Willy Wonka's factory with all the delicious raw and vegan options. I sat down at a table and waved to Cheryl so she would know where I was seated. I was chowing down the most delicious papaya I had ever tasted when I heard my name and looked up to see Rosanna running over. I jumped up to hug her.

172

"Bex, this is Joel, Joel, Bex," she said as she put her arm around a tall, handsome love child of John Lennon and Jesus, with shoulder-length dark hair and round glasses.

Joel instantly felt familiar as I reached up to hug him.

"So, we're doing it! I can't thank you enough for telling me about this place!" Rosanna said. "We wouldn't be here if you and I hadn't finally met after all these years. It was so serendipitous that you mentioned it."

"Thank YOU for giving me the extra push. It was far less daunting once I knew you would be here, too."

I hugged Rosanna again, feeling a sense of calm wash over me. Rosanna and Joel lingered by the cabanas after we left dinner but I wanted to follow the instructions we were given and get a substantial night's sleep to prepare for the first official day of the Ayahuasca journey.

"I'll see you in the intro workshop with the Shaman tomorrow morning," Rosanna said as she hugged me good night.

I waved goodbye and walked back to my room.

There were many workshops and classes offered throughout the week. The only course on the schedule listed as **mandatory** was the Intro to Plant Medicine Workshop. Despite my dislike of both the word "mandatory" and the overuse of asterisks, it seemed essential to attend. After breakfast with my roommate Cheryl, I walked into what looked like a ground-level hotel conference room, with windows framing views of palm trees and beaming sunlight. I spotted Joel and Rosanna and quickly shuffled into the row of plastic chairs next to them.

The owner of the resort, and the two female Shamans who would lead the ceremony, shared their individual backgrounds with Ayahuasca as well as key tips for those receiving plant medicine for the first time. Shane, the super tan, jovial resort owner gave some physical tips.

"If nausea or discomfort in the body strikes, it will feel far better to release and stretch out your body, breathe deeply, and surrender. Best not to fight the sensations by curling up and taking short breaths... Also, never trust a fart, if you catch my drift."

A tall, dark-haired Shaman named Baela, who seemed unimpressed with the owner's humor, followed up after.

"It is such a brave act of surrender to follow the calling here. If you can do that, you can surrender to the spirit of Mother Ayahuasca and allow her to lead you on this internal journey. More moments of surrender will be asked of you. For some, it may come in the form of relinquishing control of what you want or expect to see in the medicine. For others, a loved one or fellow traveler may struggle in the ceremony, and you may want to comfort them as you hear their cries. But it is important to remember that they are experiencing and being shown what is healing for them. Going into their journey would be like taking someone else's medication. What is healing for others could seem detrimental to you. Also, sometimes you will feel, hear, or see many things at once. Often, following the more challenging sensations or visions will result in deeper healing," she shared, pushing her braided ponytail behind her back.

"Yeah," the resort owner Shane quipped. "Like ya might see a unicorn and your creepy neighbor from childhood... and obviously, it would be more fun to jump on that unicorn... but you'll get more out of following the creepy neighbor down a dark alleyway."

A few questions were asked, ranging from extraterrestrial involvement to ideal vomit positions and postures. We were informed that we could begin entering the temple at 5:30 that evening. Baela and Shane then released us to prepare for the first ceremony at sundown.

I chose to wear another long white sundress, a Tiger's eye pendant for courage, and Justin's prayer beads wrapped around my left wrist. I also had a white "Ayahuasca prepper bag" full of supplies I'd packed myself in advance to bring into the ceremonies, including:

- Justin's scarf
- An extra pair of white sweatpants and a tank top (in case of uncontrollable "purging")
- Super plus maxi pads (for the same reason)
- Paper towels
- A water bottle
- A journal and pen
- A white eye mask with tiny rose quartz, amethyst, and tiger's eye crystals glued to where my third eye would be positioned under the mask

Cheryl was busy wrapping up a phone call, so I walked solo to the temple. I left my room promptly at 5:20 p.m. and saw that there was already a small line forming of other eagerly-punctual attendees. As we reached the temple stairs, we were instructed to remove our shoes.

I carefully slipped out of my ivory sandals while a middle-aged man with a deep voice and jolly demeanor asked, "So, what are you in for?"

"Oh wow, elevator pitch style?" I smirked.

"I guess. Well, technically temple steps style," he confirmed.

"Booze and women, mostly," I admitted.

"Wow! I did not expect that to come out of a tiny blonde in a Laura Ingles dress. I guess we've got a regular Don Draper among us," he laughed, referring to the iconic womanizing, alcoholic lead character of *Mad Men*. "Pleasure to meet you. I'm Pete," he said, extending his hand.

"I've been known to be a bit of an enigma," I admitted. "What are you in for?"

"Well, it's my second time. The first time, I re-experienced my own birth and it felt like my head was about to explode. Talked to my mom about it and apparently, I had suffered trauma at birth from too much force used with forceps. That really cleared up a lot for me, so I'm back to dive in deeper to some of my relationship patterns," he said, both vulnerably and confidently.

"Wow, that's incredible. So it can't be too awful if you're back for more?" I asked.

"Are you scared?" he questioned point blank.

"Honestly… I'm not afraid of what I'll experience, but I'm afraid nothing will change," I answered.

"You've got this," he winked and patted me on the back as we entered the temple.

Around fifty people gathered in the circular wooden arena, roughly forty that took the all-white wardrobe assignment as seriously as I had. Joel waved me over to where he had saved a mat for me next to him beside a wall. *Perfection*. The wall felt stable and Joel emitted protective brother energy. As I positioned myself on the mat and arranged all my prepper supplies, I noticed several pieces of beautiful artwork hung throughout the temple. The large framed painting facing me was the exact same pose and style as the High Priestess in Tarot: the card of intuition and sacred knowledge. I felt safer just being within eyesight of her.

We sat in meditation for around half an hour as the sun set and the Shaman prepared the medicine. I repeated my intentions in my mind like a mantra. *Please heal my addiction. Please heal my heart. Please show me anything I need to know to become who I'm meant to be.*

They called us up in sections to receive the medicine. I lined up behind Rosanna and Joel. Rosanna gave me a warm hug, and Joel gave me a high five. This was my first palpable understanding of a soul family. I knew Lindsay always felt like a sister to me, and Justin was like the big brother I never had. But this moment with Rosanna and Joel was the first time I recognized the feeling in real time: I *know* you, I *remember* you.

The procession line to receive the Ayahuasca, which was served like a viscous liquid tea, reminded me a little of communion in the Catholic Church. Still, when I reached the front, the two Shamans were much more joyful than I remembered the priests being.

"How are you doing?" one of the Shaman asked me.

"Good. Nervous," I answered.

"You have your intention?" she asked in a soft voice.

I nodded as she handed me a small, wooden cup. I drank swiftly and tried to express gratitude for the healing with all my heart. This was particularly challenging because the flavor was more what I imagined "liquid feces with a bit of maple syrup" would taste like than "magical tea."

"Thank you," I said, forming my hands in a prayer position and swallowing hard.

Thank God for my prepper bag. More specifically, *thank Mom.* I sent a massive dose of love to my Virgo mom. She was always an amazing host and prepared for almost any situation. I warmed, thinking of her as I rummaged through my bag. I used the high absorbency paper towels I brought from home (something you will not find in Costa Rica) as a tongue scraper to remove excess residue from my mouth, and then, swished with a bit of water. We were instructed not to drink too much water during the ceremony, so I spit it into my personal purge bucket.

I grabbed my mask from my bag, laid back down on my mat, and slid it over my eyes, trying to go back into meditation while the Ayahuasca took effect. I began to hear Rosanna vomiting and crying loudly. Even though she was on the other side of Joel, I could *feel* the darkness and pain she was moving through. I wanted to comfort her, but I remembered what the Shaman said about non-intervention in the healing of the medicine. Instead, I tried to send out so much love to Rosanna's heart and to Joel, who I'm sure was feeling it even more deeply than I was. Her cries softened. I wondered if I would vomit or have diarrhea. *Would that help cleanse me*? I wasn't really afraid of that part. I had all my paper towels and extra pants ready to go. I heard the spirit of the Ayahuasca answer me: *No, you don't need to purge that way. That wouldn't be healing for you.* I was shown images of myself as a little girl, and all the times that I got sick to my stomach from feeling powerless. I saw myself throwing up on tension-filled family car trips. I saw flashes of little me being badly bullied during junior high and how that developed into endometriosis with extreme nausea and vomiting later in life.

Suddenly, I felt the middle part of my forehead, where my pineal gland and third eye reside, begin to pulse. I started to see flashes of colors, mostly shades of green, appear in perfectly symmetrical, beautiful, geometric patterns. I touched my face to confirm my eye mask was still on. It was; I had been seeing the colors and patterns internally. I pulled the mask up over my head. Everything in the room had morphed. The large wooden ceiling fans shifted into cute but protective gargoyles, watching over all of us in the temple, ensuring our safety. The walls had turned colors, but the High Priestess painting was still there, unchanged.

I put my hand up against the wall next to me to view it in the beautiful colored lights, and my hand began to shape-shift. I instantly understood all the false versions of myself that I presented. One was my hand in the corporate world, one was my girlfriend hand, and another was my party girl hand. None of them were really, truly, me. I wanted to merge them all together so they would look like MY hand again. Just as I asked Ayahuasca and my Higher Self to help me show up more authentically from this point forward, a little brown and white Capuchin monkey appeared next to me. *Is anyone else seeing this freakin' monkey?* I wondered. No one else had left the inside part of the temple, but the monkey was begging me to go outside.

"OK, ya little Mofo. You better not get me in trouble," I told him telepathically.

He seemed to giggle and we walked outside together. Other people started to get up to follow.

"You're always a trendsetter," the monkey acknowledged and smiled at me.

Suddenly, ten of us were looking up in wonder at the stars. I never felt at all connected to nature before that night. All I knew was that I didn't belong in the middle of Pennsylvania, where I was bullied and unwanted. So, I learned to equate rural settings with feeling unsafe and undesired, and cities with acceptance and freedom. As I looked up at the night sky, I remembered that I *did* love nature. I did feel at home with the stars. Rosanna started to dance and grabbed my hand to twirl me around.

"Thank you, Bex. Thank you! We're here because of you," she said.

I felt the impact we all have on one another. Not just about getting to Costa Rica and to this ceremony, but when we follow our inner guidance we inspire others to follow theirs.

The following day, I met up with Rosanna and Joel at breakfast. I realized I was even hugging people differently. They were longer and more connected than my old, brief, distanced hug with a back tap.

"What a NIGHT! I don't know how I'm going to do this again. I went through literal hell last night," Rosanna said. "I wanted to join you for yoga at sunrise, but I needed the extra rest."

"Oh my god, I was sending you so much love. I felt it," I said.

"I felt you were feeling it, and I knew you were sending me white light! Thank you!" she said.

"What was it that you saw last night... if you don't mind sharing?" I asked.

"Oh god, it felt like every piece of trauma from my past, every blacked-out night, every drink and drug I ever took was being experienced all at once. The worst hangovers I've ever had, nausea, anxiety, and shame all collided together... but then, it was vacuumed out of me. Like from the inside out, and I just felt... not empty... but clean. And my intuition is already leveling way up. It's like I *know* things much faster and clearer now."

"Wow! That's incredible," I said with genuine excitement for Rosanna, although I still felt a twinge of envy that my addiction had not been vacuumed out.

"Yours is coming... tonight," she said, reading my thoughts.

A couple in their late sixties were at the end of our breakfast table and said, "So sorry for eavesdropping, but we heard you talking about addiction. That's why I'm here: opioids," the sweet redhead in cat-eye sunglasses shared.

"Yeah, that's why I'm here, too," I smiled, extending my hand, "Bex. This is Rosanna and Joel."

"Hey, Bex, Rosanna, Joel. I'm Kimmy, and this is my husband, Ted."

She smiled. Ted adjusted his khaki baseball cap as he reached out his hand to shake Joel's.

"Are you a woodworker? Do you build really cool furniture?" Rosanna asked.

"I mean, I wouldn't call myself a proper woodworker. I tinker around in the garage," Ted responded.

"Fuck right off, Ted! You're like a super skilled craftsman! Are you building some sort of desk right now?" Rosanna continued.

"I am!" he confirmed as the couple laughed in disbelief.

Damn, I want the addiction vacuum and psychic upgrades, I thought again.

"Tonight. It's coming," Rosanna confirmed with a nod.

The second night heading into the temple was a little less scary than the first because I had some idea of what to expect and had experienced the benefits of surrender. I prayed as I sat on my mat: *Show me anything I need to see, even if terrible things happened to me that I blocked out. Show me EVERYTHING I need to see to heal, even if I'm meant to leave New York and move to the jungle to live in a hut with nothing but my Tarot cards and Lola in a little grass skirt.*

The first things I started to see were the green geometric shapes again, which I heard someone else describe at lunch as "sacred geometry." Then, my forehead near my third eye started pulsing simultaneously with the right side of my stomach, where my poor abused liver was located. That's when the flashbacks started, but it wasn't like a birthday party or funeral where everyone shows the best pictures and kindest memories of you. It was the exact *opposite* of that. I was being shown movie-like visions of the most excruciating, horrible things I had done to myself and others. I saw myself doing lines of cocaine off the thigh of a D-list celebrity, nearly falling off a yacht in the process. Countless times that I stumbled home blackout drunk, barely making it to my apartment alive, were played back to me. In one of these moments, I saw little Lola licking me while I was blacked out on my living room floor, still in my heels. Her scared little soul hoped I would wake up. I saw myself hiding my addiction, lying to my parents and friends, and sneaking into Melissa's bathroom in the Hamptons to take a shot of rubbing alcohol from the medicine cabinet just to make the anxiety stop. Sobbing uncontrollably, I was drowning in sadness and disgust for how I treated myself and others. Wrapping my arms around my only friend in sight, the little orange plastic bucket, I desperately tried to vomit up the shame, but nothing came out. I was now in hell. *What if this was my life? What if I just live like this forever? Would I keep entering into toxic relationships and abusing my body by numbing myself with substances to forget the emotional abuse like a horrible purgatory loop?* I was crying and screaming so loudly that the Shaman came over and started to waft smoke from her sage over me with feathers. I looked up, and for the first time, instead of sexualizing an attractive woman standing in front of me, I saw a beautiful soul.

I repeated "Thank you," over and over again.

"Relax," she whispered to me. "If it's coming, it's going. Can you tell me what you see?"

I tried to make words through my sobs.

"It's... me... blacked out in the back of a taxi. I can't wake myself up," I said.

"It's okay. Listen to me. You have to get her," she instructed.

"I can't. She won't wake up. She looks dead," I cried and murmured to myself, "I'm so sorry. I love you. I'm sorry."

Of course, so many people abandoned me, I thought.

I wanted to leave myself. I didn't know how to get through to myself.

I somehow found the strength to carry my unconscious self out of the taxi and into my bed. I just held myself, rocking back and forth, repeating, "I love you, it's not your fault. This is going to be okay. I'm never going to leave you or let this happen again."

I saw myself open my eyes and I felt relief as the Shaman clapped her hands, trickling Florida water on my crown as I exhaled.

"It's over now," the Shaman said calmly, "You can lay back down."

"You are so powerful and amazing. Thank you," I said.

"You, too, are powerful and amazing. And you, too, are a healer," she said, hugging me before heading to assist others.

In all the temple's haziness, the High Priestess painting still remained, staring at me knowingly from across the room.

I fell asleep for a little bit. When I woke up, I tried to look at my watch, but the hands were doing a crazy circular dance. *Time is an illusion*. The next thing I knew, I felt a device being dropped over my mouth, almost like when you receive anesthesia at the dentist. Due to all the dental surgeries and procedures I had growing up, I started to fight against this familiar but traumatic sensation, but then heard a calm voice saying, *It's ok, you're safe. Trust the process.*

I exhaled deeply in an attempt to surrender, and as I did, I felt my chest opening and progressively expanding. I heard soft instrumental music playing in the background, which suddenly morphed into the theme song from the 1980's sitcom *Who's The Boss*.

My chest extended wider and I saw my heart being removed. It looked like a sad little bruised peach that had tumbled around on the back of a truck all the way from Georgia to New York City. As the music got louder, a sparkling golden heart-shaped disco ball was placed back inside my chest. *Is this my heart healing? Are those Swarovski crystals?* Before I could ask any more questions, I felt Justin's prayer beads around my wrist break apart, and a movie montage featuring all the key players in my life began to play. I saw Melissa and the great love we had shared; I apologized for the times my drinking and anxiety had hurt her in our relationship. Melissa told me she was sorry that she had hurt me so deeply. Her Higher Self explained that in doing so, she put a time stamp on my heart, forcing me to heal solo and work on myself until it was the right time for me to receive my partner, who would be equally prepared to be with me.

I was shown that Amanda and I had known each other for lifetimes! Sometimes we were siblings, often spouses, and other times, friends. I cried for what seemed like hours knowing how much I had hurt her in this life. I saw that Chloe, Amanda and I had been triplets at one point. The three of us had a pact spanning all our lifetimes to connect with each other whenever one of us experienced a truly dark time. Amanda had done exactly that for me a year ago. *I love you SO much Amanda, and I'm so sorry.*

I saw my parents and how sensitive and kind my dad is. I witnessed all the times during my early years that he comforted me when he sensed that I wasn't okay. Many past experiences were revealed from his perspective, instead of my own. I was shown parts of his childhood. I saw my stern grandfather doing the best job he could raising a son, yet teaching my father to suppress his true sensitive, empathic nature. I saw all the times I villainized my dad for his anger when, really, it came out when he was uncertain how to express fear or frustration with himself. *I love you so much, Dad. I'm sorry I didn't understand until now, and I forgive you. You're the best dad and I'm so grateful we chose each other in this lifetime.*

As I wiped away tears with my contraband paper towels, my attention drifted back to the Shaman drumming at the center of the temple while singing:

May all mothers know
that they are loved
And may all sisters know
that they are strong
And may all daughters know
that they are powerful

My mom then appeared and I was overwhelmed by gratitude. I realized I had always known what unconditional love felt like because I was raised by her. More clearly, I recognized there was a badass beneath her soft-spoken, polite nature. Her soul was incredibly strong to watch me go through the darkness I had navigated the past few years, and on a higher level, she knew it was my destined path in order for me to heal. She never gave up on me when I had completely given up on myself. She shined her light fearlessly, unwavering in her belief that I would make it through. *Thank you so much for being my mom. I don't know what I did to deserve you, but thank you! I love you.*

The strength of my sister, and how incredible she is to her children, came through. I sensed her heart and though we didn't see each other often, I felt how much we truly love each other. I was shown my niece and nephew, and all the lifetimes I had shared with my niece. A child version of Lindsay and her husband, Austin, popped up with my other friend Caroline, and a scene of us all whistling while cleaning chimneys on rooftops in the 1800s came into view. I laughed through tears at how she's had my back, literally through lifetimes. I saw Myriam dressed in a 1940s pinup-style postal worker outfit with a little mail sack, and even though she drove me batshit crazy, she was a powerful messenger that delivered a myriad of clues that led me to my healing journey.

She kissed me on the lips before saying, "Goodbye."

Wait, what? Do I have to leave Nexxus? Are we not gonna be friends? What does that mean?

"It's all perfect," she smiled and scooted off.

I saw every person who had been an impactful part of my life, and how much love we had for one another. I literally thought my sparkly new Swarovski crystal heart would burst right out of my chest from receiving so much love when I abruptly heard Kimmy, the sweet older redhead from breakfast, loudly smacking her mat and yelling, "I thought this part was over already?!"

Sofia, the petite and more introverted of the female Shamans, explained in our intro session that the ceremony songs are chosen and performed in ways to move energy, some to push you into your heart, some to make you purge. This particular song was a very loud number with lots of chanting of "AY-A-HUAS-CA." In my mind, I saw the Shamans' gowns turn into cheerleader uniforms as the lyrics morphed into an aggressive cheer:

We're gonna make you puke
Yeah we're gonna make you puke
P-U-K-E
We're gonna make you puke

Kimmy was not wrong. I also wished this part was over. As Kimmy started to yell, the Shaman moved around her, drumming and chanting louder and louder.

"You can fuck right off," the sweet sixty-eight-year-old cursed.

All at once Joel, Rosanna and I started giggling because we all knew that Rosanna had taught her that phrase just this morning. I covered my laughter with my hands as I got a quick flash of the three of us splashing around in a sink like Muppet babies. They were certainly siblings of mine.

"Are you guys kidding me right now?! Are you FUCKING KIDDING ME?" Kimmy scolded us angrily.

And like a magical orchestra, the Shaman attracted four and then eight helpers, chanting and burning sage around Kimmy. Eventually, Kimmy let out a big sigh and laid down on her mat, and seemed to go to sleep or into more peaceful journeying. It was the most beautiful visual display of fearlessly combating darkness with love.

The ceremony wound down, and we came together for a closing prayer. I methodically gathered the remaining prayer beads from Justin's necklace that broke earlier in the ceremony and placed them in my bag before heading towards the exit. I saw Kimmy and her husband on the way out and put my hand gently on her back.

"Hey, how are you doing?" I asked.

"Oh Lordy! Much better now! Rough night though," she said, glancing down at her half-full bucket.

"At least we've all been eating clean, it just looks like... a really healthy smoothie," I smiled.

"One of your most beautiful gifts is your humor, you know that, kiddo?"

"I never really thought about it, but thank you."

The next morning, I decided to skip yoga because I had too many messages to share. I emailed my mom and dad, told them everything I saw, and let them know how much I loved them. I texted my sister. And then, I called Amanda. We hadn't spoken since *that day*.

"Hey B... What's up?" she said.

"I'm so..." my voice started to break, "I'm so sorry. I love you so much and I'm so sorry. For that day... but also for everything. For the drinking, the selfishness, for all the times I didn't see you because I couldn't even see myself. You are the best human. The BEST. And I really failed you, failed us, many times. I'm so sorry. And thank you for saving me," I said through tears.

Amanda's voice cracked. "I love you, B. Thank you. You never... you never once apologized. Until now."

"I wanted to. So many times. It just felt overwhelming, like there was too much to even begin apologizing for. I love you and I'm so sorry," I said.

"Listen. Neither of us are perfect, but we've both been changed for the better because we loved each other. Thank you. I'm on my way into work, but really, thank you. I love you so much."

As I hung up, I felt like ten years had been lifted off of me.

As we walked to the temple on the final night, I told Rosanna and Joel, "I don't even know what to ask. I feel like I got everything I came for already. After everything I saw last night, I'll NEVER abuse my body like that ever again."

"For sure. Once you know, you can't unknow," Joel nodded.

"Yeah, like how I used to love chicken McNuggets when I was younger until I saw a documentary about how they genetically modify those poor chickens to have like twelve wings and three heads. I could never eat them after that."

"It's exactly like that," Rosanna grinned, putting her arm around me.

After I received my cup of medicine, I settled into my familiar spot on the mat in the corner next to Joel. There was a cooler breeze in the air, so I retrieved Justin's gray scarf from my bag and wrapped it around me, still a little disappointed that I hadn't seen him at all.

As I finished my thought, and while many individuals in the group were still in line to receive their medicine, I heard Justin's unmistakable upbeat and mischievous voice singing the catchy theme song about paths not taken and a new life around the bend.

I looked up to see him shimmying dramatically in between mats in the temple in a zigzag pattern. I hadn't even placed my eye mask on yet. *Could the medicine have even activated within my body this fast?* I blinked my eyes and looked again.

"Justin?!" I whispered.

"Who do you think broke the beads, bitch? Who's the BOSS? HELLOOO!" he laughed at his own wit, being my first boss in the fashion industry.

I began to laugh and cry simultaneously.

"Oh my God! Of course it was you! *You* healed my heart!" I exclaimed.

"*YOU* healed your heart," Justin corrected. "I'm just here to remind you of what you're capable of."

And with that, he flipped his oversized Prada sunglasses back on and sashayed off, singing the chorus to the *Who's The Boss* theme song.

I didn't know what else I could possibly see. I had received more than I'd hoped, and the singing telegram from Justin was the perfect note to end on. I mustered up the courage to ask the Ayahuasca, the Universe, and my Higher Self one remaining question:

"Ok, so if I'm supposed to be soul sister besties with Amanda, and the journey with Melissa is complete… Um, do I get a partner in this lifetime?"

Yes, of course you do.

"Is it Madonna?" I asked, making a Hail Mary pass that it would be my lifelong crush and idol.

I began to see a montage, like the most perfect music video ever made, of how Madonna served me as a teacher, a powerful guide, and a strong female role model who came from a humble background like me. She was a creative force, a sexually empowered rebel, a disrupter, a trailblazer, an undeniable inspiration… but not my future wife. *Damn, that realization stung a little.*

Oh girl, she's so much better than Madonna.

"Better than *Madonna*?" I asked, trying to wrap my head around that statement.

Then, *Wizard-of-Oz*-style, the owner of the voice that I had heard all those years, turned around to face me.

Thanks for pulling my ass out of that cab, by the way. I owe you one, and you know me, I always OVER deliver.

She was FIERCE: the smile, the warmth, the confidence. She was me, but a future version of me. She smiled genuinely, with all her teeth showing, something I never did. She stood in a beautiful modern home with floor-to-ceiling windows displaying a breathtaking view of the ocean. I didn't even notice if there was anyone else there with her, because she was just so magical. I only cared about hanging out with her. Something I never felt about myself before.

"Thank you!" I said to her, through tears of inexplicable gratitude.

As Future Me began to fade out, I heard the Shaman call us to gather around for the final closing ceremony.

The next morning at breakfast, Rosanna asked, "Are you going for the integration session?" She was referring to the opportunity to sit with the Shaman to discuss any questions that came up during the ceremonies, or concerns around integrating what we experienced.

"Yeah, I mean, most of it was really freaking clear. I still don't know where Future Me is living in that badass oceanfront home. Probably the Hamptons?" I guessed from my most recent frame of reference.

"Yeah… or maybe Miami?" Rosanna said, "I don't know why," she answered, intuiting my next question as she adjusted her sun hat.

She and Joel walked with me to the room where the Shaman was available for one-on-one consultations. The door was ajar, so I peeked my head in.

"Good luck," Joel mouthed to me as he and Rosanna headed back to their room.

"Hi, Beala," I said.

"Hey! Bex, right?" she asked.

I nodded.

"So, how was your time with us in ceremony?" she inquired.

"It was the most incredible experience of my life. I mean, hard… definitely one of the hardest things I've ever done. I thought it was gonna be like a Super Soul journey narrated by Oprah, but at points it was a little more *American Horror Story: Ayahuasca*, ya know?"

"Are you a writer?" Beala asked.

"Uh no, I mostly worked in fashion, and now I also read Tarot," I answered, wondering if there was a tiny blonde writer here this week that Beala had confused me with.

"Interesting. You tell stories like a writer. What was the hardest part for you?"

"That's the crazy thing. It wasn't seeing the worst things I did to myself and others. I mean, that was no disco dance party, but honestly, the hardest part was seeing how much love I have in my life—how it was there the whole time, even when I couldn't receive it or fully understand people's intentions. There was and is SO much love that is always around me."

I started to tear up as I pictured my parents, Amanda, and Justin.

"Oh my God. I must sound like one of those billionaire assholes that complains about all the taxes they have to pay because they have *so* much money. So hard, right?" I laughed at myself.

"Yeah, you're a writer," Beala laughed. "Also, to your point about the immense love surrounding us being harder to receive than the shameful visions, that's because love is a potent healer. Shame doesn't heal people. If it did, we'd have a much healthier society. Have you ever heard about the Bambemba tribe?"

"No, I don't think so," I said, trying to scan my memory of all the documentaries and videos I had watched to prepare for my trip.

"It's ok. Most people haven't," Baela smiled. "There's a village in South Africa inhabited by the Bambemba tribe. And when someone commits a crime there, they are placed in the center of the village. Every man, woman, and child in the community gathers around the accused person in a circle. Then, each person in the tribe, one at a time, recalls the good things the accused person has done in their lifetime. Every good deed, act of kindness, and positive attribute is shared, sometimes for days. When it's over, the individual is welcomed back to the tribe. Needless to say, the Bambemba tribe rarely have repeat offenders."

"Wow, I bet. After I had my own energetic Village People healing, I honestly feel like I love myself in a way I never have.

All that love was being reflected back to me, and for the first time, I was able to really believe and receive it," I confided.

"I'm so grateful to hear that. So, you feel like your intentions for your journey here were actualized?" she asked.

"Yes, I definitely feel like I got a massive heart-healing and clearing of my addiction. But, in terms of being shown who I'm meant to become... I guess I saw pieces of it. The healer/teacher part came through on the second night. The High Priestess painting remaining unchanged definitely reiterated that Tarot will play a big role. And maybe something with writing... if you say so," I grinned.

"The medicine just helped remind you of all the tools you have in your toolkit. Now is the fun part where you get to use them to build what comes next."

Broken Beads - Village People Healing Spell

You don't have to take plant medicine to receive heart chakra healing. The experience I had when Justin's beads broke and I felt my heart opening to so many messages of love is something I still work with today when I feel upset with myself or others.

If you have a beaded bracelet or piece of jewelry, you can use it as a physical reminder (kind of like a rosary, but with a custom intention/prayer). The intention is to observe a moment of love for yourself or for another person with each bead.

For example, when I have moments of feeling lonely or unworthy, I sit with what comes up without pushing it away. As it integrates, I begin focusing on moments of love I have received from myself or others, dedicating one bead per memory.

- **Bead one**: Invoking a memory of receiving a thoughtful package out of the blue from my mom.
- **Bead two**: Invoking a memory of my dad texting how proud he is of me.
- **Bead three**: Invoking a memory of the moment I realized I loved myself enough to face my addiction and make changes in my life.

And so on…

If I am struggling with another individual, again after acknowledging any anger, resentment, and allowing myself to sit with that as long as I need, I then assign one bead per positive memory or trait.

- **Bead one:** Invoking a memory of Melissa's open-heartedness and kindness to my niece.

- **Bead two**: Invoking a memory of how much she made me laugh on our car rides.

- **Bead three**: Invoking a memory of how, even though she's not Christian, she found a church in the middle of Hell's Kitchen that was selling Girl Scout Cookies just to surprise me with Thin Mints.

And so on…

CHAPTER XIV

THE ACE OF CUPS
STILETTOS AND (SELF) LOVE SPELLS

Ace of Cups: Love, New Relationships, Fulfillment

Less than forty-eight hours after my last Ayahuasca ceremony, I was heading back to the Nexxus office. It turns out, despite my willingness to surrender, I didn't want to actually leave everything behind to move to a hut in the jungle with Lola and a deck of Tarot cards. In addition to all my other discoveries, I learned that I am a city witch through and through. I adjusted the volume on my earphones as I headed north in my vegan leather leggings, black cape blazer, and oversized shades. I preferred walking the thirty blocks north to taking the subway, even in four-inch heeled boots.

Wearing the boots honestly felt like being back with old friends after being in flip flops for a week. Whitney Houston's *Higher Love* played as I sent so much gratitude into the grid of the city.

I missed this commute, St. Patrick's Cathedral, the looks of awe on the faces of tourists, even the angry guy selling chestnuts in front of the Plaza. Then seemingly out of nowhere, an aggressive pedestrian elbowed me out of his way in the crosswalk.

"Happy Monday!" I smiled, giggling as I raised my iced matcha latte in a toast.

"Watch where you're going," he snarled.

As I approached Nexxus, Kevin appeared in the entryway beside me.

"Kevin! Oh my God! I just need to say this before I cry all over you: Thank you!"

He seemed slightly taken aback by my newfound enthusiasm, still I stretched my arms wide open and pressed the side of my face into his chest as I hugged him tightly.

"Thank you for this job, thank you for building this company, and just... thank you for being *YOU!*" I exclaimed.

He responded with a gentle back tap that seemed to express: *"I appreciate this, but I also want to be professional."*

"I'm sorry I just..." I stammered.

"The Ayahuasca retreat, right?" he asked, remembering my strict diet at the office before my week off.

"If you need to take the day, you can work from home," he smiled.

"No, I wanna be here! I'm so grateful to be here!" I said, feeling like Scrooge frolicking through the town square in *A Christmas Carol.*

Thankfully, I left my white Ebenezer-looking cult gowns at home, or Kevin would have been even more disturbed.

I was positively giddy. I glided into the office with Costa Rican chocolates I'd picked up at the airport and distributed them to my colleagues. I gave some pieces of amethyst I found in the gift shop at LifeForce to the receptionist, who was always eager to chat with me about astrology and crystals. There was nothing from my stay in Costa Rica that would have met Myriam's luxury taste level, but I wanted to thank her for being such a powerful messenger, so I shared the vision of the pin-up postal worker with her.

"So when you say I scooted off," she repeated, cleaning her glasses, "it was like an actual scooter?"

"Yeah, it looked like a retro white Vespa," I confirmed.

"SHUT UP!" she exclaimed. "I was JUST looking at Vespas this weekend, and I think I wanna get a white one!"

"Personally, I found the whole messenger part more profound, but yeah, that's pretty cool, too," I smiled.

When I got back to my desk, I saw that I had a text from Justin's other best friend, Caroline. Justin had told us all about one another, but we never met until his passing.

Caroline told me that the last thing Justin said to her was, "Take care of Bex," and from that point on she became a protective older sister to me.

> How was Costa Rica??? I need to hear everything. I also have to tell you the dream I had about Justin the night before your flight there.
> Breakfast tomorrow? 8:30 a.m.?
> Citizens?

> OMG I can't wait to hear and tell you everything!
> See you tomorrow!

I squeezed in past the morning crowd, navigating through men in power suits on their phones and bicycle delivery boys grabbing orders to go. I instantly spotted Caroline at a table in the back. She was impossible to miss with her effortless chic style, mischievous blue eyes, and shampoo commercial-worthy, long, brunette locks. I was so grateful that Justin and the Universe assigned her big sister custody. "Oh my god, you look amazing! Tell me everything!" my fellow Sagittarian exclaimed.

"Thank you! I *feel* amazing. You look amazing, too, but you always do. Wait, before I go into the Costa Rica chronicles, tell me about your dream," I said.

"Oh right! Ok, so I saw you boarding this plane and there was no one else in the cabin. I know how strong you are, but I was just so nervous for you! I wanted to protect you, so I followed you on the plane. Then, all of a sudden, Justin boarded from the back and sat in the seat right behind you. He turned around and shot me his devilish grin and put his index finger to his mouth and said 'Shh! Don't worry, I've got it from here.' He was with you the whole time!" Caroline confirmed.

"Oh my God! I *know*! I…" I started.

"Oh wait, and one more thing. Ok, this might sound crazy…" she warned.

"Um, you're talking to a witch who now has a white cult-couture drawer," I retorted.

"Right! Ok, so I went to my energy healer last week, and she told me that me and my sister were also siblings in a past lifetime. I told her I don't have a sister. She said it is someone who is *like* a sister to me, and we were in London in the 1800s. Apparently, we were really poor and had to work as kids, but we were happy. I was really protective of you… Shocker! And Justin was our mom!" she said.

"Wait…" I interrupted. "Did your energy healer happen to tell you if we were chimney sweeps?" I asked.

"Shut the fuck up! How did you know that?" she asked, smacking the table.

I recounted the entire Ayahuasca experience, highlighting our chimney sweep rooftop dance party and Justin's cameo.

"The *Who's the Boss* theme song, though!" Caroline howled.

"It's SO Justin!" we said simultaneously.

"Do you have your cards with you by any chance? I could use some insight, and your third eye is probably more super-charged than ever," she smiled.

"Yeah, I do. I have some readings at lunchtime with some Nexxus peeps," I explained, pulling the cards out of my tote.

Even though I agreed with Caroline's observation that my psychic skills had amplified due to the healing in Costa Rica, I was still nervous to give her a reading for the first time. I shuffled and pulled out the Death card, followed by Eight of Cups and Wheel of Fortune.

"Wow, massive changes. Big transformations right now. The shedding of many old skins. I feel like this is both personal and professional."

Caroline nodded slowly and wide-eyed.

"The personal stuff, I feel like you already know what it is and what needs to be changed. You're being asked to make some tough choices. You don't have to do this overnight, but you are being called to shine light on this. The work stuff looks like it will be made clearer to you in the next couple of months. Your role is both shifting and expanding. And this," I said pointing to the Wheel of Fortune, "is asking you to use this Jupiter expansion— it's in Sagittarius right now—to get clear and prioritize *you*. You've put everyone else first for a really long time. 2014 to 2017 probably *really* showed you that, right? But it seems like now you're ready to make the changes."

I tend to only look at the cards while receiving and translating the information. When I finally looked up from the table, Caroline was quiet for a longer than usual pause. She was staring at me in a way she never had before.

Beaming with pride, she asked, "How did you do that? And how have you not been doing this your whole life?"

"I mean, I did it when I was little, and then I stopped," I explained.

"You were born to do this. I mean, first of all, all that was spot-on and it was all stuff I haven't shared with you yet. Secondly, this is it. *This* is your thing. It's so cool to watch you light up like that as it comes channeled through you. Justin would be so proud. I mean, he is. He knows. Obviously, he broke the beads, bitch," she smirked.

I jumped up to hug Caroline.

"Thank you! That means so much to me, and I feel that, you know. I never really loved what I did, like I love this. I was always trying to make it happen in fashion, but I never thrived in the same way that Andy does in cosmetology, or have the passion you do about your work," I admitted.

"That boy can talk about eyebrows for days!" Caroline, a loyal client of Andy's, agreed.

"Right? And that's why you're both so successful: the passion. I was never in love with work until now."

Caroline asked, "Do you do gift cards? I already have four people in mind that I want to gift readings to. Do you have a website?"

I tried not to squirm as I was always wanting to impress Big Sis. Up until now, everything had been pretty word-of-mouth through texts and email.

"Thank you so much! I'm in the process of setting up a website and a separate Instagram. In the meantime, you can connect us via text."

As I set out for Nexxus after breakfast, I had flashes of Justin asking our friend Trevor to work with him instead of me when he started his own denim brand. I remembered working on my lingerie line and meeting Caroline for lunch near the PR company she owned. I secretly prayed she'd love my line and want to help increase its exposure. She always congratulated me when she saw BEXnyc in the press or on celebs, but she never looked at me the way she did after that reading. I finally got it. Every rejection and closed door rerouted me like a universal GPS, navigating through detours I didn't understand at the time to guide me here.

Chloe and Sami were also dying to hear all about my trip, so we met up on Saturday for overpriced açai bowls after doing a Soul Cycle spin class together.

I told them in detail about the heart chakra healing and how grateful I was for them and our friendship. I explained the gratitude I had for Amanda and the peace I felt understanding the reasons for my relationship with Melissa. Sami took this as a cue to suggest I get on dating apps. I had gone on some dates, but no big love or true connections had formed. It had been nearly a year since I was in a relationship—and to them, more than thirty days sans relationship was an eternity. Both of my besties were serial monogamists and were mystified by my need to sequester myself after hurricane Melissa.

"You guys... I've tried ALL the apps and I've deleted them all... I really don't think they're for me."

"ALL the apps?" Sami challenged, "What about Hinge?"

"Yes. ALL the apps. Tinder, Hinge, HER, Bumble, even TinDog, that dog app where your dogs match and you go out with the owner... Lola and I liked a cute long-haired Chihuahua with a hot Japanese attorney mom, but THIS is who liked Lola..."

I held up my phone to show a screenshot of a dark brown dog named Manny with mucus coming out of its bloodshot eyes and nose that acted as a cautionary tale.

"It looks like it has the dog version of gonorr-syphil-warts!! Is that thing even REAL?" Chloe gasped.

"Yes! And that's the canine equivalent of my dating life. I'm done."

"I feel like you met a few women off of apps," Chloe persisted, trying to flag our server for a second iced coffee.

"OCDeena," Sami said with a devilish smile.

"Oh my god," I dramatically shoved my açai bowl away from me, thinking back to the separated wife of a Texas oil tycoon who showered five times a day and wouldn't let me sit on her furniture in "outside jeans."

Despite being funded by her husband's millions, she Venmo-invoiced me for exactly fifty percent of the cost of any dates she invited me on.

"NO apps!" I said firmly.

"The forty-year-old virgin was nice!" Chloe added.

"Yeah, but the nickname... was kind of the problem," I said, my head now buried in my hands in defeat.

"Because Bex is a very sensual person... which brings me to... have you heard about this Stiletto House party?" Sami held up her hand to silence my predictable dismissal. "It's that party for women who are into, or curious about being with other women. They screen so it's supposed to be high-quality members. You have to submit a photo, background info about your career, etcetera."

"For women who are curious? Yes, exactly what I need—more closet cases," I sighed.

"Not necessarily wife material, but at least it could be a way to see if you're actually attracted to other humans anymore… I don't know…" Sami reached for her purse, signaling it was time to leave. "I gotta head back, but it might be worth checking out?"

"I could go with you!" Chloe said enthusiastically.

"I can totally pretend to be bi-curious. . . I'm your straight, out of town, dick-lovin' friend Chloe… just sneaking away from my husband Marv for a big weekend in the city."

Sami stood up with a disapproving look on her face.

"No one is going to buy that. Marv? Seriously?"

"I don't know… I just watched *Home Alone*," Chloe explained.

After Chloe and Sami left, I hesitantly pulled up Stiletto House's website with a landing page of soft-core porn shots of women in lingerie with the tagline, "An Exclusive Ladies' Club for The Curious Minded."

Intuitively, I knew this was probably not a good idea, but as I scrolled through these "exclusive ladies" profiles that were attractive and seemingly intelligent, I told myself, *I could go to one party… just for market research.*

After I purchased a ticket, I received an email stating that the party would be held in a luxurious downtown penthouse and the address would be sent twenty-four hours prior. There was also a link to a Pinterest board of "Sapphire Seductress" themed outfits.

These poor women are already confused about their sexuality, and then you give them a complicated wardrobe theme to attend the event?

The following night, I put very little effort into the "Sapphire" part of the theme and just put on one of my usual deep-V, black dresses. I texted Chloe and Sami. Sami demanded I share my location in case this turned out to be some sort of sex trafficking ring.

The elevator opened into a penthouse, where a girl in a lace eye mask, bra, and blue feather capelet took my name and asked if I wanted to check anything. It was almost summer and I didn't have a coat, so I politely smiled and shook my head, a little confused.

As I stepped into the foyer, I began to understand her question. There were two separate circles of women in varying degrees of undress... Some completely nude, some in lingerie, and some in very short dresses... and of course, stilettos. They were playing spin the bottle. Everyone seemed to look like they were somewhere on a spectrum of terrified-to-drunk. I could read some of their thoughts. A gorgeous Latina woman in a royal blue nightgown was thinking about a great female love she had in college. A tall redhead debated the payoff between more calories in another glass of champagne versus the relief of nerves it would provide. The thoughts were coming in much louder, but also seemed more chaotic than ever before. I couldn't control which or whose, but when I picked up on them, they were clear. I didn't know if it was the aftereffects of the plant medicine or the mayhem of the party.

I made my way past the spin-the-bottle situation to an outdoor terrace. This was definitely not what my heart-healing was intending to let in. I was planning to get some air and text Chloe and Sami that I would have rather lit my $100 on fire and performed a heart chakra abundance ritual than waste it on the ticket to this "party," when a sexy lady with jet black hair in a very short skirt and satin tank top walked towards me.

She looked... like a younger version of Melissa. My heart leapt into my stomach. No, it wasn't her. It was just one of those, "I'm attracted to you, so you must be my ex," moments. She smiled shyly.

"Hey, how are you? I'm Bex. Have you been to any of these parties before?"

"Hi, I'm Kelly. Yes, I love these parties! I mean, my boyfriend doesn't know. I just told him it's a girls' night... Oh..." Younger Melissa abruptly put her hand to her mouth. "Excuse me for a moment."

I silently thanked the Universe for her exit as I headed back towards the entryway, past a bedroom with multiple naked women intertwined, and a bathroom with a hot tub with at least nine identifiable limbs sticking out. I turned around and Kelly nearly body-checked me.

"Oh, there you are! Sorry about that. I had too much champagne earlier and just had to get some of it up... Anyway, where were we?"

She looked up and, I think, attempted to bat her eyelash extensions at me.

"Oh, hey! I was just looking for... the bathroom."

I escaped in the direction that she motioned in while desperately trying to find my way back to the exit. I started to order an Uber. When I looked up from my phone, I made eye contact with a lanky short-haired blonde in a leather jacket who was the only other woman who didn't appear to be wasted, or in the process of getting wasted in the attempt to hook up with a member of the same gender.

She smiled at me and said, "These women... so fuckin' shy, am I right?"

It was like some inevitable law of physics that the only two lesbians at the party would spot each other.

I laughed, "Yeah... This is definitely one of the stranger parties I've attended."

She nodded and said, "So, you wanna get out of here?"

"Oh, thanks, but I have an early morning... Best of luck to you though."

Lesbian number two saluted me and took a swig of her beer.

Finally, I spotted the hallway to the exit when a drunk Australian woman, who appeared to have a bad case of pink eye (*maybe from the hot tub orgy?*) called out, "Bexxxxx... Oh my God! I saw your name on the list at the door and was like I. Know. Her! I love your lingerie line... You're not leaving NOW are you?"

She rolled away from her two companions and draped her arm around me as I strategically attempted to dodge her left eye.

"You should stay..." she cooed, "Don't be so terribly BORRRING."

"Yeah, sorry... Super early Pilates class tomorrow. Hope you have a fun night."

Making my way to the door, I was wondering where my alibi of Pilates came from when I heard a familiar, but angry voice chastising the owner.

"You CANNOT have parties of this size and volume level here! This is a CONDO building. Do you know what that means? There is a half-dressed woman throwing up right outside the main entrance!! Who is cleaning that up? Are YOU planning to?"

I peeked around the corner and it was Myriam. *Oh my God, this must be her building*. Myriam the messenger, arriving to shut the party down as if on cue. This woman loved enforcing rules more than a sexually frustrated retired cop. I tried to duck back towards the orgy bathroom before I had to explain my attendance, but it was too late.

"Bex?! What are you doing here?" Her face actually softened a bit as confusion replaced disdain.

"Myriam? Is this your building? Heeeey! I was just leaving...

I was, uh, invited," I nervously explained, "I didn't really understand the exact nature of the event…"

I bent down to pet her Pomeranian in the hallway to distract her from my cover story.

"Oh… I'll walk down with you. I was about to walk Jade when I saw the aftermath of whatever *this* is," she gestured dramatically.

She proceeded to recount her tirade and the rules of living in a condo to me, and then reenacted the speech one more time for her poor doorman. I smiled sheepishly at him while I finished ordering my Uber.

I literally leapt into the car and attempted a three-way call to Chloe and Sami.

Sami answered. Chloe's phone went to voicemail. I recounted the night to Sami on the ride home.

"Myriam lives there? Only in New York. Maybe she's on the way back to play spin the bottle as we speak! Interesting party though… I mean, I guess it's guaranteed action for these women who don't know where to find it," Sami concluded.

"I know, but I don't need guaranteed action. I can get that from one dinner. I'm a great date, and that comes with a side of sautéed shishito peppers, not a side of conjunctivitis. Ugh… Not drinking and becoming conscious makes reckless, stupid shit far less fun," I said, not even going into detail about the thoughts I could hear at the party.

"I think that's the point. You know, I'm proud of you for going… and for leaving. You're honestly killing it."

"Thank you. I love you. Where's Chloe anyway?"

"Oh you know, probably out with Marv."

The following Tuesday, Chloe, Sami, and I gathered around my coffee table, opening up our little sushi delivery boxes. Eager to dive in, I scampered to the kitchen to get plates and the "fancy" chopsticks from my cutlery drawer.

"Avocado Roll and Veggie Roll for you," Chloe said, placing my boxes at my spot.

"It's fine, we can eat out of the boxes," Sami said.

"Oh, ya know she has to plate it for us," Chloe smirked.

"It tastes better that way! We eat with our eyes *first*," I explained.

"Question…" Sami baited, "What do you do in the boudoir if it's pitch black?"

"I light a candle," I retorted.

"Speaking of which…" Chloe started.

"Oh my God, can we drop the Stiletto House disaster?" I begged.

"In all seriousness, I'm really proud of you. I remember years ago when I quit using, it was the same—you try to go into certain parts of your old life, but feel like a complete alien."

"Yeah, like I'm releasing and unlearning so much, but I'm still *me*. I still love dressing up my human avatar in cute outfits. I still love going out with you guys in the city. I still love…"

"Sushi?" Sami suggested with a mischievous grin.

"Yes… Vegan sushi," I noted, playfully shoving her.

"Ok, so Stiletto House was a bust. More clarifying data to have," Chloe comforted.

Sami stood up to grab more water, and on her way back, she opened up my infamous magical supplies drawer.

"I mean… Can't you do a spell for this?" she said dramatically, pulling out some snake sheds and a bag of mugwort.

"Well, technically, that specific combo would be more of a 'heightening your intuition to release things you've outgrown' spell," I explained. "I feel like I'm covered there."

"Where do you even get snakeskin that's not... a purse or wallet?" she prodded.

"Myriam's doorman Kyle has a pet snake. I used to order it from these witches in Nevada, but after the other night's misadventures with Myriam, I'm now BFFs with Kyle."

"SEE!" Chloe chimed in optimistically, "locally sourced snake sheds. The night was a success after all."

"You know what I mean, Bex! Can't you do a love spell?" Sami asked.

"Oh my God, no! NEVER do a love spell. It's messing with other people's free will, and it never works out the way you plan," I warned.

"Wait... That sounds like you speak from experience?" Chloe's eyes sparkled mischievously.

"Damnit!" I said, knowing the jig was up. "Ok, picture it. My best friend Evelyn's house, sophomore year. She was this gorgeous Japanese girl who had the best style and also was a math genius. I was in 'the love' with her. We were best friends, but she always had a cool older boyfriend. She went through a witchy phase too. We used to go to this little metaphysical cafe together, get our tea leaves read, and buy books and candles with our babysitting money. One night, I bought a red candle to call love in and..."

"ANNNND," Chloe and Sami said in unison.

"It's all good. Safe space," Sami said as she mock ear-muffed Lola's little ears.

"And... I carved her name and mine on the candle and got some of her hair from the brush in her bathroom, wrapped it around the candle. I burned it when I got home, envisioning that she would realize she had feelings for me," I confessed, hiding my face in my hands.

"Oh my God, what happened? How did I not know this already?" Chloe asked.

"All of a sudden, her younger sister became obsessed with me. She never even noticed me before. She was polite but other than saying hi and bye, that was it. After the candle, she started giving me little presents and wanted to hang out with me and Evelyn whenever I was there. Evelyn played the typical big sister and told her to get lost. I didn't know why until a few weeks later I was at their place and I saw her sister brushing her hair…"

"With Evelyn's BRUSH!" gasped Chloe.

"Yup, so it was hella awkward throughout the rest of tenth grade, but eventually, it faded out and I think she's happily married to some dude with two kids now. But that's the last time I messed with that stuff. It never works the way you think it will."

"Totally. But what did you carve on the candle, just your names? And does it have to be hair or any form of DNA?" Chloe joked.

"Stop it! I'm not giving any more info around that. It's something people ask me when they know I work with herbs and candle magic, and I always, always say *never* do it. It can be reckless to try to force things for ourselves, but it's downright dangerous to try to force things involving other people," I warned.

"Got it. No love spells directed at other people," Chloe said, holding her hands up in mock surrender.

"But what about a self-love spell?" Sami asked.

"I like that… Go on," I coached.

"Like, a spell giving gratitude to how you've leveled up, how you've outgrown the allure that things like Stiletto House once held, and asking for that gratitude and self-love to integrate so that you can receive the amazing partner you deserve."

"Look at you being an undercover witch," I said, putting my arm around Sami.

"YES!! I'll take one of those please," Chloe cheered.

211

My door buzzer sounded, and Sami and Chloe looked at one another quizzically.

"Amanda's coming! She had a work dinner, but I told her to pop by. We've had a bunch of really good talks since I got back, and I knew she'd be happy to see you guys," I explained.

"I'm so glad you guys are okay," Chloe said, who had become close friends with Amanda.

Amanda, thoughtful as ever, walked in with dessert in hand.

She extended the box of vegan, gluten-free cupcakes to me and Sami. Then she turned to Chloe, saying, "And some real food for us," as she offered some delicious, albeit *non*-vegan cannolis.

"I missed you! So glad to see you," Chloe said, hugging her before Lola dashed over to demand Amanda's attention.

"Me too," I said softly and hugged Amanda tightly, "So much."

"So what did I miss, kids?" Amanda said, giving Sami a squeeze, then scooping up Lola and placing her on her lap...

"The usual, sushi, witchcraft, and oh, how Miss Cleo over here is blowing up," Sami boasted.

"I actually wanted to ask you guys... Caroline sent a ton of people to me. She asked if I had a website and gift cards. Is it crazy? I mean, I have nothing established to the extent I did with my lingerie line, but after I did the reading for her, I just felt..." I paused, smiling at the rug, not wanting to sound too egotistical, "...that she really believed in me."

"It's because you're *really* good at it, B," Amanda confirmed.

"Thank you. I mean, she's sending me high-level influencers and writers, and I don't even have a website or Instagram. I'm mostly just reading for you guys and my Nexxus peeps," I explained.

"I have a guy who can help you with the website for super

reasonable prices. I'll make the intro. CCing you now," Chloe said, already typing on her phone.

"And you know I'm queen of the 'Gram. What should we call it? I think you need a new account, a fresh start... not BEXnyc," Sami guided.

"Well, sadly, Miss Cleo is taken," I answered.

Sami tapped the side of her head with her chopstick. Chloe stared out the window. I shuffled the sushi plates around as I racked my brain. Lola sat up alertly on her hind legs just as Amanda declared:

"Cardsy B."

Ace Of Cups Self-Love Spell

Timing: Best on a Friday (ruled by Venus the planet of love and beauty) during a Waxing Moon Phase

Supplies:

Pink Candle

Candle holder

Rose water or Rose Oil

A Carving Tool (toothpick, pencil, etc.)

Paper

Pen

- Anoint the candle with rose oil or rose water from the top to the base (since it is a spell for calling in/attracting self-love).

- Use the carving tool to carve your name and birthdate on the candle.

- Choose at least three things about yourself that you feel gratitude for, that inspire you to celebrate your worthiness. Use these as the magnet to call in that which is an energetic match into your life. For example, that night I chose:

  1. *I am grateful that I am generous and adore hosting people I love.*

  2. *I am grateful that I have a beautiful soul family from whom I receive graciously.*

  3. *I am grateful I am independent and also equally love sharing and co-creating.*

- You can choose to carve your gratitude and intentions on the candle itself OR write your intentions out on a piece of paper (known as a petition) and fold it underneath the holder containing the candle when you are finished.

- Allow the candle to burn fully. If you need to leave it unattended, snuff it out and relight when you are ready to resume, meditating on your intentions each time.

- As it is a spell for calling self-love in, you can choose to keep the candle wax or bury it in the earth to represent planting the seed of the intention.

CHAPTER XV

THE KING OF WANDS
BECOMING CARDSY B

King of Wands: Entrepreneur, Visionary, Creator

"I seriously think you're going to leave fashion completely and just do Tarot. You already have a decent amount of followers, and there's always a ton of people in your Lives," Lindsay said, referring to the free mini-reading hour I offered once a week on Instagram.

"Thank you so much. The new website and Instagram have definitely helped, but I'm not making anywhere near what I make from consulting at Nexxus," I admitted.

"*Yet*, but you will be, Mofo. I'm *sooo* proud of you," Lindsay said in the intentionally-cheesy voice she used whenever anything got emotional or called for vulnerability. "Hey, what about applying to one of those online psychic sites? I know a reader from a metaphysical shop here who does that and makes good money," Lindsay suggested.

"It would be nice to work whatever hours I wanted from home. Is that all she does?" I asked.

"Yeah, I met her at the Rock Shop when I bought crystals last month. She does readings there once a week because her best friend owns the store. The rest of the time she works from home for the psychic website." Lindsay explained.

It sounded too good to be true. Maybe this was a fast pass to doing readings full-time. After I got off the phone, I applied to three different online psychic websites. I heard back immediately from PsychicAngels.com and was asked to do two blind readings over the phone without knowing anything about the individuals. The first call took place while I was at my "second office," Soleil Cafe, since it was scheduled on a Tuesday at lunchtime.

"Hello, is this Cardsy?" The caller asked flatly.

"Yes, hello, how are you?"

"I'm okay, are you ready to start reading?" She asked through a yawn.

God, this is gonna be tough. "Yes, totally, what did you want to look at today?"

"The usual, work, love, whatever you see." She answered.

It didn't take a psychic to know that she obviously wasn't in love with her current job, but I did see via the Three of Swords and Eight of Cups reversed that an ex was trying to return to the picture.

"Yeah, that asshole texted me last night!" she confirmed, her voice displaying a fluctuation in tone for the first time on the call.

"I would be cautious, it looks like he's gonna keep trying to reach out, but it doesn't seem like his patterns have changed much since you ended things," I gently guided.

"Thanks. That's actually really helpful," she noted.

Silvio, a tall, olive-skinned server at Soleil with salt and pepper hair who knew my lunchtime routine well, winked as I wrapped up the call. I took that as a good sign.

The second blind reading was for a man who was much more upbeat and energetically open than the first call, and a week later I was offered the job. They advised employees not to use actual surnames, so it was convenient; I had already been dubbed Cardsy B. After I uploaded my photo and a short bio, I was told I could log on whenever I was available and would make $2.99 per minute. Customers could choose audio or video calls through the site. As a natural night owl, I often found myself awake at odd hours. This was a way to practice my reading skills and earn money, all while wearing pajama pants. It seemed too good to be true.

I excitedly logged in, and in less than five minutes I got my first client request from SanDiegoScorpio77. I clicked "invite to reading" and took a deep breath.

"Hi, how are you doing tonight? I take it you're a Scorpio?" I smiled.

"Oh yes, we'll get to all that, but do you mind if I do an energetic release to start?" SanDiegoScorpio77 asked.

"Um, sure," I answered, assuming some people must like to start with some sort of meditation.

SanDiegoScorpio77 closed his eyes, so I followed suit, closing mine, and took a few deep breaths. When I opened them, he stood, his jeans already off, pulling down the elastic waistband of his navy boxer briefs.

"What the *actual*...?" I screamed, slamming my laptop closed and crawling under my coffee table. Lola ran over, sensing my stress, and positioned herself to guard me in the makeshift fort.

I caught my breath and called Lindsay.

"What the actual fuck, indeed! Men are disgusting. I'm sorry that happened, Mofo. That is *not o*kay. I don't think anything like that ever happened to the reader I know. That's awful and so invasive. Who goes to a psychic site for that, and who asks to start with that? Jesus!"

Lindsay was more comfortable expressing affection for those she cared for as rage directed towards anyone who might cause us harm.

"He probably likes the shock value, disgusting asshole!"

"But you got that's what he meant… from 'energetic release?'" I asked, dumbfounded.

"I mean, yeah, but I'm also highly skeptical of everyone," Lindsay admitted.

"Honestly, I think it's a sign that it's not the right fit for me. The ability to make extra money between laundry loads and when I can't sleep would be nice, but I was also looking forward to practicing and developing my abilities more, not getting flashed for money," I admitted.

The next week, I came home and opened my mailbox to my first *and* final check from PsychicAngels.com for $2.99. I threw it in my tote and looked down at my phone to see Chloe calling. The more readings I did, the more I found myself intuiting little things, such as what elevator door would open first and when the phone was about to ring, even though my phone was always set to silent.

"Hey, lady, what's up?" I answered.

"Whatcha up to? Wanna come down to Go Ask Alice? I'm meeting up with a few work peeps, but Sami is gonna join in like an hour. Did you eat? We're putting our order in."

"Amazing, I'll feed Lola and head down."

I speed-walked the twenty blocks south, feeling badly in need of a social outing. I squeezed through the heavy wooden door of what looked like a nondescript brick storefront with a dimly lit glass window and glowing red neon sign. I was quickly stopped for ID by a super tall bouncer before he directed me through a bulky scarlet brocade curtain to the speakeasy-style lounge. I made my way through a maze of plush velvet booths and candlelit round mahogany tables. Chloe instantly spotted me and waved me over.

"You should frame that check!" Chloe howled as I recounted the story to her and Sami.

"They have a psychic here," Sami noted, pointing to the neon sign in the storefront window which served as the mysterious entryway to the West Village speakeasy bar and restaurant.

"Wait, I know her! I'm gonna go say hi," I said, recognizing a reader with Bettie Page bangs, winged eyeliner, and bright red lips who I followed on Instagram and met at a metaphysical shop in Union Square. I squeezed my way through the trail of banquettes, past the narrow bar, and back through the heavy red curtain into the tiny psychic nook.

"Hey Vivian! How are you?" I asked, hugging her.

"Oh my god, Bex! Or should I say Cardsy B? Your Instagram is blowing up!" Vivian smiled. "Actually, are you looking to pick up some gigs? It's really hard to get in here, because you make straight-up cash - like $400 to $600 for a couple of hours. I don't want to lose my slot, but I need some time off. I know you're good, so if you wanna cover for me, I'll vouch for you so you won't have to bother to come in to do a sample."

I learned that psychics and readers are usually required to audition or provide a "sample reading" to get hired for locations and events if they aren't yet known by reputation.

"$600 a night? Whoa, that's great!" I exclaimed.

"Can you start Thursday? The shift is ten 'til two and you get free dinner. I usually bring water and extra snacks. You can charge what you want for the readings. I usually do $25 for ten minutes, that way they don't linger too long. Make friends with the bouncers, they will keep an eye on you and keep the drunks away."

When I got back to the table, Chloe had already picked up the tab for my roasted beet salad and Virgin Mojito.

"I didn't mean for you to grab that while I talked to Vivian. I'm so sorry!" I grabbed my phone to Venmo her.

"She would have done it whether you were here or not! Thank you, Chloe, you're too good to us," Sami said, hugging her.

"You know, I'm just gonna Venmo it right back to ya if either of you tries anything sneaky," Chloe warned, pointing to my phone.

"King of Pentacles!" I exclaimed, referencing the king of abundance, Chloe's Tarot doppelganger.

"Look at you, making moves King of Wands style, did you just land another job in the last five minutes?" Chloe asked lovingly.

"I think so actually, it's all cash, and it seems like I will make more than $2.99. There's also a bouncer present, who will keep any flashers at bay."

"Are you...I don't know, nervous that you might run into old fashion industry contacts coming in?" Sami asked cautiously, always looking out for future landmines.

"I hadn't thought of that, but it wouldn't really bother me. If they're out drinking after 10 p.m. on a weeknight, how is that somehow above me working on my reading abilities in exchange for money? I feel like anyone I'm meant to see I will, and the rest just won't cross paths with me anymore," I answered honestly.

"I want to feel more like that about many things. I love that and I love you." Sami said, putting her arm around me. "Get those *Dolla Dolla bills*, y'all."

I returned to Go Ask Alice that Thursday and was greeted warmly by the same 6'4" bouncer who had carded me the week before. He promised to keep an eye on me, but also encouraged me to get up and come over to him if need be. I nestled into the little storefront window. The window, transformed to psychic HQ, was just to the left of the entry's mysterious scarlet curtain, which magically muffled out much of the music booming from inside. A small wooden table and two chairs were dimly lit by the red glow of a neon psychic sign that hung at the top of the window's edge. I sat in the chair closest to the wall and unpacked my Tarot deck and my seven small chakra stones, which I began using when doing back-to-back readings to help clear and balance the energy of the cards. I closed my eyes and took a deep breath, silently reciting my intentions to bring helpful, healing and empowering information to anyone who needed it, and asking that only those truly seeking clarity and guidance find their way to me. Just as I opened my eyes, I heard the backbeat of Stevie Wonder's *Superstition* playing over the clinking of glasses as the curtain parted ways from inside, revealing a petite, dark-haired woman named Penny. She was waiting on a guy she matched with on Bumble, who was twenty minutes late, so she came to me to pass the time. She fidgeted with a gold chunky ring on her middle finger as I shuffled and began to pull her cards.

"Okay, first of all, it looks like he's coming," I said, flipping over the Knight of Pentacles with a smile. "Delayed, I think, because of work..." I hesitated as I pulled over Four of Cups, "Not sure if it's a great love connection. I think he's definitely more into you than you are of him, so don't force yourself to stay longer than you want if that's the case."

"I was already kinda feeling that!" She admitted.

Then I pulled over Ace of Pentacles, "Ooo good work news though, did you recently apply for a new job?" I asked.

"Yes! I just interviewed on Monday," she said.

"Yeah, I feel really good about that," I confirmed.

Penny looked up and whispered "That's him," regarding the frazzled-looking man unbuttoning his collar at the front door. She said, "I need the job more than a boyfriend, so thank you!" She quickly pulled out cash to pay me before greeting her date.

Go Ask Alice, just like the OG Wonderland, was a mixed bag. There were some clients, like Penny, who I could assist. There were also a lot of tipsy Tonyas and Messy Marys, whose attention spans for the information coming through in readings were shorter than their skirts. The worst were the drunken dudes who tried to hit on me with innovative lines like "Where are we going after this? You must know already since you're psychic, right?" Luckily Greg the bouncer was good on his promise and quickly escorted them out. The lucid clients who actually remembered the readings usually followed me on Instagram, and many booked one-on-one sessions with me outside of Go Ask Alice.

Two Thursdays later, after work at Nexxus, I answered a call from Lindsay and yawned a sleepy "ellllo" into the phone.

"Mofo, you sound like you're in a coma. Are you OK?"

"Yeah, sorry, I'm just really tired. I've been taking shifts reading at that speakeasy I told you about, and by the time I get home and in bed, it's usually three in the morning. Then I have to be at Nexxus by 9:30, so I haven't been getting much sleep," I explained.

"I know you said the money is good, but you've already turned down a bunch of full-time fashion job offers since you started getting more Tarot work. If this doesn't feel good, maybe it's time to move on from this too."

"I know," I admitted. "It's clear to me now that Nexxus will be the last place I work in fashion. But this is a job where I'm getting paid well to do readings. It feels ungrateful to walk away."

"You said you want to practice your reading abilities and help people. Do you feel like you're able to do that there?" Lindsay, a master of directing me back to my inner guidance system, asked in a neutral tone.

"Dammit, I know you're right. Most people are not seeking guidance, and the ones that are, end up booking with me separately afterward. Yeah, I would rather focus on building my individual client base. I'm also not learning much," I sighed. "But I did create a secret hand signal system with the bouncer to request the removal of sleazy drunk guys from the area."

"Secret hand signal?" Lindsay asked.

"Oh yeah. I raise my hand, index and middle finger to make a two, then an L shape with my thumb and index finger to let Greg the bouncer know that it's a *Too Legit* situation. When he sees that, he signals the two and L back and then a quick wave to let me know he's on his way to handle it."

"As much fun as that sounds, I feel like your creativity could be used for things you would enjoy more than these intricate cheer routines… Have you given any more thought to the Tarot deck idea?"

Lindsay was referring to a seed she planted on a trip we took to Amsterdam together. I'd flown in from New York and landed before Lindsay arrived from Toronto. I was walking to grab a coffee when I got an Instagram notification: *@LindsayKJablonski tagged you in a post*. It was a photo of the altar I set up at our shared hotel room desk, complete with protection crystals, copal, Tarot cards, a pendulum, and rose petal encrusted macarons, which she captioned "How you know you found your best friend's hotel room." I instantly texted her:

> OMG you're heeeere!!!!
> Headed back to the hotel
> now.

> I can't believe you brought a whole
> crystal shop in your carry-on. Also,
> are these macarons with the roses
> an offering or for us to eat? Cuz I
> may or may not have eaten one...

It was Lindsay's first time visiting one of my favorite cities in the world. I took her through the winding canals of the Negen Straatjes to all my go-to metaphysical shops before we were meeting my old boss and good friend Mark for dinner. Our heeled black boots did their best to navigate the cobblestone sidewalks.

"I really want a new Tarot deck," I explained as I walked through a beaded curtain into a small corner shop that smelled of frankincense.

"You have so many, Mofo," Lindsay said as she picked up an orgonite triangle from the table beside me.

"I know, but I want one that's all strong, badass women..." I said, "but all I can ever find is:" I mocked a show-and-tell gesture of the multiple fairy, goddess and angel decks.

"What about this?" Lindsay said, picking up *Tarot of the Red Light District*.

"Alright," I said with a smile, "I'm getting that one for Chloe. But seriously, there are none."

"Have you ever thought of creating your own? You're a good illustrator, why not just make it if it doesn't exist? Plus, it's an awesome way to dive deeper into the cards, and you know how to do all the design and layout yourself."

I remember thinking that was a good idea in theory, but also seemed like an intense amount of work to hand illustrate, color and layout seventy-eight Tarot cards and write a guidebook. I hadn't given it much more thought since that trip, but when Lindsay brought it back up, it seemed less daunting than before.

"Did you ever find the perfect deck you've been on the hunt for all these years?" She asked rhetorically, bringing me back to the present.

I brainstormed out loud, "I mean... maybe that is a better use of my time than PsychicAngel.com and the Too Legit hand jive. Even if I just create a deck for myself to read and teach from. I could draw them the way I teach you, Sami and Chloe. The Hierophant is like Oprah because it's the teacher of life lessons."

"This is amazing, I love this. Yeah, Justice should be inspired by RBG!" Lindsay added, always the best partner-in-crime and hype woman. "I love the way you teach. I think that's why your Instagram grabs people, because you're not just doing the usual sage plus crystals plus tarot card shots like everybody else."

"Yeah, I guess there's something to the 'Tarot card plus healing elixir in a martini glass shot.'" I laughed.

"There *is* something to it because it's really *you*. You are fun and extravagant and New York City. But you're also magical and soulful. And you share messages and teach in your real voice with your ridiculous humor and style," Lindsay said.

I thought back to all the iterations of my hands I saw in the Ayahuasca ceremony. Cardsy B was the most genuine version of my handprint that I'd ever shared with the world. Alone at home,

I scribbled meditations into bedside spell books in my serial-killer handwriting, and frequently created healing elixirs from recipes that came to me in dreams. I usually drank those elixirs out of martini glasses. I pulled Tarot cards for myself daily, and often on a bath caddy in the tub while listening to Cher. I also created space for deep, raw, vulnerable conversations with my best friends.

And when comic relief was needed, I would pause the conversation to dial zero on a rotary phone with a photo of Oprah affixed to the center to ask, "Oprah-ator, can you patch us through to ask the Universe this one?" Sami once asked me where one gets an Oprah-ator phone. I explained that because my apartment had an old landline phone jack on the wall, which was a complete eyesore, the best way to cover it was to order a stylish retro phone from eBay and use it as a quantum line to the Universe. I imagined Oprah would be behind the switchboard.

Now I shared the silly, playful, mystical me publicly as Cardsy B. All the sides that didn't quite fit into my corporate executive identity or sexy lingerie line founder persona, were being set free. I knew I wasn't sharing messages in the same way as everyone else in the spiritual world, or even how those in the niche Tarot community were teaching, but I didn't care. I wanted to make that little outcast girl in the occult section of the bookstore proud. It was easier to be authentic when there was no guidebook, no degree in Tarot, and no rules required the way there were in the corporate world. So maybe Lindsay was right; maybe there was a reason I was being guided to create my own Tarot deck.

After I got off the phone (my cell, not the Oprah-ator rotary), I grabbed a notebook and a pen to list the titles of the seventy-eight Tarot cards and the keywords I associated with each. Then I began to fill in the names of iconic female celebrities, athletes, artists, and entrepreneurs that would serve as the inspiration for each card. For someone considered hyper-organized, that list was the only strategic part of the whole undertaking. From there, I uncharacteristically let the process flow. As I worked, I didn't think about bills, rent, or meetings coming up the next day. I didn't even give much thought to the next steps of the tarot deck itself. I just decided to sketch one leading lady at a time, and then color the drawing with watercolor pencils. The first card I chose to sketch was the card I cast myself in. I put a checkmark next to number fifty on my list.

- 50. King of Wands / Element of Fire / Entrepreneur, Visionary, Creator / Cardsy B ✔

I had no idea that picking up my pencil that night was going to change everything. I just knew I had to do it, and it was the first time I remember fully surrendering to the process of creation with no plan, end date, or goal. I just wanted to teach people Tarot in the most accessible way I knew how.

Tarot Card Embodiment Spell

As I illustrated the deck, I got to know each card much more personally. I cast myself as King of Wands due to the card's elemental ruling of fire, its creative and entrepreneurial qualities, and the contagious ambition of the Fire King. I illustrated my card with my "kingdom" of the New York City skyline in the background, and my loyal fur baby, Lola the Dom Pom, by my side. I drew a mystical Harry Potter-style wand in my hand, in place of the traditional wooden rods used in the Smith Rider Waite Tarot.

If you were going to cast yourself as a Tarot card, which card would it be?

Would it be a specific archetype, like the High Priestess or Justice? Or would it be tied to an element? Or does a certain number resonate strongly?

Are there specific colors or items you would include in the background? How would you portray yourself in the card?

This is a powerful visualization exercise and can be used as a journaling prompt.

I also invite my fellow art nerds out there to try it as an illustration, digital collage via Canva, or old-school cut and paste (vision board style) montage.

CHAPTER XVI

THE HERMIT
CUTTING BACK THE SECURITY BLANKET

The Hermit: Introspection, Solitude, Insight

"Hey Bex, can you come into my office and bring the spring and summer swim silhouettes binders?" Myriam popped her head out of her corner office and called to me as soon as she saw me settle into my desk.

"Sure, no problem." I said, trying to wipe marker smudges off my hands from outlining the illustration of the Hermit card the night before. Even my morning shower didn't remove the stubborn Prismacolor marker stains, and I knew Myriam would be distracted by even the smallest perceived imperfection. I pulled my sleeves down to my knuckles before heading to the shelf outside Myriam's office where the massive pile of binders lived. She liked to keep them for every possible category and sub-category. Binder making was my least favorite part of the job. Initially, all the printing and hole punching of things that could be easily digitally accessed and archived was almost therapeutic, like The Karate Kid waxing Mr. Miyagi's car. But after over a year of playing "binder-open/binder-closed," I began to empathize with stories I heard of cab drivers who were surgeons in their native lands, but drove taxis to make a living in New York. I was so grateful to have a steady job again, but printing, collating, and binding was far from the creative design work I had done in the past at Playboy, DKNY and NIKE. Going home at the end of the day to my creative outlet, illustrating the tarot deck, felt like being back in the artistic operating room again.

I laid down two overstuffed binders on Myriam's desk. Since Jessie had returned from maternity leave, I shifted into a Fashion Director role, reporting to Myriam. The ongoing work at Nexxus allowed me to stop freelancing for other companies in order to make ends meet as I rebuilt my life over the past year. I'd even turned down two full time Creative Director roles with other brands, because it became apparent that fashion was no longer my purpose. Reading and teaching Tarot felt different. I was thankful for Nexxus, but intuitively knew this was my last stop in the fashion industry. The contrast between the reward of providing channeled information through readings, and collating and hole punching, was becoming more pronounced.

"We'll have to update women's spring swim," Myriam said, narrowing her eyes on the top binder. "Also, I wanted to ask you about your schedule," she noted, adjusting her glasses as she looked up at me.

When I was little, I had a white and pastel-yellow quilted blanket I took everywhere with me. My mom said I had no problem weaning off of my bottle and other objects from infancy and childhood, but I wouldn't go anywhere without that damn blanket. She tried to hide it, but I always found it. Eventually, she started cutting it back and hemming the edge, slowly making it smaller and smaller until it became just a tiny handkerchief sized square. This was it, my moment to cut back the security blanket of Nexxus Brands.

"Actually, I wanted to talk to you about my schedule," I started.

"Great, can we bump you up to five days a week?" "I need to decrease it to two to three days max."

We spoke over each other.

"You want to work *less* days?" Myriam, the workaholic, was trying to compute.

"Yes. I mean, I love it here. It's just that I have other clients," I explained. "So, two to three days is the most I could be in the office, with possibly some additional work from home," I said strategically, choosing to cloak my tarot business and personal well-being as "other clients" knowing Myriam wouldn't understand. I knew the "work is life" code of ethics all too well from my VP days. Back then, I prioritized work over my marriage, my sanity, and even my physical health. My assistant at the time kept extra hair ties in her drawer for me when my endometriosis flared up to the point of vomiting. On more than one occasion, she helped hold my hair back in the bathroom like a sorority sister, so that I could lead a presentation immediately after. Her support and the well-stocked hair-tie drawer ensured I never missed a meeting. So much had changed in and around me since then, and as much as I didn't want to let Myriam down, I knew I didn't belong in the "Sisterhood of Corporate America Burnout" sorority anymore.

"Ok, if that's the absolute maximum amount you're available... I guess we'll work it out." Myriam sighed.

I walked home that summer evening after confirming my new decreased schedule, feeling much lighter. I usually chose to walk home to my apartment in Chelsea from Nexxus via Fifth Avenue, even though it wasn't the most direct route. I loved sneaking glimpses of the ornate Tiffany windows and the well-heeled guests exiting the St. Regis Hotel, before passing Bryant Park's lawn full of Millenials sprawled on blankets with cheap wine in Solo cups. In the busy intersection at 41st Street, I noticed how many fellow pedestrians missed out on the magic of 5th Avenue, their heads buried in phone screens, or yelling loudly into receivers to answer work calls. As the pedestrian light turned green, I heard *This is What You Came For* by Calvin Harris blaring from the speaker of an off-duty taxi with its windows rolled down. I smiled at my Radio Guides. This *is* what I came for. I came to be part of the city, to feel, experience and connect with the people in it, not to dismiss it as an expensive backdrop to a job and an iPhone.

I looked down at my bag to see my dad calling.

"Hey dad!"

"Hey Sweetie, I'm not interrupting you at work, am I?" He asked.

"Nope, just walking home now. How are you?"

"I thought I'd try to catch you now since I'm headed on a fishing trip for the next couple of days and might not have good service. So how's Nexxus going? Any big projects? Have they offered you full-time yet?"

"Actually they have, it's just..."

"That's fantastic! I knew they would, congratulations!" He beamed.

"Uh yeah, thank you. I'm not exactly certain that it's gonna work out, but thanks, dad! I hope you have a great trip."

"Thanks, sweetie! Don't worry, I'm sure it will work out. Love you!"

"Love you, too!"

My dad and I had become much closer from all the healing work I'd done over the past couple of years. The more understanding and kindness I offered myself, the more I was able to give to those in my life. But that didn't stop me from continuing to crave the approval that all those A's and academic trophies had earned me growing up. I wasn't yet ready to let him down by explaining that I planned to leave fashion and corporate America entirely to become a full-time Tarot witch.

On some levels, it still seemed crazy, like perhaps I should just put my head down and stay put. Maybe I should be grateful for any full-time employment offer, especially after knowing the darkness that came with losing all my money. Somehow even that painful memory compiled with my dad's potential disappointment didn't motivate me like it once did. The freedom that came with not being tied to a full-time employer and the autonomy I had over my schedule outweighed the fear of the unknown. Besides, many friends in the fashion industry and I had sold our souls to companies in the past, and that still did not grace us with guaranteed lifetime employment. The more I opened up to my intuitive abilities, the more aware I became of how little control we really have over other people and their free will. This made it easier to choose what felt good over debating fear-based choices.

I began to look forward to coming and staying home. Instead of rushing back out to meet up with Chloe or making phone calls to distract myself from being alone I excitedly set up my home "office" each night. With my legs crossed under my glass coffee table in the middle of my small studio apartment's living room, I set up piles of white 8.5 x 11 paper, Prismacolor markers and watercolor pencils.

My coffee table office became more elaborately decorated

over time. Sami gifted me a pillar candle of Madonna to help inspire the creative process. As my savings account grew from increased Tarot clients, I treated myself to a cushy gamer chair that looked like it belonged in the bedroom of a fifteen-year-old boy. I collapsed it and hid the unsightly gray lump in the closet when I wasn't working, but oh my God, it felt like heaven to my tiny ass which ached from sitting on the hardwood floor for hours on end.

I didn't have a set schedule of when or what I would illustrate. I usually worked with the energies that came up. On the day that I felt like work was successful, but a little bit of an uphill battle, I drew Ten of Wands. The evening that I was feeling grateful for the increased balance of my finances, I chose to draw Two of Pentacles. Before I began illustrating a given card, I looked up all the information I could: the meaning behind the original symbolism and imagery, the numerology and its astrological ruling. It was like obtaining my own self navigated Ph.D. in Tarot.

Because illustrating mostly requires the right, creative side of our brain, I was able to listen to podcasts or videos in the background while I sketched and colored. I mostly chose astrology and Tarot podcasts as well as Eli Vate's energy updates. On the hard days when I felt run down from the office, or lonely and in need of energetic comfort food, I listened to Summer and Anna fighting over the adorable nerd, Seth Cohen, in old episodes of *The O.C.* as I shaded swords and pentacles. The teen soap opera, which I practically memorized from when Lindsay and I binged it in college, felt like a soothing noise machine when I wanted to turn the analytic side of my brain off as I sketched into the wee hours of the night. Sometimes I would forget to eat dinner until 11 p.m. or midnight, inadvertently shifting my body to Pacific time. The only thing reminding me that I was still in New York was my view of the Empire State Building whose lights shut off at two each morning. This became my new signal to clean up and put myself to bed. One night I didn't pay attention to my skyscraper night light going out and woke up on the rug under my coffee table. Lola was curled up next to my left hand, a red pencil still in my right.

One sunny Saturday morning, after getting up to stretch and stare out my window enviously at the people brunching on patios on 27th Street, I answered the phone to Sami chipperly declaring,

"Oh hey, I'm looking for my friend, the Bex-cluse... ya know, the former extrovert known as Cardsy B."

"Omg HEY!!!! I miss you!!!" I gushed, thankful for the reality check.

"I miss you too, but happy to see the Blonde Ambition candle is working over there. What are you up to today? I'm working from The Dream Hotel prepping for a conference."

"I would love to see you, but I am seriously down to the last twenty cards and I have this feeling like I'm supposed to finish by the fall equinox..." I explained as I shaded in the dark golden shadows on the Six of Pentacles.

"Mmm hmmm, I figured, that's why I'm headed to your place now to kidnap you out of the Tarot lair for some much-needed vitamin D," Sami answered.

"That's so sweet but..."

"See you in five!" Sami chirped, hanging up the phone.

My buzzer sounded and Sami arrived at my door with an iced matcha. "I know I know, you don't wanna stop the flow, but let's just pack up all the pencils. You can sketch by the pool you know, maybe get some access to the *outside* world, that thing you used to love so much..." she said in her maternal tone, scooping up my pencils into her Valentino bag.

"Okay, okay!" I laughed. "You're impossible."

"And that is why you love me! Grab a swimsuit and some sunglasses."

Sami ordered us two virgin mojitos as I continued to color in the Six of Pentacles next to the rooftop pool. I thanked her as I adjusted my oversized black sun hat to strategically create shade on the area of my Casper white chest exposed from my black plunge neck bathing suit.

"Do you need some SPF 200, my little Vampire Vixen?" Sami smiled, alluding to the fact that my skin hadn't even seen Manhattan's version of the sun for months now.

"But seriously, though, isn't this better?" she asked.

"Undeniably. What would I do without you?"

"Let's hope we never find out. So what is that one all about?" She asked, pointing to the drawing balanced on top of the Vogue magazine in my lap.

"Six of Pentacles is the card of balance and fair energetic exchange: the ability to give energy and resources out to the world, save some, and spend some on yourself," I explained.

"Like being able to work on what you love AND also connect with your bestie?" Sami asked with a huge grin.

Cutting Back the Security Blanket / Releasing Spell

This is for when you don't necessarily want to banish something entirely or rapidly, but you're ready to begin to release yourself from an unhealthy attachment to the comfort it brings.

Timing: Best on a Tuesday (ruled by Mars for action), during a Waning moon to work with clearing energy.

Supplies:
The Hermit Tarot Card
The Six of Pentacles Tarot Card
Black Candle
White Candle
2 Candleholders
Frankincense Oil
A Carving Tool (toothpick, pencil, etc.)
Paper
Pen

Tarot Cards:

Place at the center of your table or altar space

The Hermit - Working with invoking comfort in solitude with what comes up

Six of Pentacles - Working with calling in a balanced energetic exchange

Candles & Oil:

Place beside The Hermit and Six of Pentacles

- Anoint the black candle from base to top (as we are using the black candle to release) with the Frankincense oil. Anoint the white candle from the top to the base (since we are using the white candle to call in protection and purification) with the Frankincense oil.

Because of Frankincense's association with the sun and the solar plexus, it helps us release parts of our ego which hold us back from connecting with our soul, as well as release feelings of unworthiness and insecurity.

- Use the carving tool to carve your name and birthdate on the white protection candle.

- Declare what you want to begin to release attachment to. For example, in releasing the security blanket of Nexxus I chose:

  1. *The amount of days I am working in an office*

  2. *The attachment I hold to the identity of this job*

  3. *The belief that this is the best/only source of abundance possible at this time*

  4. *The belief that my dad will think less of me if I leave this job*

- You can choose to carve your intentions on the black candle itself OR write your intentions out on a piece of paper (known as a petition) and fold it underneath the holder containing the candle.

- Allow the candle to burn fully. If you need to leave it unattended, snuff it out and relight, meditating on your intentions each time.

- As it is a spell for releasing attachment, it's best to remove and release the remaining wax and petition at the completion of your spell, either burying it in the earth or disposing of it.

CHAPTER XVII

THE FOUR OF CUPS
TINKERBELL RETURNS

Four of Cups: Contemplation, Reevaluation, Discernment

"How many more of these are we gonna print, Bex?" Allan, the night clerk at the Kinkos on 23rd Street asked, running his hand over his buzz cut.

"Fingers crossed, Al. Fingers crossed." I exhaled.

Al and I became well acquainted because after I finished all seventy-eight illustrations, designed the back repeat print, wrote and laid out the guidebook, and formatted the cards, I printed countless proofs on the serve-yourself machines at Kinkos to check for any errors.

"Where's my girl, Lola, tonight?" Al asked as he eyed the clock. It was 10:55 p.m., five minutes before close.

"Had to leave her at home so I wouldn't get distracted... Big night, Al. If this one is correct we can print the final on glossy paper." I checked the cards methodically. They were... all error-free!

"AL! WE DID IT!!!" I squealed.

"Yes, girl!! You going out after? Poppin' bottles?" He smirked.

"Hardly," I laughed, pointing to my black sweatpants and Village Witch graphic hoodie.

I arrived home with my unofficial first edition of The Badass Bitches Tarot Deck. I immediately cut all seventy-eight cards lovingly by hand. I cleared my laptop and colored pencils from the glass coffee table, laid out a black reading cloth, and returned my chakra stones to their place, ceremoniously transforming my workshop back into a reading parlor. I shuffled the freshly cut cards and began the very first reading from MY deck.

The top card revealed the Eight of Cups, the card of bittersweet endings. Lola looked up at me from the ivory rug under the coffee table and tilted her little head to the side.

"I know Lola, you think I'd be thrilled to be done with twenty-hour days," I sighed as I scratched her chin. I looked down at the cards, taking in what I had created over the last six months. I thought about all the healing that occurred during that time. In my creative incubator, I learned more about Tarot than I ever thought possible. I spent more time solo than I had in my entire adult life and finally understood what "channeled work" felt like. I knew I would even miss the war paint of marker stains on my palms, watching the Empire State Building's lights go out, and the rush of printing a successful proof to Al's applause.

As I navigated the creative equivalent of postpartum depression, I tried to dip back into my social outings. Chloe and Sami were both consumed by new relationships, so I ventured out to find other magical weirdos who might relate to my Tarot obsession, as well as the insights and spells that I had begun intuiting in unusual ways.

I attended a few moon circles tucked away in back rooms of retail shops, but found they were mostly a space to share intimate stories. I completely respected the need for this, but I already had a comfy living room where the goddesses that were Sami, Chloe and Amanda communed together. And that came with vegan dessert samplings. I decided that maybe I should specifically seek out other practitioners of magic, and typed "magical gatherings nyc" into the Google search bar on my phone. A Harry Potter-themed bar came up along with various magic shows, *No, I mean real magic.* I thought, petting Lola's back.

I added a "k" behind the c to emphasize the legitimacy of my search: "magicKal gatherings nyc." This retrieved some pagan festivals and sabbat rituals. *Okay, now we're talking.* Scrolling down further, I found a link for a Spiritualist seance that was taking place in Midtown in two days. From what I read about Spiritualism in the past, the core belief is that death is not the end. Not only can we communicate with those who have transitioned, via mediumship and seances, but we can learn about higher aspects of this life through doing so. I clicked through the link to the full event description:

WEEKLY MESSAGE CIRCLE/SEANCE - WEDNESDAY 9PM

- The message circle follows our nightly service. All are welcome to attend both the service and circle, but each may also be attended independently. Services will start at 8 p.m. Message circles begin promptly at 9 p.m.
- Message circles are led by psychic mediums and certified seance conductors.

- The circles utilize the flow of the group's energy to open communication with spirit.
- Late admission is not allowed as it interrupts the flow of messages.
- There is no guarantee of receiving a message, but every effort will be made to receive and translate as many messages as possible.
- There is a charge of $20 for all Message Circles to be collected before the start of the circle, payable in cash.

"Wait, hold up. You literally didn't want to leave your apartment for months, and now you're headed to a seance in the middle of the night?" Sami asked as I switched my phone to the speaker setting.

"Ok so first of all, 9 p.m. isn't exactly the middle of the night. And I don't know, I'm just trying to open up to meeting new people who might be into this stuff too."

"I know I've been in the honeymoon stages of this relationship the past couple of months, but I'm here. You don't need to replace me with dead friends!" Sami laughed.

"You, my dear, could not be replaced by anyone, dead or alive," I assured her before hanging up.

Was I being a forcer again? I thought back to when I had a big fight with Justin years ago and heatedly posted a Craigslist ad for a new bestie:

—

FAB FASHION DESIGNER LIPSTICK
LESBIAN SEEKING GAY MALE BFF

Ideal candidate is located in Manhattan, lovably bougie, has impeccable style and a fierce sense of humor.
Madonna fans to the front of the line.

—

I got some interesting responses to that ad, and went on some painful "friend dates" as a result. At the end of the day, all I learned was that you can't capture the perfect bestie; they're discovered, not recruited through Craigslist. I never did tell Justin that story. I'm sure he knew being on the other side, but just in case he didn't, maybe I should go to the seance… Perhaps Justin had something to say.

I decided not to attend the service. My Catholic upbringing had created an aversion to organized religion, even of the ghostly kind. I arrived ten minutes early, taking the "no late admission allowed" bullet point very seriously. I texted Sami to calm my nerves.

Walking in now 👻
It's up a stairway to a
secret room above the
church. It's a bit creepy but
I think it's legit.

I'm sure it is, but you know the drill:
Drop a pin so you don't end up in
a bin! Love you.

I shared my location with Sami as requested and walked through a white door with chipping paint to reveal a small room. Old books with worn cloth covers were crammed into bookshelves that lined every wall. A handful of participants were already gathering around a rectangular table, shuffling metal folding chairs around it. A tall man with a neatly groomed beard introduced himself as Reverend Williams and explained that he would be leading the circle. He turned off all the lights except for several small battery-operated candles clustered together in the center of the table. We were then asked to turn our cell phones off.

"Let's start by closing our eyes. Envision any of the chaos or heaviness from today exiting your body like a dark cloud, drifting further and further away, above the building, up into the ethers."

I pictured the binders I compiled all day at Nexxus floating up to the skyline like the random objects depicted within the tree in a *Highlights* magazine.

"Once everything has been released, envision a white light moving through you from the crown, all the way down until you are filled with light. Start opening up to your loved ones from the other side and prepare to receive messages from them," Reverend Williams guided.

Hey Justin. I'm here. Thanks for the cameo in the Ayahuasca ceremony. I love you so much. I'm sorry I posted an ad on Craigslist to replace you when we were in that dumb fight and didn't speak for a whole summer.

"Slowly bring yourselves back into the room and open your eyes. I will do my best to open and deliver as many messages as possible, first asking for your consent to share the information," the Reverend explained. He began sharing messages as they came through, some incredibly specific involving upcoming dates and locations, others more general about worthiness and confidence. Towards the end of the hour, he fixed his eyes on me and asked:

"May I share a message with you?"

"Yes, absolutely," I responded.

"Wow. This one has a lot to say. He's very... sassy. He wants me to tell you to stop paying to connect with friends, including me. I'm always with you." Reverend Williams paused, seeming uncomfortable. "He says... I'm always with you, bitch. Go buy yourself a handbag with that money. I know that the admission to this show wouldn't buy a great one, but even a vinyl clutch from H&M would be a better investment." The Reverend shook his head. "I'm sorry for the language, does that make sense to you?"

I laughed, wiping a tear from my right eye, "Yes, too much."

As the night was wrapping and no more messages appeared to be coming through, Reverend Williams looked at me knowingly and said, "Wait, Bex, was it? Do you have something to share? Are there messages that you are receiving?" Instantly, I heard the opening beat and vocals of Cee Lo Green singing *Crazy* while Raphael the red Teenage Mutant Ninja Turtle surfed by.

"Hey guys," I said, softly clearing my throat, "I'm Bex aka Cardsy B. I do intuitive Tarot readings, but this is my first seance." My hands began to clam up as I experienced flashbacks to the one and only twelve-step meeting I attended.

"As I step deeper into my own energy work, I've been receiving messages in different ways. I'm trying to understand them, so that's why I wanted to come tonight... and of course, to meet other people who get that. I don't normally do readings without my cards but I did get a message just now. And I think it's for you," I said to the Reverend. "Okay, this is gonna sound weird."

"Nothing is weird. Don't overthink it," Reverend Williams instructed.

"I just heard a Cee Lo Green song and saw Raphael the Teenage Mutant Ninja Turtle. It seems to be a message about childhood and music and your relationship to music... Does that make sense?"

"Yes! I sing in the choir here but I'm getting back into R&B and playing the keyboard which I learned as a kid. I actually love Cee Lo. Also, it's funny that you narrowed in on Raphael. He's one of my guides—the archangel, not the Turtle!" he laughed.

On the way out, a petite woman with a bright red pixie cut who appeared to be around my mom's age, smiled as she stopped to hold the door for me.

"That was pretty impressive, especially for your first time here."

"Oh, thanks. Yeah, it was cool. The message that he shared from my friend was spot on."

"I'm Penelope, by the way. If you're looking for more of us, you should come to the Order of the Golden Dawn's New York Chapter."

"Oh, amazing. I didn't even know that existed. I am so fascinated by the Order of the Golden Dawn and its ties to the Tarot. I just finished creating my own deck, inspired by the Smith-Rider-Waite origins. Do you guys have a website or Instagram?" I asked, taking out my phone.

"No, dear." She laughed. "We meet this Saturday at midnight under the terrace by the Bethesda Fountain." She reached for a pen in her overstuffed black satchel and began to write her number on my right forearm like it was 1985. "That's me, in case you get lost."

"Your cell or your landline?" I asked what I thought was a logical question given the sequence of events.

"Cell phone, dear. I'm not THAT old," she giggled as she shuffled out into the night.

The latter part of the week was now reserved for my favorite client: me. I finished the final authorization of the digital proof of my Tarot deck and ordered a small batch of 100 copies. My main intention was to use it myself to read and to teach, so I kept the production run small and affordable, learning from all the dollars

I unsuccessfully dumped into my lingerie line. Just as I clicked send, I saw missed texts from Sami and Chloe.

> Hey Ladies my work dinner
> got canceled but I'm still in
> Chelsea from this conference.
> Any chance either or both of
> you are free around 6:30?

> Free as an overworked but
> eager-to-see-you bird.
> The Smith?

> Totes. See you soon!

I walked through the glass door of The Smith in Nomad to see Chloe and Sami at our usual spot. Chloe had already ordered truffle fries for the table.

"Wait, what is that?" Sami pointed to the residue of the ink on my arm from Penelope's number.

I recounted the seance details to the girls which caused Chloe's romantic optimism to perk up.

"That's kind of an adorable meeting story," she gushed.

"Yeah… I mean maybe, if she weren't my mom's age, but no, it wasn't those kinda vibes."

"Oh, come on, Lego!" Chloe laughed, trying to bring back a nickname she created for me since my last girlfriend was in her fifties and I also accidentally went on a date once with a nineteen-year-old.

"Are we still trying to make Lego happen?" I shook my head.

"Come on: Lego means fun for all ages," Chloe mocked.

"In fairness, the nineteen-year-old told her she worked at *Vogue*, she didn't say she interned," Sami said, coming to my defense with her eidetic memory.

"You're not actually going to the Central Park midnight seance are you?" Chloe asked.

"It's not a seance, it's more of a ceremony I think. Plus I'm really interested in the origins and the magic of the Order of the Golden Dawn."

"She's totally going," Chloe said, shaking her head lovingly to Sami.

"As long as you drop a pin…" Sami started.

"So you don't end up in a bin." Chloe and I recited Sami's safety spell in unison.

In the Uber, I asked the driver to take me as far through the 72nd Street entrance as cars could go, so I wouldn't have to walk too far into Central Park at 11:50 at night. As we neared the destination, I meditated, asking my Higher Self to put a shield of white light around me for protection so that only those with good intentions could see me. I also asked Justin's spirit to have my back. For additional human physical world insurance, I chose to wear my most aerodynamic vegan leather leggings and combat boots, as well as carry a makeshift Mace—a travel size hairspray—in an easily accessible pocket. Luckily it wasn't too much of a trek.

As soon as I got to the terrace behind the Bethesda Fountain, there was a group of people in black cloaks forming rows. Two other cloaked attendees were draping a folding table with a dark red tablecloth to create an altar for wine and bread.

"I knew you'd come." I turned around to see Penelope's bright red lips smiling under her black hood.

"Hey! Yes, I'm so excited! Are the ceremonies always at this terrace?" I asked.

"The Bethesda Fountain is built on powerful energetic ley lines, so we hold a lot of services here, yes. Cleopatra's Needle is often used as well, which also holds a lot of power."

"Cleopatra's Needle?"

"Yes, the big Egyptian Obelisk in Central Park right near the Met. It was created in Egypt in the 1400s. There are ties that run back that far for Tarot, you know. And it was delivered to New York in 1881, right around the time the Hermetic Order of the Golden Dawn began."

I was intrigued that there were still more magical secrets that I had yet to learn about my great love, New York City. I was about to ask Penelope another question, or twelve, about the ley lines and magical artifacts that had apparently always been in the city without my knowledge, when a blonde on roller skates wearing angel wings whirled right past us.

"We must be starting soon," Penelope said, looking down at her watch. "That's Katrina, she serves the communion and sometimes also plays the harp."

Katrina whirled to her center position behind the altar as two cloaked figures stood on either side of her and began speaking in Latin. Ominous choir music played on bluetooth speakers while they began chanting something that the majority of the crowd joined with in unison.

I spent most of the first half of the ceremony wishing they had the translation prompters used in Opera houses because unfortunately, my Latin was limited to that of the Pig variety. The chanting halted and after a prolonged pause, the front two rows of the forty or so attendees moved closer to the center and created a line towards the altar. When it was our turn, Penelope seemed to sense my nerves and advised:

"It's best to go up and accept the sacrifice. But be aware that they, not always, but often, lace the bread with LSD. The wine is just cheap wine. Seems counterintuitive, I know. You can take it in your hand and discard it, or feel free to partake. I don't think I can go on that journey tonight myself, maybe next time." Penelope seemed to be having that debate more with herself than with me.

I followed her advice and took a fake sip of the red wine, then held my palms out to accept a small square of bread, pulling it into my sleeve when I felt confident no one was watching. Once everyone received their bread and wine and returned to their standing horizontal lines, more group chanting and singing in Latin resumed. I was about to write the whole thing off as an underground church with cooler costumes, basically a Catholic Burning Man, when I looked to my left to see an equally bored-looking woman around my age pull out a spoon from her pocket. She continued to fixate on it through the rest of the ceremony. She covertly returned it to her jean pocket as the two cloaked leaders bowed down and said, this time in English, "Thank you, until we rise again."

I thanked Penelope for her invitation and hugged her goodbye, not wanting to lose sight of the spoon girl. She was honestly the most intense and magical part of the evening. She was heading towards the 72nd Street Central Park entrance as well. I caught up and asked,

"Hey, sorry if this is weird, but I was next to you in the ceremony. I wanted to ask you… the spoon. Is it a divination tool? Or were you trying to bend it with your mind?"

"Not trying," she said with a smirk, as she produced a spoon from her back pocket that upon closer examination had a notable curve in its neck.

"Damn, Gina!"

"My name's Shaundra," she said flatly.

"Yeah, sorry that was a lame Martin Lawrence reference... how do you do that?"

"How do you do what you do? I mean you obviously singled me out as legit in that mixed crew tonight. Are you a witch as well?" Shaundra asked, still holding the spoon in between us.

"Yeah, I guess I am. I mostly do energy readings with Tarot for others, but I work with herbs and candle magic for myself as well. I don't know how to bend anything with my mind, though," I said, still in awe.

"I haven't mastered the spoon thing. I just thought I'd try tonight because there's a lot of powerful energy in this location, and I thought the frequency of the ceremony might amplify it. I mean, I guess I made a little dent," she said, rubbing her finger over the curve. "My teacher is really amazing. She has a whole collection of spoons and other heavy metal items she bent."

"Is there a telekinesis school somewhere?"

"Yeah, kind of. They don't just focus on moving things with the mind, we work on all kinds of psychic abilities: remote viewing, telepathy, psychometry. It only opens once a year. I went last year. I think they are starting auditions for the next class soon. They only take thirty-three people and you have to test to get in. I can send you the info. What's your instagram?"

"C-A-R-D-S-Y B"

"Wait, you're Cardsy B? I already follow you. You'll get in no problem."

I grinned. *The spoon-bending wizard thought I was psychic-school-worthy.*

When we reached 72nd Street, I waved to Shaundra as she turned right towards the subway entrance while I veered left to meet my Uber.

Even though I got home just before 1 a.m., I was wide awake from my encounter with Spoon-Bender Shaundra. I clicked on the link she DMed me through Instagram to check out the psychic school. I had heard of the founder. He was a famous psychic known for being able to acquire knowledge from books by sleeping on them. I remember my grandmother telling me stories about that ability. I felt a bit like Goldilocks when none of the groups I tried to fit into felt quite right, so I decided to give one last try to the psychic school. Interviews for the upcoming class were starting in a couple of weeks and even if I didn't learn how to bend spoons, maybe I would at least meet some other magical misfits like me there. Two Saturdays later I woke up to a text from Sami.

We're still meeting at ABC V
for brunch, right?

Totes. I may be 5 min
behind because I'm
coming from that
Psychic thing. See
you soon!

OMG! Right! Can't wait to hear
about it.
See you soon. Xx

I shoved my way into a small, overstuffed elevator in a rundown building on 36th Street in Herald Square. The downside of being 5'2" is that I often found myself at armpit o'clock on the subway and in crowded elevators, but I wanted to make sure I was on time for my official interview for the Psychic Institute. Half of me expected to hear a sad sales pitch of why I should invest in psychic school courses, while the other half of me hoped I had just found Hogwarts. The welcome email confirming my appointment explained that the first part was an individual interview to see if I was a good fit for the program, a measure taken to "make the best use of everyone's time and energy." I walked onto the designated, nondescript floor. It was one of those aging Manhattan high-rises where each room was being rented by the hour by a different instructor or organization. Some were being used for classes, some for interviews, and some for acting workshops. I asked at the front desk which room Sydney was interviewing in, and made my way down the hall in the direction the receptionist pointed.

I walked into a room where three apathetic individuals were seated facing me, at a long folding table. Various empty metal folding chairs were arranged in a semicircle.

"Hi, Sydney?"

"Yes. Name?" The thin hipster in the middle with 90s bleached tips demanded flatly.

"Hi. I'm Rebecca Szymczak."

"Ok Rebecca, give us what you've got for Georgina."

What the actual fuck... am I supposed to just channel on demand? Is this the interview process?!

"Well, I... I mostly work with Tarot cards. But... um... sure, just give me a minute..." I said as I rifled through my purse for my deck.

"I think she's in the wrong room." The tall woman with a severe bun on the far right said with an eye roll.

"Is this not the room for the Psychic Institute interviews?"

"Did you pick up on that? Without your cards?" the bitter Kurt Cobain-hipster asked before yelling, "NEXT!"

Apparently I wasn't psychic enough to know I had been in the wrong room the entire time. *Off to a great start,* I thought. I shoved my Tarot deck back in my bag and returned to the small desk that served as a makeshift reception.

"Hi I'm looking for the *other* Sydney... with the E.C. Psychic Institute?"

"Oh yes, that's room 104."

Sydney was in her late fifties with a serious demeanor but had much kinder eyes than the first Sydney. She walked me through the outline of the program, starting with an introduction to the science of intuition and psychic abilities. Then, she moved into more hands-on modalities including field trips to work with locations and objects to practice psychometry. The last section included advanced exercises like divination, mediumship and psychic investigation. It felt like I had indeed found a magical school of enchanted education! Sydney then explained we would start with a test on precognition. I would be shown an image on the computer screen, but before it appeared, I was instructed to draw a plus sign to indicate a positive feeling, or a minus to indicate a negative feeling about it. The images ranged from war photos (negative) to a box of puppies (positive). I marked my answer next to each number and then told Sydney when I was ready to be shown the visual. Out of twenty images, I got sixteen correct. Sydney could tell that the straight A student in me was beating herself up (obviously, because she's a psychic school professor) and she assured me that sixteen was a very high score. We then moved on to a series of strange interview questions and exercises, all of which were far less horrifying than my unintentional audition for the part of Georgina. At the end of the interview, I was told I qualified and that if I was interested I could sign up to reserve my spot for this year's class.

"It's the 'Sure, give me a minute' for me," laughed Sami, as I recounted my failed unintentional acting audition.

"Beyond humiliating... ugh I need a matcha like whoa." I reached for the menu.

"Well in fairness, I'm sure they see all kinds of weird NYU drama students who are way crazier and have worse auditions than that," Chloe added diplomatically.

"Should I do the brunch bowl or the blueberry waffles? I should be good and do the brunch bowl." Sami agonized over the choices.

"We can always get pancakes for the table!" Chloe added decadently, as we all placed our orders.

Chloe was not at all vegan and therefore assumed consuming plant-based pastries and sweets was the same as eating kale.

"But how was the actual interview?" Sami prodded.

"Oh weird for sure... but I guess I did well. They gave me a blindfold and then placed a card in my hand, telling me the color. They did the same with a black and a yellow card. Then I needed to determine how each felt or looked like in my mind while blindfolded. Once I went through the colors, they mixed up the cards and asked me to determine the color of whichever card they put in my hand. Apparently, I got it right seven out of ten times so that was good. Then they paired me with another candidate and gave us a card with a shape or image on it, asking one of us to telepathically send the image to the other across the room. And then you switch."

"Could you do it?!" Chloe and Sami asked at the same time.

"I guess so. It feels like meditating... with intention. When it was my turn to be the 'sender' I had to send the image of a butterfly to the receiver. At the end of our time, she got 'sideways hourglass' which I guess counted as close enough. Then she had to send me her image and you know how I always hear songs as messages, I heard a bum drunkenly whistling and bottles clinking. At first, I was trying to decipher if it was actually happening outside. But eventually, I just went with it and guessed 'wine.' It was a bunch of red grapes so we got points for that."

"Dude! You're psychic AF," squealed Sami, always my biggest cheerleader.

The term psychic always made me anxious, like I didn't deserve it, or that it would set me apart in a bad way. I believed we all had access to these abilities. I thought back to the bold san serif font of the mission statement painted on the entryway of my first employer, NIKE.

OUR MISSION IS TO BRING INSPIRATION AND INNOVATION TO EVERY ATHLETE*

*IF YOU HAVE A BODY, YOU ARE AN ATHLETE.

I felt like psychic gifts deserved a similar asterisk: *If you are a human, you have intuitive abilities.*

"I mean... we all are," I said. "I think it's like meditating or working out... the more you dedicate time and energy to it, the easier and more effective it gets. I just spend a lot of time trying to understand the crazy voices from the Universe."

As I finished talking I looked down at my phone to see an Instagram notification.

"Oh my God, you guys!! Eli Vate just followed me on Instagram!" I squealed with a joy matching that of a teen Justin Bieber fan who just scored floor tickets.

Sami attempted to explain my outburst to the waitress who just arrived at our table. "Sorry, it's a big moment. Eli Vate just followed her."

"Oh, cool! I love him. He's like a young, sassy Eckhart Tolle." She smiled as she organized her tray. "Ok one avocado toast, one chia bowl, pancakes to share and one order of gluten-free blueberry waffles... wait that's not right is it?" she asked.

"Omg, that's what I *really* wanted!!" Sami smiled at the waitress. "It's cool, I'll take them."

"See! You totally just sent a telepathic message to the kitchen, Sami!" Chloe smiled.

"I love you guys so much," I gushed, soaking up the signature blend of playfulness and connection that we experienced when we were together.

"Because we ordered communal pancakes AND waffles?" Chloe winked.

"No, I mean, I was trying to go to all these circles and ceremonies and schools..."

"And seances!" Sami added.

"Yeah...and I already have my magical mofos. It's you guys," I smiled.

"We can learn more about Tarot!" Chloe offered eagerly. I put my arm around her, smiling as she continued. "No I mean I get it, it's like when you go into high school or college and you go through all these different groups trying to find your people. You were just doing the Hogwarts version of that."

"But it was here all along, Toto," Sami said dramatically, blinking her eyes at me. "We've always seen how magical you are. And so does Eli, and so will all the people that are meant to come into your life."

It took me such a long time to find a true sense of belonging. I thought back to being an awkward little loner kid who stowed away in my big sister's closet, peeking through the shutter doors to catch a glimpse of her and her and her best friend watching my favorite show on her rabbit ear antenna TV. Once I accidentally blew my own cover as I leaned in a little too far to try to see the screen, causing the closet door to creak.

"REBECCA!"

"Hey guysth" I said with a slight lisp due to my retainer and headgear. "I love Melrose Plathe too! I want to be justh like Amanda Woodward when I grow up," I said, referring to Heather Locklear's ruthless, blonde, boss lady character. Turns out that didn't end up being too far off from my Playboy years. *Be careful what you wish for…* But I *was* glad I had always wished for amazing friends because the Universe outdid itself by delivering Chloe and Sami.

"I'm so sorry about this but our computer system is down and we can't process credit card payments. There's an ATM on Park Avenue at the corner if you don't have cash," The waitress explained as she laid the check down on our table.

"It's okay. I have cash from readings. And I owe the generous King of Pentacles about thirty meals," I said, smiling at Chloe. I placed the money in the plastic check folder and passed it back to the waitress.

The waitress returned with the change and Sami pointed excitedly at one of the singles.

"Ooo we got a fancy one!"

"Oh. My. God," I gasped.

"Is that the…" Chloe looked at me wide-eyed.

I picked it up and inspected it. It was in fact *the* dollar, with my sketch and my signature.

"The Tinkerbell dollar!" I exclaimed, holding it up like I had just won the golden ticket in Willy Wonka's Factory.

"Shut. The. Fuck. Up. Ok, you have to guard that with your

259

life. No more recklessly putting it in circulation! See that B?" Sami declared, pointing to the heart-shaped B bubble I drew being blown like a kiss by Tinkerbell. "B is for Cardsy motha fuckin' B. THIS is where this love belongs. And it came back when you began to really love yourself."

Everything I was looking for *was* right there with me all along.

Four of Cups / That Which is For Me Cannot Go By Me - Tinkerbell Spell

This spell is for letting go of an attachment to a person or situation, but making an intentional effort to leave the door open if it is meant to come back around at a more aligned time. Usually best cast with the intention of having the item circulated to a specific person, it can also be for a specific location or setting. For example, this occurred with a book that a friend of mine sold on Amazon when she was questioning whether she was in the right place career-wise. Someone who worked with her bought that exact book and showed my friend her name written inside.

Timing: Best on a Monday (ruled by the Moon for intuition and change/travel).

Supplies:

An item you can put into circulation:

I used a dollar bill for mine. There's a law about defacing currency but from my personal research into this, the law is aimed at 1. changing the denomination 2. advertising a business on it 3. shredding, burning, or otherwise rendering it unfit for circulation. That being said I am not encouraging anyone to draw on a dollar. Friends of mine have had books, vintage clothing, jewelry, and other accessories that they've sold come back to them or someone they know, in a short period of time.

A tool to mark/customize the item:

This can be a pen to draw an initial, small custom sign or symbol. If you have metal accessories or jewelry, a knife or etching tool would work well.

Ethically-sourced smudging herbs

I use sage from my friend Christina's garden for this.

1. Sit with the item in your hands until you come to a neutral charge/feeling of detachment to the item. Cleanse the item you plan to circulate by lighting the smudging herb(s) and wafting the smoke around it to clear any previous energies or attachments.

2. Draw, etch, or carve the initials or symbols of your choosing somewhere on the item that you will be able to clearly identify later.

3. Take a picture of the unique markings you created on the item for later reference.

4. I recommend repeating something along the lines of:

That which is for me, cannot go by me.

I release you now on your journey.

If you choose (enter name) as your home,

I will open-heartedly trust the outcome.

If you find yourself on a different track,

I'll see this as clearing, not as lack.

CHAPTER XVIII

THE KING OF PENTACLES
TUMBLEWEEDS OF TRANSFORMATION

King of Pentacles: Success, Abundance, Groundedness

Through my fashion industry colleagues, I was invited to the house of a high-profile food-lebrity I lovingly refer to as Auntie Em. Though her home was only an hour outside of the city, it seemed like I had entered an entirely different world. It felt surreal, as if I were being transported into the pages of a magazine. Her estate had been photographed extensively and featured on her various television shows.

When we arrived, Auntie Em greeted us in the horse stables located at the center of the property. She thought it would be fun for us to go on a treasure hunt to get a taste of some of the highlights of her one-hundred-plus acre estate. We were given a checklist of items to either bring back in her sustainable, logoed tote bags or to snap photos of on our phones.

Even though I was sweating through my signature black-on-black uniform, I couldn't help but be in awe of the pure architectural perfection of the sprawling manor. The excitement I felt as a new vegan when I saw her elaborate vegetable gardens reminded me of entering the Hershey chocolate factory as a child. I began to fade after an hour of hunting for flowers I'd never heard of, and fruit I couldn't identify without their neatly printed Whole Foods name tags. I strayed a little off course to locate some shade when I happened upon the most beautiful pool I had ever seen. This gorgeous aquatic oasis made the pools I'd seen in my former life at Hamptons estates and the Playboy Mansion look like they belonged at a Days Inn. I took out my phone and photographed my freshly manicured toes stretched out in front of Auntie Em's pool and texted the picture to Sami and Chloe.

Oh hey, I live here now.

HOLY SHIT! Where are you?
I'm headed into a meeting
from hell. #Jealous

Me too, I'm on a never-ending
conference call.
Where is that?

Auntie Em's house, She's my new girlfriend. We can't wait to have you both over for Thanksgiving dinner. 😜

Get it, Lego!

Just as I was composing another selfie, a guard tapped me on the shoulder and informed me that the treasure hunt was wrapping up and prizes would be announced before lunch was served. I clearly would not win the grand prize after veering off from the field trip. Part of me felt a twinge of guilt that I let my inner top student down because I usually worked hard to excel at these challenges. But another part of me was proud of myself for practicing presence—and for getting the perfect toe selfie.

We were seated for lunch when a couple of my colleagues asked me if I had my Tarot cards on hand. Over the past few months, word continued to spread and I expanded into reading for other people in the company, including a couple of private equity dudes that sat on the board. This was the first time I showed up to a high-profile fashion event as both Bex *and* Cardsy B.

"I just need a quick look at whether or not this deal is gonna close by the end of Q3," Jordan, Director of Investments, said while unbuttoning his collar, surrendering to the afternoon sun.

Billy, a young jovial marketing executive chimed in from the other end of the table, "Yeah, then me! My wife and I are trying to get pregnant and I heard you're really good with predicting time frames."

"Ok boys, but keep it on the DL. I don't want to re-create the mob situation that occurred at the holiday party and upset Auntie Em."

"So you're the Tarot reader?" Auntie Em said, towering over the end of our table at an impressive height. She was a model in her youth and had a beautifully formidable presence.

"Yeah, she's really good! She created her own deck and everything," Billy touted.

"Well then I'd love for you to read for me," she said.

I began to sweat profusely but luckily the heat disguised my nerves. I needed a way out. It was going to be downright dangerous for me to read for Auntie Em. My deck was inspired by iconic women. and I'd chosen her as my muse for the Four of Pentacles: the card of miserliness or in my interpretation, "energetic hoarding." Auntie Em spent time in prison for charges related to insider trading a while back, which is a very literal translation of Four of Pentacles.

I could feel everyone's eyes on me while I pretended to fumble through my purse, a distraction while I attempted to do the math in my head:

The probability of one card out of seventy-eight, while pulling a nine-card spread… maybe a ten to twelve percent chance? That is too damn high.

"Ugh, I'm so sorry. I thought I had them but I don't," I said.

"You always have them with you!" Billy exclaimed in disbelief.

"I changed purses and they must be in my other bag," I lied.

I was still so bummed that I received, and then declined an invitation to read for Auntie Em, when Lindsay called me on the way home.

"Hey, how was the big field trip today? Did you milk a cow?"

"No, but my worlds are starting to officially collide," I explained, recounting the lunchtime Tarot debacle.

"Ok, but why didn't you just do it? If the card came up, couldn't you have found a positive way to spin it?"

"Mofo, the image on the card is wearing an ORANGE JUMPSUIT!"

"Oh my God! I'm dying, I'm putting you on speaker," she said, so I could relay the story to Austin.

They both laughed before Lindsay thoughtfully offered insight, "I mean it's pretty hilarious, but also maybe it's a sign that your fashion days are on the way out. Maybe don't hold on too long in Four of Pentacles-style, when you know where your passion lies."

"And also," Austin chimed in, "maybe remove unflattering cards if you're attending the home of their celebrity inspiration in the future."

"I can't believe you sold out of the first order of decks already! You should have a launch party!" I could feel Chloe's convincing CEO smile through the phone.

"I mean it was a *small* first round of decks because I don't really have a budget for big production runs, or for a launch party," I said, feeling my stomach tighten as I thought back to all the money I had lost on my lingerie line.

"You're in a really different place than you were with your line. And the fact that the first production run is already sold out says a lot. So does the fact that you're not trying to force it," Chloe added.

"No more maniforcing!" I declared.

"No more maniforcing. On that note, what if you got a sponsored venue? Between you, me, and Sami, I bet we could find one. That way you wouldn't be shelling out money for it." That was why Chloe was the King of Pentacles. She had mastered the codes for acquiring abundance and for the worthiness of receiving it.

I made a list of all the places I had read Tarot over the past year. First, there was the OG speakeasy I started at, Go Ask Alice. From there, I'd done everything from the VIP area for a Lizzo concert, to corporate events for big brands, media and editor events for magazines, and a horror-themed vintage trolley tour called Mistress Mortuary, where I read Tarot for morbid tourists on Friday nights. I scratched Mistress Mortuary off the list of potential launch party venues. Not that it wasn't cool, just that the mobile nature of it didn't lend well to the fashionably late crowd.

Two days later I received several replies. The first email I opened was from The Ace Hotel. I was one of their featured readers in their Psychic Sundays series. The Ace was a chic boutique hotel chain that had locations in all the hip North American cities. The New York location hosted art and music events in a dimly lit communal lobby with photobooths, typewriters and a craft cocktail bar.

From: **Bill Halsey <bhalsey@theacehotel.com>**
Date: Wed, Sept 26, 2018 at 4:30 PM
Subject: Inquiry for Tarot Deck Launch Event
To: Rebecca Szymczak

Hey Cardsy
Congratulations on the completion of your Tarot deck! This is really awesome, so the short answer is yes. We do book launch-type things pretty often; those usually include a DJ or playlist in the 6 p.m. to 8 p.m. range on a Tuesday night. We could do Oct 30th, perfect for when the veil is thin right before Halloween. Low key; lobby is per usual but you'd have a reserved section for friends and press, and being in the Lobby is great because there's more opportunity for the general public to see your stuff.

We could also do a feature of select cards on our blog, posts on socials, etc.

LMK when we can jump on a call to firm up the details.
-Bill

I turned right on 29th Street towards the Ace Hotel's lobby entrance when I noticed neon pink stenciled graffiti on the sidewalk that declared: "Sometimes The King is A Woman." I nodded in agreement as I pushed the heavy glass door into the entrance of the hotel. I noticed my Tarot decks on display in the windows of the boutique, and a sign displaying artwork from the cards, along with my photo in the Lobby. *Oh my God. This is really happening.* I arrived early to help set up stations for two of my favorite readers in the city who I met through metaphysical events over the past year. I hired them to offer readings with my Tarot deck for attendees, who according to the RSVP list, included a lot of my friends, several bloggers and a few magazine editors. I nervously sipped on a virgin ginger mule adjusting the plunging neckline of my J Lo-meets-Morticia Adams black lace dress when I heard Amanda's infectious laughter. The first attendees were, of course, the royal court: Amanda aka The King of Swords, known for her fierce intellect and being the ultimate truth bomb, Chloe aka The King of Pentacles, known for making abundance look effortless, and Sami, The Queen of Cups, the emotionally intuitive nurturer. Amanda held up a toy sword in her right hand while Chloe jangled some change to represent pentacles. Sami donned a Swarovski tiara and explained she intended to retrieve her chalice from the bar.

"I... I love you guys so fucking much," I said, wiping at the corners of my eyes.

"Eye makeup!" Sami cautioned, reaching for a tissue in her clutch before embracing me.

"We love *you* so much, B," Amanda said, hugging me.

"We're so proud of you and have a little something for you." Chloe pulled a gift bag out of her YSL tote.

I reached into the black tissue paper to reveal a well worn

dark green copy of *The Tarot of The Bohemians* by Papus with the wheel of fortune embossed on the front.

"Is this?" I asked with my mouth still hanging open.

"Yeah, it's a first edition," Chloe smiled.

The Tarot of The Bohemians is considered one of the most sacred and comprehensive texts on Tarot that delves into its history and esoteric origins from Egypt, to Kabbalah, to the Order of the Golden Dawn. The original edition was published in 1889, making it impossible to acquire. Sami's, Chloe's and Amanda's powers combined proved that like the pink graffiti outside stated: sometimes the king *is* a woman, and when that's the case, nothing is impossible.

Amanda pulled me aside. "Hey I got you something else too," she said, as she handed me a small gift bag.

"You didn't have to do anything else! What is..." I asked pulling out what looked like dried-up tumbleweed. "Thank you, but what is it, exactly?"

"It's a Rose of Jericho. When I was in LA last week, I was drawn to them for some reason in this shop and asked the store owner about them. Apparently, they are known as resurrection plants because when you place them in water they blossom and become all vibrant and green again as the bowl of water cleanses and transmutes the old energies. I thought... well this feels like your resurrection night, opening up to this whole new path and whatever opportunities and abundance awaits."

"Wow! That is... so incredibly thoughtful and magical. Thank you. I love you so much." I said, hugging her tightly.

A few bloggers filtered in behind a couple of my Nexxus colleagues. Myriam arrived in a Gucci belt wrapped around a chic snake print dress that I knew was her homage to the witch motif. She had perfected the art of dressing "on theme" in just the right amount for every occasion. As she hugged me, she said "I'm so proud of you." This meant more to me than any binder or trend board she had ever approved. I walked Myriam over to where I saw Chloe chatting with Andy. They'd met before and were good company, so I didn't feel guilty continuing my way around the lobby in an attempt to thank everyone who showed up.

I was wrapping up a conversation with a writer from Nylon Magazine about the potential for podcasting, when Lydia, a friend I had met through Chloe, arrived looking elegant in a black wrap dress with her long dark brown hair pulled back in a low ponytail.

"Bex!!! Congratulations!!! I can't stay long, but I wanted to thank you in person."

"Thank YOU!" I said as I hugged her, uncertain of what I was being thanked for.

"Remember when you did that reading for me on the balcony of the William Vale? And you said I was going to meet my person through work in five weeks?"

I squinted trying to recall the reading, "Wait, yeah I do remember… you said that you work on a super small team and everyone was married or fugly."

"Yes, and true," she laughed. "But he's from the Paris office!! I didn't think about the overseas team! We met exactly five weeks to the day that you told me that! We're madly in love and I'm moving to Paris!"

"Wow! Congratulations to YOU! Champagne and plant-based, non-alcoholic elixirs are at the bar, and Chloe is right over there." I waved at Chloe and Myriam. As I turned around to greet the newcomers, I noticed a missed text on my phone and checked to make sure it wasn't someone who was trying to find their way to the launch party.

Hi Cardsy. I'm not sure if you
remember me, my best friend
Jill had a reading with you and
recommended you so highly
that I booked a session with my
daughter last week. I meant to
write you sooner but it's been a
crazy few days. I want to thank you
for sharing your insights with my
precious girl who is going through
such a dark time. When she came
to me and broke down saying she
didn't want to be here anymore,
my heart shattered. I sincerely
mean this when I say... you helped
save my daughter's life. I know
you did. When she came out of
her bedroom after the session she
was in tears but with her shoulders
UP, smiling and showing a sense
of relief, some hope, and some
confidence. You are a blessing
and I can't thank you enough.

I stepped into a corner to respond immediately. I definitely
remembered her. Aside from the occasional mother-daughter duo
that came to an event, I only ever read for adults unless a parent
booked a session. Kyla's mom told me nothing other than that
she was going through a tough time and then walked the laptop to
her daughter's bedroom. I remembered feeling Kyla's darkness.
It was one of the only times that the Eight of Cups and the Death

Card showed up as literally contemplating death in a reading. I didn't say that outright, instead, I told the nervous, soft-spoken tenth grader that though things seemed incredibly dark right now, she wasn't alone. She obviously had an amazing mom who was there for her, and who was willing to help get her any tools and support necessary. And now I was part of her soul squad too. After seeing the Eight of Cups and the Death card in her recent past, I saw some conflict and cruelty around her with the Five of Swords. I explained that, though it felt like this card represented the whole world, Kyla was much more powerful than her current circumstances (aka high school) often allowed, and she would be shown glimpses of that power until she could fully embrace it. I also saw the Magician and The Page of Swords. These cards showed me that she had immense gifts with her throat chakra and with music. She nodded shly when I described this, telling me she was interested in pursuing music in college. I explained that I saw massive success in her future career as a result of this pursuit. Although it was tough right now, I guided her to tap into the tools she had in the vein of the Magician: not only her gifts, but the support from those who cared about her, because there were a lot of us. At the end of the reading, I candidly shared that I felt exactly like her once. Following my own gifts was the reason that we were together for her reading on Zoom, and I was thrilled that I got to connect with the most amazing people every day because of it. She also had a big mission, even larger than mine in a lot of ways. Before I said goodbye I told her, "You've got some powerful stuff to do, Kyla, and I can't wait to see it."

Tears welled up in my eyes as I typed my response, just as they did after that reading.

OMG yes of course I

remember you both! Most of all I remember Kyla's powerful soul. I sensed the darkness in her but also all her internal strength and the excitement on the horizon. I'm so happy to hear this and beyond grateful you reached out to share it with me. She is so blessed to have you as a mother.

I wiped the corners of my eyes when Amanda, Chloe and Sami spotted me.

"You ok, B?" Amanda asked, putting an arm around me.

"I'm SO Okay! I love you guys so much." I embraced all three of them in a Golden Girls-style group hug. "You guys... I can't believe I get to do this! I think I'm actually helping people."

"Of course you are. You're really good at it," Chloe smiled.

"You know, in all the years we've known each other, I never saw you *that* moved over anything in your fashion work," Amanda said.

"I never felt like I made this kind of a difference. The best thing that happened to me tonight isn't this awesome venue, or the tarot decks in the window, or that big sign with my face on it. It was the most touching note from a mother of a girl I did a reading for. It's crazy but sometimes people just send me DMs that say 'thank you for being you' or send me Venmo donations because of things that I shared that help them. No one in fashion ever said to me, 'Hey, thanks for picking that perfect Pantone color of coral, can I give you a donation of gratitude for that?'"

Amanda, always the sage of the group, said, "I think some people in fashion, and every industry, receive a version of that if it is their true passion and calling. It just wasn't yours, B. I think this is yours. I know you thought you were destined to be a CEO but I think you're meant to be—"

"A C*W*O," Sami finished, smiling. "Chief Witchy Officer."

"Cheers to that!" Chloe raised her glass and the rest of us followed suit.

I went home that night, and before curling up with Lola in bed, I placed a rose quartz and a citrine crystal inside my little tumbleweed from Amanda before placing it into a glass bowl of water on my window sill. I placed my hands above the bowl and said:

I am opening to whatever opportunities allow me to stand in my purpose, to activate others to receive the most amount of healing, love, and abundance, possible, and allow me to receive the most amount of love, abundance, and healing possible in exchange.

"I feel like a ton of people at the launch asked if you had a podcast," Sami noted as we stood in line the following week at the vegan fast-food chain, By Chloe.

"I think there was *one* editor who said that," I smiled. "But I know, it's something I've been thinking about. It seems like the set-up and work would be super technical though... When we were married, Amanda's nickname for me was Nana due to my level of tech-savviness," I admitted.

"I mean, you managed to figure out how to create and produce a Tarot deck from the living room floor of your apartment. Also is the taco salad or the caesar better here?" Sami asked, weighing the menu.

"Both are good but I would go with the Tac... Whoa!"

"TacWhoa? Is that a special?" Sami looked down from the menu.

"Wait Wait! Look at this," I said, pointing to my instagram notification which distracted me from my previous role as menu advisor.

I held up my phone to show Sami a comment under my most recent post of the Moon card from my deck:

Hi Cardsy, I'm from Gold River
Publishing and I'm in love with
your cards! I sent you a DM with
my email. I would love to talk with
you if you are seeking a publisher.

Sami immediately stepped out of the line to give this news ample processing time. A woman behind us let out an intentionally audible sigh.

"Sorry! My client has a pressing issue and needs her agent's advice! You can get in front of us," Sami directed. "You know I'm down to be your agent, but you may need to be repped for real. Don't just sign with the first publisher. This is huge, Bex!" We hugged, further holding up the line.

I took Sami's advice and sent an initial response to the publishing inquiry before researching and reaching out to agencies who repped authors or thought leaders I admired. All three responded right away to schedule meetings. The first two smaller agencies announced that they wanted to represent me on the spot. I told them I still had one other meeting scheduled and would be in touch after. On my way to Paradigm, the third and largest agency located in a skyscraper in the financial district, my Uber driver jolted to a forced stop when I looked up to see what caused the near-accident. A bus with an ad for *House of Cards* with Robin Wright looking fierce as hell had cut in front of us. *House of Cards?! Paradigm must be the one.*

I waited in the massive white lobby in a cushy banquette next to a colorful Jeff Koons-looking sculpture. Nervously, I eyed their roster of clients, an impressive range from Danielle Steele to Neil Patrick Harris to Toast the famous Cavalier King Charles Spaniel. *Okay, I might not be as cute as Toast, but I think if they published her book, they might be down with my Badass Bitches Tarot Deck,* I convinced myself.

"Cardsy B? I'm Rose and this is Alicia," a stylish strawberry blonde said, motioning to her petite brunette colleague.

"Yes, hey!!! So nice to meet you!" I said, shaking both of their hands.

After being led to a small conference room. I gave them each a copy of the Badass Bitches Tarot Deck and a quick explanation of my hand-illustrated iconic ladies representing the seventy-eight major and minor arcana.

"We love it!" Alicia squealed excitedly.

"We love it and we *get* it," added Rose. "We love your Instagram! Also in your email you said you were starting a podcast? That would be really good for the demand for the deck as well."

"Yes, totally. I'm right on top of that, Rose." I smiled.

Between their infectious enthusiasm and nearly getting hit by the sign on a bus, I signed with Paradigm the very next day. In place of the celebratory drink (or nine) that I would have purchased myself after a successful big meeting in the fashion industry, I celebrated by heading to B&H Audio on 9th Avenue and 34th Street. I walked in and instantly experienced a state of overwhelm. I grabbed my phone to Google "equipment needed to start a podcast." All kinds of microphones, headphones and gadgets came up.

"Shit," I accidentally said out loud.

"Can… Can I help you? I'm Abe." A soft-spoken sales associate with curly hair and glasses smiled nervously at me.

"Oh, man I hope so!" I sighed. "Hey Abe, I'm Bex. I'm starting a podcast and I'm legit the least techy elder millennial."

"Ok so are you hosting solo? Taking calls or only having guests in person? Are you looking for just a mic or a production console as well?"

I stared at him like he just asked me to solve a calculus equation in mandarin after three glasses of wine. "I want to talk about Tarot and astrology… and for it to sound clear enough for people to want to listen," I answered honestly.

"Okay, so why don't we start you out with a Blue Yeti microphone. What program are you using to record your podcast?" he asked.

"Um, can you just tell me what I should use?" I said, feeling a lot like my dad anytime a new phone model came out.

"Well, a lot of people use Garageband but some people who like Adobe Creative Suite prefer Adobe Audition," Abe explained.

"Okay! Yes, that one! I use Adobe. I can probably do that one! Can you help show me how to set it up? Is there a fee or a way I could hire you to do that?" I begged.

"Listen… I'm not supposed to, but if you want to come by tomorrow with your laptop around 6 p.m. and I'm not with any customers, meet me in the corner by the headphones and I'll do my best to get you started."

"Yes! Totally! Keep it on the DL! Secret Society!!" I nodded enthusiastically.

"I'll try to get you set up tomorrow then," Abe said, trying not to laugh.

A week after the very patient lesson from my new B&H Audio BFF, I recorded and released my first episode. I started with weekly cosmic energy updates and teaching the cards associated with each month and astrological transit. After a couple of months of solo episodes I started reaching out to guests and was shocked and flattered when authors, spiritual leaders and celebrity psychics I admired, accepted invitations to come on the podcast.

My favorite guests were still the ones I knew and loved: those who were a part of my personal journey and who were on healing journeys of their own. My Ayahuasca soul sister Rosanna was my guest for an episode and talked about her work as a CEO in the finance world and her desire to instill consciousness in economics. Andy invited me over to his condo to record his episode in which he spoke about infusing wellness into his beauty line, as he recently introduced a rose water mist and soy wax meditation candle as part of his product line. As we wrapped the episode he looked up at me proudly and said,

"You're killing it, Bex. It feels like you really found your thing."

"I mean, I really love what I do and I feel like I'm helping people. But after everything I've been through, I just want to do things as long as they feel aligned without attachment. So I guess I'll keep doing it as long as it feels right," I said for the first time ever.

Tumbleweed Transformation / Rose of Jericho - Opening to New Pathways Spell

For transforming and transmuting current circumstances in order to open to receive abundance: fulfillment of love, financial prosperity, or abundance of other opportunities.

Timing: Best on a Thursday (ruled by Jupiter for expansion and opportunity), or on New Moons.

Supplies:

Rose of Jericho

The resurrection plant. A lot of metaphysical shops sell these and they can be ordered online as well.

A Large Bowl

This will be used as the container for the plant to blossom and transform. The Rose of Jerichos open to double, if not triple the size, so go big or go home with the bowl.

Water

Regular water is fine but if you have moon water prepared this is a perfect use for it. (see the spell at the end of Chapter VIII on how to prepare Moon Water)

Crystals for Chosen Intentions (Optional)

You can add intentional crystals inside the dried rose of Jericho before placing it to blossom in the bowl if you want to charge it with additional intentions. Rose Quartz is great for love, Citrine for Abundance (more examples are listed at the end of Chapter VII - Undercover Crystals Spell).

Tarot Cards Chosen Intentions (Optional)

If you like working with Tarot cards, you can also select a card or cards to place under the bowl along with your petition. I like using King of Pentacles for Abundance, Ace of Wands for opportunities related to Work/Purpose, and the Lovers and Ace of Cups for Love.

Paper and Pen to Create a Petition

Write out your intentions for what you are opening up to. For example, when Amanda gave me the Rose of Jericho at the Tarot Deck Launch, I used it that evening and wrote out a petition intending:

> *I am opening to whatever opportunities allow me to stand in my purpose, to activate others to receive the most amount of healing, love and abundance possible, and allow me to receive the most amount of love, abundance, and healing possible in exchange.*

1. Create your petition, fold it, and place it under the bowl along with King of Pentacles or other chosen Tarot cards.
2. Place any crystals you want to add into the dried Rose of Jericho, focusing on your intention.
3. Place the Rose of Jericho in the bowl.
4. Fill ¾ full with Moon Water or regular water.
5. Meditate on your intentions in silence or with a playlist. (I have multiple spell playlists, including one for the Rose of Jericho Spell, on my Spotify which can be accessed on www.cardsyb.com.)
6. Leave the bowl overnight (longer if desired).
7. You can dispose of the water, or if opening to abundance

for a home or business space, you can use the water to mop/clean the front hall or entry space floors.

8. Allow the Rose of Jericho to dry/curl back up for future use.

CHAPTER XIX

THE WHEEL OF FORTUNE
BURY, BIND, OR FREEZE

Wheel of Fortune: Transformation, Evolution, Change

When I told Andy that I now only do things as long as they feel aligned for me, I didn't know that statement would be put to the ultimate test less than a year later. Just as I made peace with surrendering the attachment I once held to my identities—girlfriend, wife, future-wife (of Madonna), designer, and executive—I began to feel a shift around the one remaining title I still believed defined me.

For as long as I can remember, I always wanted to live in New York. My uncle lived there and even after he passed away, my mom used to take me once a year to see a play or visit the Christmas tree at Rockefeller Center. It was as if she knew I needed that exposure to something other than our small rural town. I needed to experience a place I could belong in the world, a place where everyone was accepted for who they were and what they believed. She told me as an adult, in a TMI conversation, that I was conceived in New York City when she and my dad were visiting my uncle one weekend, and that I had gravitated towards returning to the city seemingly ever since.

In grade school, my chosen subject matter for any research project or report was always New York. My favorite movie growing up was Breakfast at Tiffany's. By high school, one of my greatest manifesting tools hit the small screen, the HBO masterpiece, *Sex and the City*. My teenage self knew beyond a shadow of a doubt—*that* was the life I was going to lead. Throughout college, I walked the streets of downtown Toronto near my University campus listening to my "NYC Life" playlist on my iPod. It started with Dolly Parton's *9 to 5*, during which I would picture myself rushing to catch the subway to my design job in the garment district, and ended with Joan Jett's cover of the *Mary Tyler Moore Show* theme song. I even threw my hat in the air at the end if I was wearing one, knowing I *was* going to make it to New York after all. Even in the darkest days, in that gas leak and rodent-infested SoHo-close-to-Chinatown apartment, I insisted on staying on the island of Manhattan. I was nothing, if not a New Yorker.

The shifts I felt were small at first. I couldn't tell if it was because of all the changes over the past couple years that had occurred from my own healing, or because the city itself was changing, but I felt an ominous dark cloud looming. It began with the voice that was now coming in louder than a National Weather Service Alert. ***The time is coming to get up and out.*** I heard it on more than one occasion. *I am out.* I thought. *Where is up? Canada? A higher floor in my building?* I contemplated the latter as my once immaculate view of the Empire State Building was now obstructed by a new high-rise going up one street north of me. I also considered the former option because I was spending more time in both LA and Toronto due to Tarot deck pop-up shops and events. But as much as I enjoyed visiting both, neither felt like a home to me the way New York always had.

On my birthday in December of 2019, the voice sternly advised: *You need to get super clear, so get clean. REALLY clean.* Up until that point, I was vegan-curious and allowed myself an occasional glass of champagne at a birthday or wedding. From that day on, I became plant-based and completely alcohol-free because I knew my Higher Self was asking me to prepare my body for something big. I didn't know exactly what it was but I had learned by now to trust the voice.

On Valentine's Day of 2020, I found myself single, yet again, while all my friends were partnered up. Sami was looking to buy a home in New Hope. Amanda had moved to L.A. to be with her girlfriend. Chloe had fallen madly in love with a girl who was in Australia. I was always a sucker for cheesy holidays, whether I was coupled or not, so I asked Chloe if she wanted to go to dinner as Galentines. We walked through the dimly-lit ornate hallways of the refurbished McKittrick hotel, now an immersive theater venue and meticulously designed restaurant intended to transport patrons back to the 1930s. Over the past two years, in addition to hearing "the voice" and other people's thoughts more clearly, I started occasionally seeing auras as well. Sami and Chloe knew this about me but that night was the first time I noticed Chloe's aura was almost blindingly yellow. I blinked slowly to clear my field of vision as Chloe looked up knowingly.

"Uh oh… whatcha seeing over there Oda Mae?" She asked, referencing Whoopi Goldberg's psychic character in *Ghost*.

"I know this might be the hippiest shit I have ever said, but your aura is REALLY bright right now," I explained.

"Oooo what color?" Chloe asked, always game to learn about my weird world of witchery.

"Bright yellow. I mean I think that's a good thing. Yellow represents solar plexus, confidence and empowerment. Very indicative of your Leo Rising and King of Pentacles vibes. Nothing bad, just seems... way crisper than usual."

"Yellow for the win!" Chloe said, squeezing her lemon wedge into her water glass. Suddenly, that shadowy cloud I felt looming seemed like it was hovering directly over the dining room floor of the McKittrick hotel. I felt a jolt, like the power went out but without the visual loss of light, just the feeling. When I looked down at my phone it had gone from displaying full battery when I left my apartment thirty minutes prior, to the twenty percent low battery warning. I bit my lower lip as I looked up slowly, knowing the answer to the question I was about to ask.

"Chloe..."

"Now you're freaking me out. What?"

"Is your phone dead?"

"Holy shit! It's at ten percent. It was charged when I left the office," she said, double tapping her screen. "How did you know that?"

"Something's going on," I said.

"I know. I feel a little trippy but this place always has a bit of that effect on people," Chloe said, referring to the intentional time travel theme of the McKittrick. Underneath her logical, executive demeanor, Chloe was a superstitious Catholic Italian, and one of the most low-key intuitive friends I had.

We both turned our phones off in an attempt to save what little power remained, and when I looked up, I realized I could see tons of auras, all at once. Not everyone's though, maybe twenty to thirty percent of the patrons in the restaurant and bar. Intuitively I knew that the ones with the visible auras also felt the shift. After we finished our dinner and used the remaining twenty percent of my phone's battery to split an UBER, I was still disturbed by the shift in frequency we experienced inside.

"I just have this feeling that this is the last time we're going to be doing this," I shared.

"You mean you think the McKittrick is gonna close?" Chloe asked.

"I don't know, I can't figure it out. It just feels off."

"Maybe it's because you're going to be so successful with your podcast and Tarot that you won't be able to go to stuff like this without being harassed by fans," Chloe, always the optimist, suggested. I think we both knew that wasn't the root of the premonition.

I scooped up Lola and crawled into bed, looking up at the Empire State Building behind the sprouting construction. The roof, which looked like a little lit-up top hat, was now the only part visible. That was the night when the dreams started. They were in black and white which was odd because I normally dream in color. It looked like something out of an old movie and felt very unsettling. I was perpetually trying to get out of the city, something I had never wanted to do before. In every dream, I had to slink through alleyways and strategically avoid dark energy authority figures. In one dream I specifically saw army tanks rolling down fifth avenue and signs for mandatory curfews.

Over the next month the darkness expanded and descended over Manhattan, and in March the ominous cloud opened up to a torrential downpour. The wealthy were the first to leave. They fled to their Hamptons and Berkshires homes within days, if not hours, of news breaking that all non-essential businesses were closing. Then the middle classes departed, finding refuge in spare bedrooms of suburban friends and family members. A tradition of banging pots and pans for front line workers began at seven each night. It was the best part of the day because I was reminded there was still life in the city besides me and Lola. The banging became progressively quieter until it stopped completely around May. It seemed like very few of us remained by then. I called my parents each night to check on them. They continued to attempt to convince me to come stay with them in Pennsylvania, and while part of me knew I would need to leave eventually, I still believed that if I stayed, I could somehow energetically nurse my great love, NYC, back to health.

Limited hours and a drastic increase in crime made the subway far less desirable. I walked everywhere I needed to, taking a backpack and the supplies required to line up for hours just to get groceries. Many homeless people in need of support would often congregate near the grocery store lines. I started withdrawing extra cash before I went out to share what I could, and when I forgot to stop at the ATM, I would take requests to add to my shopping list. The homeless people were the kindest and the least fearful, presumably having faced so much trauma and adversity already, they had gained wisdom we didn't yet have. A man named Rafael, who camped out beneath scaffolding on 5th and 28th, sold cardboard signs that he created with sayings like "Choose Love over Fear" and "Interrupt Anxiety with Gratitude." I asked him the cost, paid him the requested $10 for each, and took photos. He seemed confused when I didn't want the physical artwork. I explained I was more than grateful for the digital photos that I would post to share his beautiful messages. It was kind of like an unofficial NFT.

I wore an "I Heart NY" t-shirt when I went on my healing walks. It was my superhero costume that I wore whenever I left my apartment. It was the last purchase I made in a non-essential store before the lockdown. I felt pulled to go into a tourist shop in early March and purchase a fitted tee to display my love of NY. I went on those walks every day, choosing different routes and neighborhoods so I could tap as much love as possible into the grid of the city. When I returned home, I sat on my living room floor trying to create and share as much unifying content as possible for my podcast and Instagram, and continued to offer virtual readings.

The hardest part wasn't the solitude. I had spent the better part of 2018 on that very living room floor by myself. The part that was unbearable was the cruelty of the city's inhabitants towards one another. The occupants of a city that once stood for the celebration of diversity of beliefs now existed in constant a state of xenophobia, fearing anything different than their own views. Everyone's individual trauma was bubbling up to a breaking point and the human desire to connect for comfort was the one thing we were forbidden to do. On my walks and in the grocery store I found that I could hear people's thoughts louder than ever. And nearly all of them were extremely unkind.

I consciously curated my media intake with the same mindfulness I applied to my diet. I had unsubscribed from cable years prior, so while others were glued to the 24/7 media fear fest, I chose to watch inspiring documentaries and comedies. Louise Hay's meditations and Eli Vate's videos became more nourishing than ever. It felt like my past self had prepared a metaphysical prepper bag of tools that I now needed. My friendship with

Eli began around that time, through DMs and voice notes on Instagram. He shared his experiences in Los Angeles and I described the energies of New York City. He encouraged me in those incredibly dark days, reminding me:

> You got this Cardsy, you were
> placed exactly where you're
> supposed to be, you're the NYC
> ground crew—you're a warrior.

And for six solid months, at a time when the majority of Manhattan's occupants had departed, I embraced my assignment. I wanted to serve my city and tap healing and light back into its grid, but the signs were getting increasingly louder. Restaurants and businesses I had frequented for the past fifteen years closed permanently, one by one. I continued my daily walks past all the once beautifully-designed storefronts that were now ominously boarded up. The only stores that remained uncovered by plywood were abandoned months prior with "For Lease" signs in their windows. By late summer, restaurants had received permission to create open seating outside with makeshift booths. While I admired the tenacity of one restaurant's chalkboard sign that announced they would provide patrons with marathon foil blankets in cooler weather, it only increased my awareness that my time left in New York was about as durable as those creaky plywood benches.

As I looked up from the sign to check my phone, I saw that I had three missed texts from Sarah, a friend I had worked with years ago in the fashion industry. She was also one of my only other friends who had remained in the city. The first two messages were screenshots from Citizen, an app that alerts users of nearby danger based on their zip code.

3:10 p.m. Nearby Incident: Report
of Person Wielding Metal Bar at
5th Ave and E 19th.

4:52 p.m. Two Women Slashed
with Knife (Chelsea, Manhattan).
Officers are investigating near 8th
& W 23rd. Suspect description has
not yet been provided.

I'm not sure if you have this app but you
live right between these two incidents so
I wanted to give a heads up. I'm out.
I can't pay these prices to live like this.
Movers come Friday, I'm headed to
Austin and then will see what's next.
Good luck girlie, stay safe Xo.

As I added Sarah to the running tally in my head, I calculated
that she was the twenty-fourth personal friend who had
permanently left the city. When I got home with my groceries,
I opened my email to see my rent renewal. The apartment was
actually increasing by $500 per month. *In these conditions? Ok, I
hear ya. Up and out.*

A week later, after having made the decision to finally listen
to my inner guidance system, I decided to go for what would be
my last long walk down to my favorite organic grocery store. It
seemed a miracle that it had managed to remain open for business
in SoHo for so long. The once-bustling streets had been desolate
now for months. I occasionally passed two to three people per
block where dozens used to congregate. Despite the sunshine

beating down on Sixth Avenue, the cloud of despair remained, lingering over the city. I no longer walked wearing headphones. Instead, I took inventory of my surroundings far more than I used to. Yet, while making a left on Broome Street, I was still extremely startled by the man in front of me, appearing seemingly out of nowhere.

"Give me your fuckin' phone," he demanded, standing six inches from my face.

There were two reasons I was incredibly lucky. First, I wasn't on my phone. He just assumed I had one. Fortunately, it was tucked away in a pant pocket hidden under my shirt; thank God for the designer of those Free People yoga pants. Second, I often had cash on me in case I saw someone in need. *I guess the person in need today is this asshole,* I thought, reaching into my other pocket to grab the three twenty-dollar bills. I threw them on the ground. As he hunched down to grab the cash I ran like Forrest Gump to the closest bodega. I ordered an Uber, no longer feeling safe to walk back home, even though it was a bright and sunny August day barely past 6 p.m. When I got home I grabbed Lola, silently thanking God/Source/The Universe that she wasn't with me and that I had arrived back unharmed. I collapsed on the living room floor in tears. When I sat up, I called Chloe, wanting to talk to someone but not wanting to scare my parents or Lindsay until I was safely out.

"Oh my God. Are you okay? Do you need me to drive in and get you?" Chloe asked, currently staying with her parents in New Jersey. "Did you report it?"

"What would be the point? My friend Sarah recently sent me Citizen app updates about metal bar-wielding maniacs and random knife slashings, you think the police are gonna be able to help with a gentle mugging?"

"Gentle mugging? Did he have a weapon?"

"Honestly I have no idea what he even looked like. He was in a hoodie and his mask covered the whole lower half of his face. I don't think he did but I didn't wait to find out, I just threw the money and ran... kinda like a bad ex-girlfriend," I said, weakly attempting a joke.

"I'm so sorry. I can't even imagine how scary that must have been."

"It's just... this was the place I used to feel the safest in the world, safe to be myself freely, safe to hold whatever beliefs resonated, safe to express myself, and safe to be out and about at any time of day or night. Now it's just so fucking clear that I don't belong here anymore," I said, my voice starting to break. "I'm just pissed that this happened after I already decided to leave, it's not like I needed the extra push! The movers are coming Saturday and my mom is driving up to get me and Lola. It reminds me of being in a club when you're already tired, wanna head home, and your rowdy group of friends get kicked out, leaving you stuck paying the tab. Then as if that's not enough, the bouncer comes over yelling, telling you to leave with them and you're like 'Dude, I'm REALLY trying to get out of here!'"

"I'm sorry about the asshole bouncer today," Chloe said.

"I think I need to do a final bind, burying or freezing spell before the movers come."

"How do you know which one to do?"

"Binding is for stopping someone or something from doing you, or themselves, harm. Freezing is a kind of defensive magic, to stop or freeze someone's negative actions against you."

"That seems risky in a rental though because it could be unknowingly defrosted if you leave them when you vacate," Chloe noted wisely.

"True. I think this calls for burying, which is for when you wish to release and transmute something. I do hope New York can be transmuted and rise again from the ashes. I think I, like many of us, may still take a while to process what this dark time did to us, but one of the biggest lessons I've learned throughout the past couple of years is the importance of *surrender*. I don't know for sure where I'm headed, but I know it's time to go. No more maniforcing."

"No more maniforcing," Chloe said, somberly this time.

On the final day before the movers arrived the only things that remained unpacked were the large pieces of furniture, Lola, and a little purple and red Madonna lunchbox I'd held on to since childhood. I used it over the years to house meaningful letters, cards and small mementos. Due to my aversion to visual clutter, I stored that tin box away in a cabinet, but I liked to open it from time to time, especially in times of intense hardship. It had an effect similar to the Village People Gratitude Spell I learned during my time in Costa Rica. I always loved the smell when I opened that box. All of the cards and papers from the past two decades combined to emit a scent reminiscent of the back section of a library. I flipped through thank you notes from interns and designers who worked for me, the first letter Lindsay wrote me from freshman year of college, a thoughtful birthday card from my parents, and various Madonna concert tickets. I began to pull out a few items that represented my New York life: my old Playboy business card, my first apartment lease, and a photo of me posing proudly with the giant gold sewing man statue in the middle of the Garment District. I folded them together in a small square. I grabbed some of Kyle's snake sheds that I still had from my "essential items" in a nearby suitcase, and wrapped them around the folded papers before sealing them into an envelope. I asked my Radio Guides via Siri to play a song I needed to hear. Siri selected *Landslide* by Fleetwood Mac.

I played that damn song three more times while holding the little envelope to my heart, crying as I listened because I *had* built my life around New York. Eventually, I got up to unpack a spoon from one of the kitchen boxes and walked the two blocks east to Madison Square Park. I departed while it was still early in the day, but left my phone at home and took two twenty-dollar bills in my pocket just in case.

I dug a little hole in the corner closest to the entry of the park, placed the envelope inside, and quickly scooped small spoonfuls of soil on top to seal the contents of the envelope in the ground to be released and transmuted. I put my hands on top of my tiny landslide of earth, compressing it gently and intending out loud:

"I'm so sorry this happened to you, New York, but it's clear we don't belong together anymore." I wiped my eyes and placed my hands back on the earth before declaring, "I fully surrender any and all people, places, and situations that are no longer serving me, in order to enter the highest timeline so that the Universe can work with and through me to create what is in the highest good for all."

As I got into bed that night, I looked out the window at my now almost-completely-obstructed view of the Empire State Building—a reminder that my night light was out for good—and I said a final goodnight to my greatest love and home of fifteen years.

Bury, Bind or Freeze

As I explained to Chloe, each of these rituals are powerful in different ways. It's important to choose the method best suited to the situation.

1) BURYING: *for surrendering and transmuting*

Timing: Best on a Friday (ruled by Venus for love and surrender), during waning moon periods or a full moon.

Supplies:

Items to Surrender

These can be photos or mementos like I selected, or a handwritten list of emotions and/or experiences that are ready to be released and transmuted.

A Sealable, Biodegradable Container

A cardboard box or paper envelope.

Snake Sheds (Optional)

Snake sheds are powerful symbols of release and rebirth. I realize they are hard to come by, but they are a potent optional addition. Seek sheds from a snake-owning neighbor or an online source.

A Digging Device and Outdoor Space

If you're a city witch, a spoon and a park can do the trick.

Tarot Cards Chosen Intentions (Optional)

If you like working with Tarot cards, you can also select a card or cards to keep on a table or altar in your space for twenty-four hours after burying the items. I like using the Death Card for Transformation and Rebirth as well as Wheel of Fortune for evolution and expansion.

1. Select your items or write your list.

2. If working with snake sheds, wrap them around the list and/or items.

3. Place everything in a box or envelope.

4. Hold them to your chest/heart chakra while envisioning the gratitude you hold for the experiences and the lessons they brought you. Envision releasing them lovingly back to the earth to be transmuted.

5. Bury and cover them completely with soil.

6. Place your hands on the ground to show gratitude for the Earth's support in transmuting the energies.

7. Share your intentions. Mine were:

   I fully surrender any and all people, places, and situations that are no longer serving me, in order to enter the highest timeline so that the Universe can work with and through me to create what is in the highest good for all.

2) BINDING: *for stopping someone or something from doing you and/or themselves harm.*

Timing: Best on a Saturday (ruled by Saturn the planet of responsibility and discipline), during a waxing moon.

297

Supplies:

A Representation of What it is You Wish to Bind

A photo of the person, place or thing is ideal. If you cannot acquire one, you can write out the name or explanation.

Tape or Ribbon

I believe this originates from using ribbon or twine but I prefer tape (those of you who saw the OG version of *The Craft* will know this one).

Black Candle

For psychic protection and clearing of negativity.

1. Light the black candle next to where you will be performing the binding.

2. Begin wrapping the photo or paper with the name, in a loop with the ribbon or tape, clockwise/from left to right in order to call in the binding and call in protection.

3. While binding repeat:

   I bind you (name) from doing harm, harm against me, harm against others, and harm against yourself.

4. Picture the negativity you have experienced from this person or situation moving away from yourself like a dark cloud dissipating, drifting further from your body, further from your home, from your location, etc. Picture it moving increasingly further away with each circle of binding that is completed.

5. Repeat until the image is covered.

6. Allow the candle to burn down.

7. Take the bound photo and the remains of the black candle and dispose of them, focusing on sending the negative energy away and binding this person or situation from harm to others and themselves.

8. As an extra step, you can choose to bury to further alchemize any negativity, or freeze for additional defense and protection against the person/situation. On extreme occasions, I recommend both binding and freezing.

3) FREEZING: *Defensive magic to stop or freeze someone or something's negative actions against you.*

Timing: Best on a Saturday (ruled by Saturn the planet of responsibility and discipline), or Tuesday (ruled by Mars, the planet of action), during a waxing moon.

Supplies:

A Representation of What it is You Wish to Freeze

As with binding, a photo of the person, place or thing is ideal. If you cannot acquire one you can write out the name or explanation.

A Container

Make sure it's large enough for the photo to be completely covered in ice and frozen within. You don't want little pieces popping up. This has happened to me and I had to transfer to a bigger container and add more water.

Salt

For purifying the container.

Water

Moon Water is best (see Chapter VIII for Moon Water recipe), otherwise, you can use whatever water you have access to.

Seal

This can be as simple as a Tupperware lid or the top of a Mason jar. If you want to get really serious about success, you can also duct-tape the lid after closing, or seal the lid with wax.

1. Salt the container first for purification and protection.

2. Fill with water.

3. Add the photo or representation.

4. Picture the person or situation being frozen energetically, unable to access you, unable to permeate your thoughts or energy field.

5. Add more water if the container is not full.

6. Seal and place in a freezer.

7. If you're a homeowner, you can just leave this tucked away in the back of a freezer. If you rent your space, you can leave it behind when you move and roll the dice that the new owners leave the weird container frozen. Note of caution: I had one defrost and pop up after a long silence as a result of my old apartment being rented. To avoid this, you can transfer the frozen container with you or discard it at a crossroads. Crossroads represent transition, choice and consequence.

CHAPTER XX

THE LOVERS
POSTCARDS TO MY PAST SELF

The Lovers: Love, Harmony, Alignment

I stepped off the stage at the Life To Paper Book Festival in Miami and hugged Tabitha, the festival's founder, with immense gratitude for hosting the *Tapping Into Intuition Through Tarot* event, where I spoke about the creation of my deck, my healing journey with the Tarot, and answered questions from the audience.

"That was brilliant! You're a natural storyteller and I feel like so much of your journey is relatable. I hope I didn't cut in too soon at the end but the questions would have gone on all night," she said as we embraced.

I was pleased to hear that because, in all honesty, that evening went by in one huge blur. I didn't remember what I said and just hoped I answered the questions somewhat eloquently. I hadn't done a big in-person event for a year and a half and I almost forgot how to do it. As I stepped into the foyer, I was met with an incredible reception of some new friends, a couple of fellow New York refugees, several podcast listeners, and a few long-term clients who happened to live in the area. I did my best to hug and thank everyone before I headed out, juggling two bouquets of white roses, my favorite flower, that were gifted to me. One of my friends asked if I wanted to share an Uber ride home. I gave her another big hug and told her I was good to walk the ten-minute trek, feeling grateful for the seventy-five-degree temperature in November. I also needed to process the gratitude overload I felt from the turnout and engagement of the event.

As I headed south on my way home, I looked down at my phone to see a bunch of missed texts. There was a good luck text from Lindsay and a message from Eli Vate who visited me the week prior. In addition to being a quantum rockstar and magical wizard, Eli also became a dear friend. He held up a mirror for me, surrounded by lights that rivaled those in the dressing room of *RuPaul's Drag Race*, in times when I wasn't able to see my own magic.

> Hey Boo, Congratulations on your
> first live event since New York! I
> know you're gonna be amazing. I
> feel like there's another big door that
> might open from this as well. Also
> big hugs to my girl Lola. Love you.

I noticed I also had a text from my parents asking how the event went. I juggled my roses into one arm and called them back.

"I'm so proud of you sweetheart!" my mom gushed. "Your dad wants to talk, hold on."

"Hey Sweetie, how was the speaking engagement?"

"So good! I was surprised at how many people showed up and how excited they all were."

"You're amazing! You know that? Hey, the guys are coming over in a few minutes for poker. Do you see anything in the cards for me? You can wait until you get home, no rush!" he said.

"Don't worry I have them right here from the event," I laughed. I took a little detour and sat down on a stoop next to Versace in the Design District, ogling the handbags in the window while I dug out my cards. I shuffled and pulled the top card over to reveal Temperance.

"Okay Dad, so we got the Temperance card. Be patient. Looks like you come out on top but it comes later in the game."

"Will do! I love you!"

I continued walking towards my apartment, passing my favorite metaphysical shop, the House of Intuition. My Tarot deck was on display and could be seen from the window. I took my phone out to take a photo and send an energetic postcard to my past little-self, sitting in the occult section at the back of the bookstore in her holey leggings.

Hey you, Greetings from Miami!

Don't worry, you do ALL the things you ever want to do in New York... some things you shouldn't, but then again they're all part of the journey. Guess what? Not only are Tarot and esoteric books super cool now, but there are also entire shops dedicated to them, and they are everywhere! And the best part... wait for it... you create your own Tarot deck that a ton of people use and it's on display in the

front *window. Stay strong, my love. I'm with you the whole time. P.S. People pay extra for slashed knee leggings in the future, ya little trendsetter.*

As I walked through the lobby of my building, I realized that these postcards I sent to my past self may be a part of the Voice I'd been hearing all this time. I silently thanked my Higher Self and all the aspects of me—the whole damn squad—for helping to deliver the messages, dreams and spells over the years. I smiled, opening the door as Lola scampered out to greet me.

"I'm sorry I didn't take you, little one. But lots of people asked about you! Uncle Eli says hi too." Her ears perked up at that. I picked her up and scratched her chin as I looked out at the water. That beautiful apartment with the ocean views I saw my future self hanging out in, back during my Ayahuasca journey, was now my home. And Rosanna was right. It *was* in Miami, not the Hamptons.

A boat with twinkling lights wrapped around its deck caught my eye, reminding me of Saturn's rings as it sped full steam ahead towards South Beach. *It's time to finish the book.* I had a couple of projects I put on hold as a result of unexpectedly leaving New York, but something in the synergy I felt tonight told me it was time to start writing again. I was just about to text Tabitha that I wanted to talk to her about publishing when I noticed I had a message from her.

Thank you again for tonight! No pressure to work with us, but I honestly feel you have a powerful story that is worth sharing one way or another.

I was JUST texting you to
say exactly that! I really
want to work with you.
Thank you for everything
and for being you!

"Can you believe we get to live this life, Lola?" I asked, feeling like my heart was literally going to explode with gratitude from the past three hours. As I walked into my bedroom, I looked up at the three Tarot cards painted in gold on large black canvases that hung above my bed, representing the most important elements of my journey. On the left was *The High Priestess* who appeared in Costa Rica in the temple and never left my side since. I knew I had to work with her to access my intuition and Higher Self through intrinsic examination and shadow work before truly being able to help others. *The Sun* hung in the middle, reminding me of healing my relationship with abundance and working on my ability to receive financial prosperity. It also hung as a reminder that I deserved to receive joy and happiness, especially in my work (also hello, Florida the SUNshine state). When I chose the order of those paintings on my wall, I knew it was important to work with *The High Priestess* and *The Sun* before opening to the energy of the third painting, *The Lovers*.

"What do you think, Lola? I think it's time."

Postcard To My Past Self Spell

In times of extreme joy, accomplishment, or gratitude, many of us have been conditioned to not share feelings for fear of appearing egotistic, igniting reactions of lack, or causing jealousy in others. Even if we have amazing soul families who celebrate us, we don't always allow ourselves to fully bask in the deliciousness of these experiences. Giving energy to these instances not only charges them but attracts more as a result. I find the best people to share these moments with are versions of our past selves that would benefit from encouragement and inspiration. Now when I experience moments of intense joy and self-gratitude, I often close my eyes and consider:

Questions:

1. What version of my past self would be psyched to hear this right now?

   - *Is it my awkward, little, bullied self in grade school?*
   - *Is it the version of myself that was struggling in a misaligned job?*
   - *Maybe it's the version who lost all her money and was fearful of how she would pay the rent that month.*

2. What details would my past self want to know the most?

Applications:

Much like the Tarot Card Embodiment Spell, this is a powerful tool that can be used in many ways

1. <u>Visualization:</u> in seated or walking meditation.

2. <u>Journaling prompt:</u> writing out the questions and free

writing the response to your past self.

3. <u>Spoken word:</u> leaving a voicemail for your past self as a voice note on your phone.

4. <u>Actual Postcard:</u> you can even get a little creative with this one and send an actual postcard from a location your past self would love to know you made it to. You can either address it to your past self located at your current address and save it or do the letter-to-Santa-style drop-off in a public mailbox with no address listed to be sent out to the ethers.

In addition to this book being a spellbook and a diary of the transformations I experienced since my Saturn Return, it is also a collection of energetic postcards sent to many of my past selves. And more than anything, I hope it reaches some of yours.

WITH GRATITUDE

A special thank you to the team at Life to Paper Publishing, you are true magicians of the written word. Tabitha, I knew we were meant to do big things together from the moment we met, your talent and passion continue to inspire me. Michelle, your mastery of editing combined with your knowledge of the esoteric world has made my work so much stronger. Jennifer, thank you for the late nights of tag-teaming edits with me and for your word-wizardry and technical knowledge.

ABOUT THE AUTHOR

Rebecca Szymczak—aka Cardsy B—is a writer, intuitive tarot card reader, and healing catalyst. Her work has been featured in MTV, Nylon, Shape, Bustle, and The Zoe Report. After experiencing a dark night of the soul, she exited her career in fashion to dive deeper into her intuitive gifts. She now uses the Tarot to guide clients, including celebrities, C-suite executives, artists, and entrepreneurs, to their own inner knowing and healing abilities. In addition to creating her signature deck, Badass Bitches Tarot, Cardsy B is also the host of the *Hex and the City* podcast. *The Saturn Diaries: A Modern Day Grimoire* is her first book.

Instagram: @cardsyb
TikTok: @cardsyb
Website: www.cardsyb.com
Podcast: Hex and the City

9 781990 700088